THE TAROT

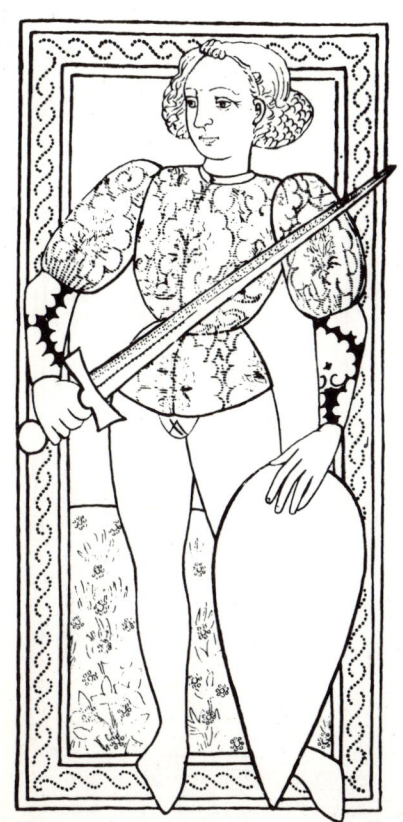

THE TAROT
Richard Cavendish

CHANCELLOR
PRESS

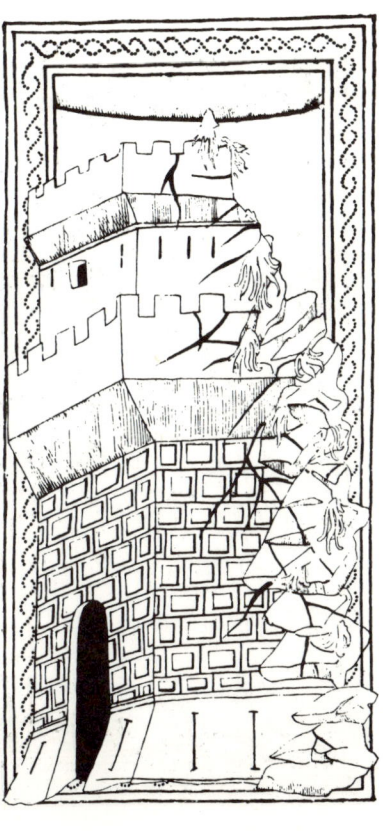

First published in Great Britain in 1975 by
Michael Joseph Ltd

This edition published in 1986 by
Chancellor Press
59 Grosvenor Street
London W1

This book was designed and produced by
George Rainbird Limited
40 Park Street
London W1Y 4DE

Reprinted 1987

© Richard Cavendish 1975

All rights reserved.
No part of this publication may be reproduced,
stored in a retrieval system, or transmitted, in any
form or by any means, electronic, mechanical,
photocopying, recording or otherwise, without the
prior permission of the publisher.

ISBN 1 85152 021 X

Printed in Hong Kong

CONTENTS

Author's Note 6
SECTION ONE   History 9
1 Origins and Legends 11
2 The Universal Key 26

SECTION TWO   Interpretation 47
1 The Cabala 49
2 The Twenty-two Trumps 59
3 Meditation 145

SECTION THREE   Divination 149
1 The Cards and Their Meanings 154
2 Layouts and Readings 173
Notes to References in the Text 185
Bibliography 186
Illustrations Acknowledgments 187
Index 189

AUTHOR'S NOTE

I am very grateful for assistance generously given by Ronald Decker, Francis King and Sylvia Mann: and to my wife, who read the book in manuscript and made many helpful suggestions and criticisms. I am also heavily indebted to the authors of previous books in this field, listed in the Bibliography. Responsibility for the views expressed and for any errors, however, remains mine.

R. C.

From the 'Charles VI' pack: the seventeen surviving cards.

COLOUR PLATES

The Judgment of Paris *page 41*
Italian minchiate cards *42–3*
The bull of Pope Alexander VI *44*
Paradise Garden *93*
A tarocco card of the Lovers *94*
The Chariot driven by a queen *95*
A modern Magician *96*
The Etteilla Devil *121*
The Tower of Babel *122*
Four cards designed by Aleister Crowley *139*
Cards from the 15th century *140*
French Revolutionary court cards *157*
The Knight of Cups from nine packs *158*
Four Aces designed by G. M. Mitelli *175*
The King of Coins *176*

DIAGRAMS
1: The Tree of Life *50*
2: The Twenty-two Paths *54*
3: The Hebrew Alphabet *57*
4: Correspondences of the Paths and Trumps *58*
5: *Le Grand Jeu* *184*

SECTION I

HISTORY

Cards were early used for gambling, as shown in this 15th-century German woodcut, where a suit corresponding to the modern Hearts is in play.

The Tarot is a pack of mysterious cards which are related to our ordinary modern playing cards and are often said to be their ancestors. Card games were played with them and still are, here and there in Europe, but they are now far more widely used in fortune-telling and for mystical and magical purposes. All sorts of theories and legends have gathered round the cards, because of their puzzling but enticing symbolism and the uncertainty of their origin. It has been said that they came from China or India or Persia, that they were brought to the West by the gypsies, or by returning Crusaders, or by the Arab invaders of Sicily or Spain, or alternatively that they had nothing to do with the East at all and were invented in Europe.

It has been claimed that the Tarot preserves the wisdom of ancient Egypt, the mystery religion of Mithras, pagan Celtic traditions, the beliefs of medieval heretics, or the teachings of a committee of learned Cabalists who supposedly designed the pack in Morocco in the year 1200. Or again, the imagery of the Tarot has been traced to the collective unconscious, or to the symbolism of Dante's *Divine Comedy*. The name Tarot itself has been derived from Egyptian, Hebrew or Latin, and by one ingenious writer from Astaroth, the great fertility goddess of Syria and Palestine, condemned in the Old Testament for the sensuality of her rites.

What stands out among the welter of conflicting theories is that the Tarot cards have something peculiarly fascinating about them. Most of the modern packs are painfully ugly, but some of the older cards are very beautiful and have an air of profound significance. They tug at half-buried memories and obscure connections and intimations in the mind, at associations with mythology, legend, magic and folk belief. They give an impression of holding the key to some vital secret which cannot quite be put into words, which is almost in the mind's grasp when it slips elusively away. It is because they do this that so many different meanings have been read into them.

The standard modern Tarot pack has four suits: Swords, Cups, Coins (or Pentacles) and Batons (or Sceptres, Wands). These are the usual suits of Italian and Spanish playing cards and correspond to the Spades, Hearts, Diamonds and Clubs of the conventional English and American pack. The Tarot, however, has fourteen cards in each suit instead of thirteen. There are four court cards – the King, Queen, Knight and Page – and the numbered cards from the Ten down to the Ace. But the main difference between a Tarot pack and an ordinary one is that the Tarot has twenty-two extra cards, which have their own names and numbers. In the usual order they are:

0 The Fool	11 Strength
1 The Juggler	12 The Hanged Man
2 The Female Pope	13 Death
3 The Empress	14 Temperance
4 The Emperor	15 The Devil
5 The Pope	16 The Tower
6 The Lovers	17 The Star
7 The Chariot	18 The Moon
8 Justice	19 The Sun
9 The Hermit	20 The Day of Judgment
10 The Wheel of Fortune	21 The World

Interest in the Tarot centres on these extra cards, the 'trumps'. Sometimes, to emphasize their importance, they are called 'major trumps' or 'major arcana', and the other cards are the 'minor arcana'. Different authors have interpreted them in different ways, arranged them in varying order, changed their names and altered their designs. Most of the leading modern interpreters of the Tarot have redesigned the cards to fit their own explanations of them, a process called 'rectifying' the pack if you agree with it, and obfuscating it if you do not.

Two cards from the Tarot pack long believed to have been made for King Charles VI of France, but now thought to be Italian and to date from about 1470: the Page of Swords, and Temperance represented by a woman pouring liquid from one vase to another.

1 ORIGINS AND LEGENDS

The original meaning of the Tarot trumps is still in doubt, and so is the initial relationship between the trump cards and the minor cards, because the early history of playing cards is lost in a fog of obscurity. The first definite references to them in Europe date from the 1370s and 1380s, and even at that time it was not clear where they had come from. Brother John, a monk of Brefeld in Switzerland, wrote an essay on them in which he said: '... a certain game called the game of cards has come to us in this year of Our Lord 1377. In which game the state of the world as it is now is most excellently described and figured. But at what time it was invented, where, and by whom, I am entirely ignorant.' He goes on to describe, not a Tarot pack, but a pack more like a modern one, with fifty-two or more cards in four suits.[1]

The household accounts of King Charles VI of France show that in 1392 a payment was made to 'Jacquemin Gringonneur, painter, for three packs of cards, gilded and coloured, and ornamented with various devices, supplied to the King for his amusement'. A priest named Menestrier suggested in 1704 that Gringonneur was the original inventor of cards and that he devised them to divert Charles VI's mind during the unfortunate king's recurrent fits of madness. Other authors repeated this suggestion and another legend was added to the Tarot's rich store of them. It is now clear that cards were known in Europe before 1392, and by 1397 they were sufficiently common in Paris for a regulation to be issued forbidding people to play with them on working days. In the Bibliothèque Nationale in Paris there are seventeen magnificent cards, sixteen of them Tarot trumps, which were long believed to have been made by Gringonneur for Charles VI, but which are now thought to be Italian and to date from about 1470.

Cards are not mentioned by Petrarch in his essay on gambling, or by other fourteenth-century authors, like Boccaccio and Chaucer, who would probably have referred to them if they had known of them. There is no sign of cards in numerous earlier medieval denunciations of gambling, though dice are frequently mentioned and have a much older known history. A French decree against gambling in 1369 does not mention cards, and it looks as if they first appeared on the European scene in the later fourteenth century.

Where the cards came from is still a vexed problem. The Chinese had playing cards at least as early as the tenth century, and before that they were using paper money which their cards closely resembled in design. Cards are also said to be of great antiquity in India, though whether this is true is doubtful. In any case, Chinese and Indian cards are not much like the European varieties. Theories that cards were imported into Europe by Crusaders or Arabs or hordes of invading Mongols probably put the entry of cards into the West too early. On the other hand, the popular belief that they were brought in by the gypsies dates them too late, because the cards were in western Europe before the gypsies. It seems likely that cards were invented independently in Europe, in the north of Italy. It has been suggested that they may first have come into use in the valley of the Taro River, which is a tributary of the Po: hence the Italian name for cards, *tarocchi*, and the French name Tarot.[2]

OVERLEAF The trumps from the Marseilles Tarot pack.

The standard modern Tarot pack is descended from a type of Italian pack known as the Venetian or Piedmontese Tarot, which has the twenty-two trump

LE MAT

LE BATELEUR

LA PAPESE

L'IMPERATRISE

LE CHARIOT

IUSTICE

L'ERMITE

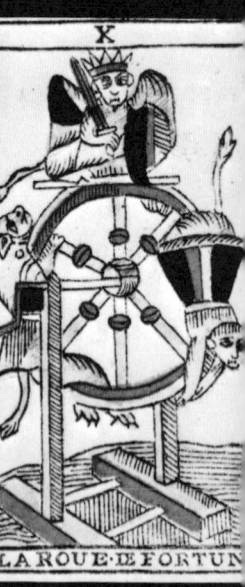
LA ROUE DE FORTUN

TEMPERANCE

LA MAISON DE DIEU

LES ETOILES

LA LUNE

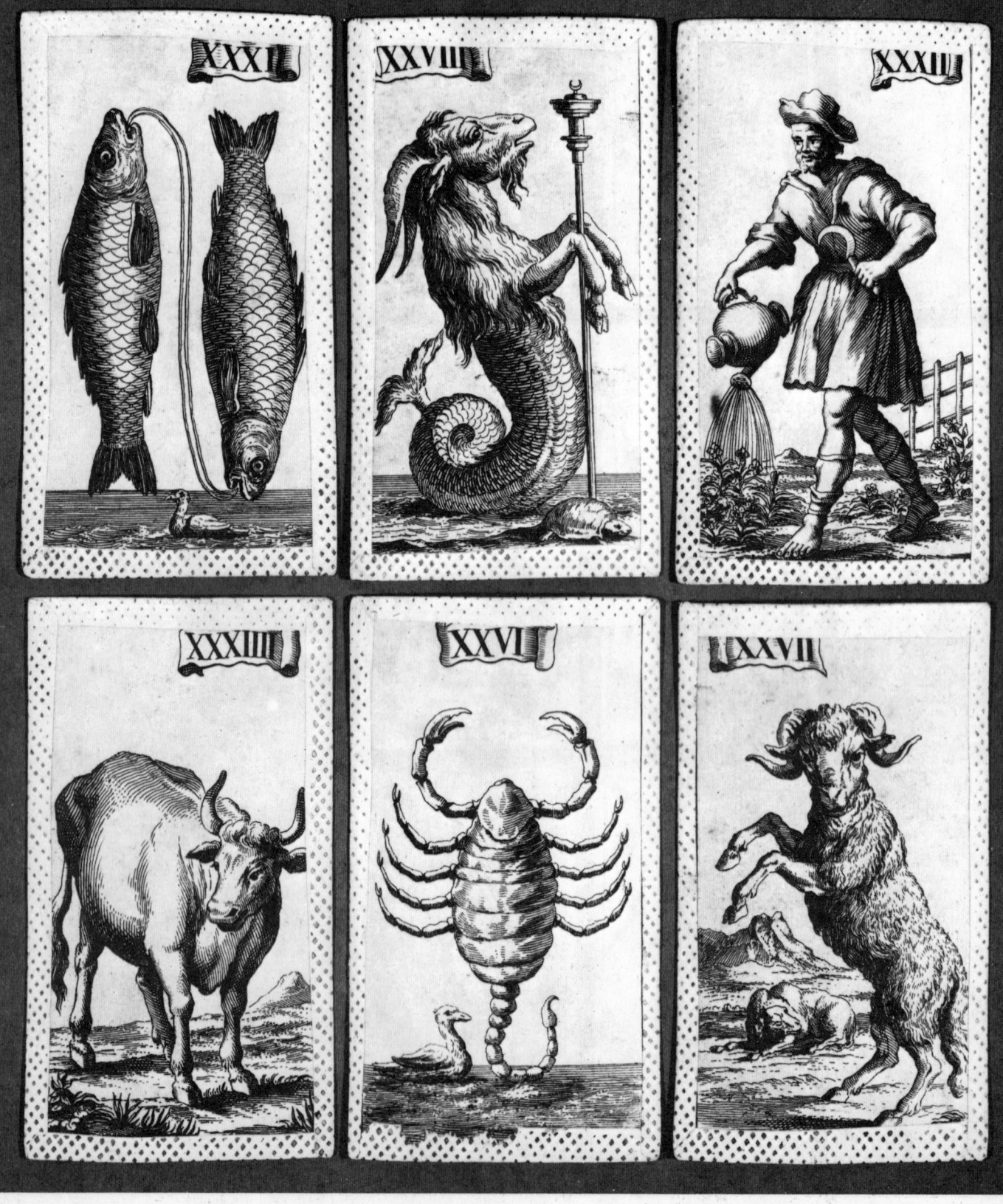

cards listed earlier. This is the same as the French pack called the Tarot of Marseilles. The designs are those which were generally accepted by about 1500 in northern Italy and France. Another Italian variety, known as the Florentine or minchiate pack, has ninety-seven cards altogether, the fifty-six minor cards in their four suits and forty-one trumps. The trumps are the Venetian ones, in a different order and leaving out the Pope, plus the four virtues of faith, hope, charity and prudence, the four elements of fire, air, earth and water, and the twelve signs of the zodiac. Yet another Italian type of Tarot is the Bolognese pack, which has sixty-two cards.

The Venetian or Marseilles pack of seventy-eight cards, with twenty-two trumps, became the standard one, but the names, designs and order of the trumps varied. Under pressure from the Church, the Pope, Female Pope, Empress and Emperor were sometimes replaced with other figures. In Sicily, where the Tarot was introduced from Italy in the seventeenth century, the Pope, Female Pope, Devil and Day of Judgment were replaced by a card showing a beggar and named Poverta or Miseria, a female standing for Constancy, and the cards of the Ship and Jupiter. German card-makers in the eighteenth century printed many Tarot packs in which the trump cards have little or no relation to the older designs. They show animals, legendary monsters, scenes from popular operas, elephants with howdahs, intrepid explorers riding on camels, and anything else which the designer's fancy might suggest. Tarots of this kind went on being produced in the nineteenth century. One of 1879, for instance, has scenes from history on its trumps and the court cards have turned into Shakespeare, Louis XIV, Marlborough, Kepler, General Gordon and other notable figures.

Ordinary packs of playing cards, without the extra trumps, also varied considerably in design. Many different emblems were used for the suits. Italian and Spanish card-makers generally remained faithful to Swords, Cups, Coins and Batons. The standard marks on German cards became hearts, bells, leaves and acorns, and on French cards hearts, pikes, lozenges and trefoils. The court cards were frequently characters from history, mythology or legend. In French packs the four kings might be Charlemagne, Caesar, Alexander and David, the four queens Judith, Rachel, Pallas and Argine (apparently an anagram of Regina, 'Queen' in Latin) and the four jacks Lancelot, Hector, Hogier and La Hire. Hogier is Ogier the Dane, a hero of medieval romance, and La Hire was a famous soldier of the fifteenth century, a supporter of Joan of Arc, said to have invented the game of piquet. Many other real or imaginary people appeared on cards. In a German pack of 1815 the Duke of Wellington is the Jack of Diamonds and Marshal Blücher the Jack of Clubs.

For a long time it was quite widely believed that cards had been invented by the Devil. St Bernardino of Siena, a celebrated Franciscan preacher, denounced them as a creation of Satan in 1423 and the puritanically-minded all over Europe followed suit. In an attack on gambling and theatre-going published in England in the the 1570s, John Northbrooke anticipated the modern theory that cards contain the pagan wisdom of the ancient world: 'The play at Cards is an invention of the Devil, which he found out that he might the easier bring in Idolatry amongst men. For the Kings and Court cards that we use now were in old times the images of Idols and false Gods: which since they that would seem Christians have changed into Charlemagne, Lancelot, Hector and such like names . . .'[3] In England in the

Signs of the zodiac from a minchiate pack: Pisces, Capricorn, Aquarius, Taurus, Scorpio and Aries.

Modern Viennese cards with different pictures for the two ways up.

eighteenth century John Wesley referred to cards as 'the Devil's pops' and they were called 'the Devil's books' on into the nineteenth century in Scotland.

Cards were fiercely attacked because people enjoyed playing with them when they should have been thinking about the welfare of their souls or getting on with their work, and because they were notoriously conducive to gambling, cheating, hard drinking, ill-temper and bad language. But a deeper reason for disapproving of them was the Christian doctrine of Providence. In Christian belief, God is working his purpose out as year succeeds to year. Everything which happens is part of the divine plan, which God may and frequently does alter in detail as time goes by. All games of chance and all methods of telling fortunes, by card-reading, astrology, palmistry and other popular techniques, imply the existence of a different, impersonal mechanism behind events, much closer to pagan ideas of Fate than to Providence.[4]

Like the pack seen by Brother John of Brefeld in 1377, the cards denounced by St Bernardino do not seem to have been tarots but ordinary playing cards. But

ORIGINS AND LEGENDS 17

sometime between about 1450 and 1480 another Franciscan friar, preaching in northern Italy and also condemning cards as the Devil's invention, distinguished between the ordinary minor cards and the Tarot trumps themselves, and described the trumps as the rungs of a ladder which led to the depths of hell.

It is significant that Brother John said that the cards he saw pictured 'the state of the world'. Unfortunately, he failed to write down most of the things about the cards that we would like to know, but he did say that because they portrayed kings, nobles and common people they could be used for moral purposes. He may have believed, as many people did later, that the four suits stood for four classes in society: swords for the aristocracy, lords and knights; cups or chalices for the churchmen; coins for the merchants; and batons or clubs for the peasants. He certainly thought that the cards could be used 'to teach noblemen the rule of life' and to instruct the common people in 'the way of labouring virtuously'. In other words, they could be used to demonstrate the structure of society and to inculcate the lesson of knowing and keeping one's appointed place in it.

The court cards have frequently been turned into historical figures: from a German pack of the 19th century.

Among the many subjects included on cards for educational purposes, propaganda or satire, are the Old Testament, as in the card ABOVE showing Nebuchadnezzar eating grass: OPPOSITE, LEFT TO RIGHT, TOP Latin grammar, expounded in the form of a garden; virtues, represented by Modesty; a supposed amour of Oliver Cromwell: BOTTOM zoology, with a mammal and a bird; James II's Queen producing a son; and American political geography.

Teaching became an important function of cards and it may be that the Tarot trumps were devised separately from the minor cards, and rather later, as a means of conveying more complicated teaching about the world than the game of four suits could provide. They may then have been combined with the minor cards for playing games, and later for telling fortunes. On the other hand, some authorities on the history of cards believe that the trumps were initially designed for games-playing though, if so, there still remains the problem of why these particular subjects and figures were chosen.

Many special packs of cards have been invented for educational purposes as well as, or instead of, for amusement. In 1509 Thomas Murner designed a pack of sixteen suits intended to teach logic, and later another to teach law. There are scenes from the Bible on a German pack of 1603 and scenes from Greek mythology with explanatory notes on a pack produced in Paris in 1644. The young Louis XIV was taught history, geography and other subjects with packs of instructive cards, apparently on the initiative of Cardinal Mazarin, himself a devoted card-player, notorious for cheating, who was still enthusiastically playing a hand on his deathbed. A pack printed in England in 1692 taught the art of carving meat and fish. The King of Hearts is shown dealing neatly with a sirloin of beef and the King of Clubs dissects a pickled herring. Early in the eighteenth century the firm of Lenthall's in London advertised forty different packs which instructed ladies and gentlemen ('and others', the notice adds, rather pointedly) in various arts and sciences. The subjects included heraldry, travel, sea battles, astronomy, geography, history, mathematics, cookery, carving, grammar, proverbs and sayings, fortune-telling, strategy, fortification, glories of the female sex, fashion, acrobatics, and reading and spelling for children.[5]

Special packs for teaching children history and geography were still being sold in France in the late nineteenth century. Heraldry, geography and the art of war were always favourite subjects with card-makers, but many other branches of knowledge were exploited, including theology, ethics and politics. During the First World War the Austrian firm of Piatnik published a Tarot pack of battle scenes, which optimistically included a picture of a U-boat in New York harbour.

From education to propaganda is a short step and many packs have been designed to promote political attitudes, satirize and caricature opponents, or teach partisan versions of history. Seventeenth-century English cards show the misdeeds of the Rump Parliament, the wicked machinations of the Popish Plot, and the tyrannical follies of King James II. During the French Revolution, card-makers in Paris prudently removed the crowns from the court cards, sometimes leaving the unfortunate figures with no tops to their heads, and special revolutionary packs were printed with the court cards replaced by approved philosophers, moral qualities and proletarians. In one of these the four kings have become Molière, La Fontaine, Voltaire and Jean Jacques Rousseau. The queens are the four classical virtues of Prudence, Justice, Temperance and Fortitude, and the knaves are soldiers and workers. In an American pack of about 1800 the four kings are Washington, Franklin, Lafayette and John Adams. The queens are Roman goddesses – Fortune, Ceres, Minerva and a modestly draped Venus. The jacks are Indian chiefs.

Earnest attempts to purge playing cards of all traces of the old regime were similarly made in Russia after the Bolshevik Revolution. 'A pack satirizing religion

ORIGINS AND LEGENDS 19

20 HISTORY

MISERO·I·

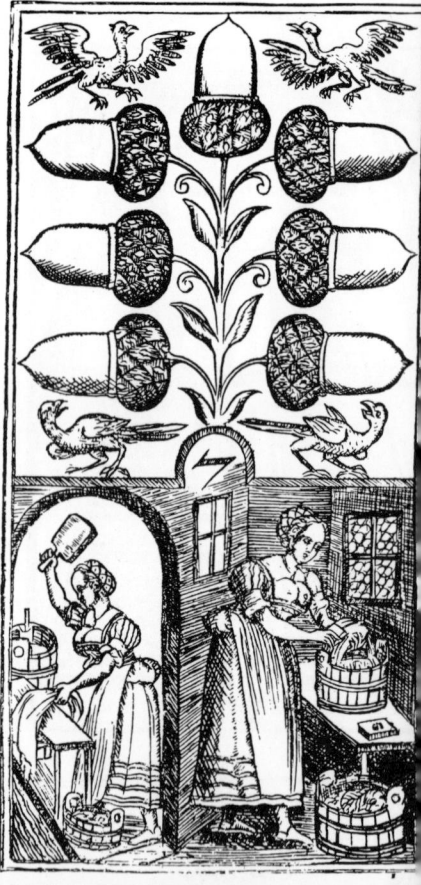

was published in Russia about 1930. The court cards show priests and nuns indulging in scurrilous behaviour such as taking bribes or dreaming of a mistress whilst celebrating Mass, or imagining the embraces of a lover or the joys of the table whilst lighting votive candles.'[6]

There was a popular story, long circulated in penny pamphlets, about a soldier who used his pack of cards as a combined Bible, prayer-book and almanac. The pips on the cards reminded him of events in the Good Book and articles of the Faith: one for the One God, three for the Trinity, four for the four gospels, five for the five wise virgins, and so on. The fifty-two cards stood for the weeks in the year, the four suits for the four seasons, the twelve court cards for the months, the thirteen cards of each suit for the weeks in each quarter. These apparently coincidental correspondences between the cards and the calendar have impressed some modern occultists as suggesting that the cards are connected with the structure and arrangement of the universe. It has been pointed out, for instance, that there are thirteen cards in each suit, and if you add the numbers from 1 to 13, the total is 91. Multiply 91 by 4, for the four suits, and you get 364, and add the Joker and you have 365, the number of days in the year.[7]

Much earlier, however, at the beginning of their history, the Tarot trumps may have been meant to teach something less simple-minded about the nature and structure of the universe, or at least they emerged from a background of enthusiasm for putting instruction of this kind in visual and schematic form. An interesting set of fifty instructional picture-cards, produced in Italy in the fifteenth century, was formerly attributed to Andrea Mantegna, the great painter who was employed by the Gonzaga family at Mantua, though the attribution is now considered false. One theory is that the 'Mantegna' *tarocchi* were devised at Mantua in 1459 by Pope Pius II, Cardinal Bessarion and Cardinal Nicholas of Cusa, to while away the time during a Church council which lasted for six months.

These cards do not form a Tarot pack as we now think of it, but they are evidence of the background from which the Tarot came. They were meant for playing a real game, apparently, but their main purpose was educational. They are divided into five groups of ten cards each which, placed in the correct order, show the organization of the world. The first and lowest group depicts ten conditions of life in which a human being may find himself. Reading from the bottom up, these are beggar, servant, skilled workman, merchant, gentleman, knight, doge, king, emperor, pope. The next group consists of Apollo, the Greek god of beauty, poetry and philosophy, and the nine Muses who preside over the arts. The next group shows the ten sciences which man can acquire and which raise him above the other animals: grammar, logic, rhetoric, geometry, arithmetic, music, poetry, philosophy, astrology and theology. Next come the seven virtues of temperance, prudence, fortitude, justice, charity, hope and faith, plus three cosmic principles, of the earth, time and light. Finally, in the highest group are the seven planets known in antiquity, with the eighth sphere or heaven of the fixed stars, the Prime Mover and, at the summit of the whole arrangement, the First Cause.

These cards, each of which is numbered and lettered to show its correct place in the system, form a symbolic ladder from heaven to earth. 'From the summit of this ladder God, the *Prima Causa*, governs the world – not directly, but stepwise, *ex gradibus*, by means of a succession of intermediaries. The divine power is thus transmitted down to the lowest level of humanity, to the humble beggar. But the

FAR LEFT Misery, a beggar, in the series depicting the ten conditions of life which is part of the 'Mantegna' pack; LEFT, TOP a 16th-century card of the suit of acorns, with two scenes showing a household wash; BOTTOM a card of the same period, in which leaves are shaped into Hearts.

ladder can likewise be read from bottom to top; seen in this way it teaches that man may gradually raise himself in the spiritual order, reaching at last the heights of the *Bonum*, the *Verum* and the *Nobile* – and that science and virtue bring him closer to God.'[8]

Exactly the same thing is said of the Tarot by its modern interpreters. The trumps form a symbolic ladder which leads up to the Good, the True and the Noble, and the human being who makes the arduous climb comes closer to God, in Christian occult systems, or in Hermetic systems eventually becomes God. The scheme of the Tarot is not remotely as clear and straightforward as that of the 'Mantegna' cards (if it were, it might now be of little more than antiquarian interest), but it may have been a product of the same intellectual climate, of Renaissance humanism.

'Humanism' is a word which has many shades of meaning, but which basically implies a conviction of the worth and dignity of man, a view of man as godlike. Humanist philosophers, scholars, poets, painters, princes and churchmen in the Renaissance were in love with the civilization of the ancient world. They looked back to Greece and Rome for truth and beauty, rather than to medieval culture, which they dismissed as dark, barren and primitive. The term 'Middle Ages' itself was originally used with this derogatory connotation, for the period between the submergence of classical civilization under the barbarian invasions in the fifth century and its reappearance in the glories of the fifteenth. The humanists thought that the myths and legends of the ancient world concealed sublime truths which had been cloaked in fable to hide them from the common herd, 'showing only the crust of the mysteries to the vulgar,' in the words of the Italian philosopher Pico della Mirandola, 'while reserving the marrow of the true sense for higher and more perfect spirits'. If you were a higher and more perfect spirit, you could discern the same profound truths behind Christianity, pagan mythology, the classical mystery religions, the Orphic hymns, the Jewish Cabala, Plato, Pythagorean and Neoplatonist philosophy, and the Hermetic and gnostic texts of the late pagan world. The humanists wanted to reconcile these traditions and isolate the true religion which they believed had existed from the beginning, veiled in these various forms. They were helped by the fact that their sources, many of which were later in date than they realized, did have many ideas in common, but they had an uneasy relationship with the Church, which half approved and half disliked the attempt to reconcile Christianity and paganism.

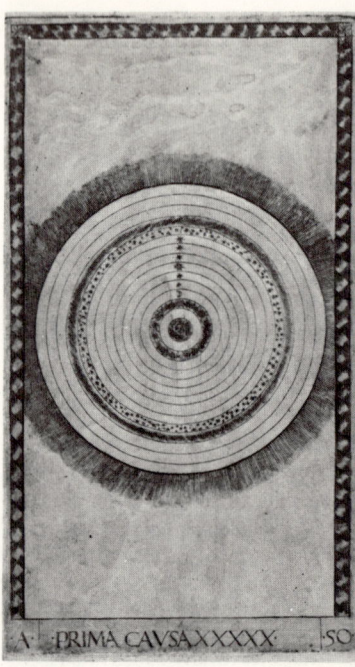

Renaissance artists took pagan myths as subjects and treated them in a way which would hint at 'the marrow of the true sense'. The story of the Judgment of Paris, for instance, was believed to teach the lesson that the world is made of opposites. The One, the supreme ultimate unity of which all things are part, displays itself to our eyes in pairs of opposites, each with a common centre. The three goddesses, to one of whom in the Greek myth Paris had to award the prize, were interpreted as the opposites and their centre, standing for three kinds of life – contemplative, active and passive – or for three human goals: wisdom, power and pleasure. Similarly, the classical myth that Mars, the god of war, and Venus, the goddess of love, had a daughter named Harmony, showed that progress comes through the reconciliation of opposites in a higher unity. Veronese's *Mars and Venus United by Love* and Mantegna's *Parnassus* are exercises on this theme. Another is Botticelli's *Mars and Venus*, in which the gentle love goddess has put the violent war god to

ORIGINS AND LEGENDS 23

Primavera by Botticelli, an example of the Renaissance liking for using pictures to convey spiritual truths; and OPPOSITE the First Cause, from the 'Mantegna' pack.

sleep and baby satyrs are using his lance and helm as toys, but the opposite element of hostility remains present in the equation, shown in the wasps buzzing round the sleeping god's head. Botticelli's famous *Primavera* contains several examples of the theme of the reconciliation of opposites, and the painting as a whole has been described as a talisman of Venus, a device for capturing in the mind the influences of love and beauty associated with Venus as goddess and planet.[9]

The humanists took a lively interest in astrology and magic. The Florentine philosopher Marsilio Ficino, translator of Plato and the Hermetica (a group of gnostic texts of the early centuries after Christ), published in 1489 a medical textbook, *Libri de Vita*, in which he recommended the use of 'images', which could be real or mental pictures, for attracting healthful planetary influences. He said, for instance, that students sometimes become ill or depressed after working too hard, and this is because academic study is ruled by the baneful planet Saturn. They can gain relief by attracting strengthening and cheerful influences from the sun, Jupiter or Venus: for example, by holding in the mind an image of Venus as a beautiful young girl carrying flowers and apples.

Giordano Bruno, who was burned alive as a heretic and magician at Rome in

1600, also recommended image-magic of this kind. He supplies various images of the sun: a laughing Apollo with a bow; a bearded and helmeted man, riding a lion, a golden crown above his head; an archer killing a wolf. These pictures are symbols of the sun's nature and by meditating on them the sun's influence is brought down into the human mind and personality. (This kind of magic interestingly resembles more direct modern systems of self-improvement through appropriate thoughts: 'Every day and in every way I am getting better and better.') Various medieval and Renaissance textbooks of ritual magic supply similar images of the spirits and demons which the magician attempts to control, apparently on the theory that by taking the spirits' characteristic forms into his mind he can master them there.

During the Renaissance there was also great interest in the art of memory, whose purpose was to work out ways of arranging ideas and groups of ideas in tidy patterns so that they could be compared, related and remembered. Attempts were made to reconcile classical techniques with the methods of Raymond Lull, the medieval pioneer of mnemonic systems. Lull was a Spanish philosopher, visionary, scientist and missionary to Islam. He was killed in 1315 by irritable Muslims in Algeria who resented his efforts to convert them to Christianity. Lull was influenced by the Jewish Cabalist practice of meditating on letters and their combinations and permutations. In his books he used letters and diagrams to represent

Botticelli's *Mars and Venus*, in which the opposites of War and Love are shown reconciled.

ideas and the connections between them, hoping to assemble all knowledge in a clear and convenient scheme which would compel Muslims and Jews to recognize the truth of Christianity. Like the 'Mantegna' cards, Lull's system is a ladder arrangement, showing how the world is arranged in a descending and ascending hierarchy, with God at the top and the angels, stars, man, animals, plants and everything else suitably disposed on the lower rungs.[10]

The Tarot trumps seem to have emerged, though on a much humbler level than that of a Lull, Ficino, Bruno or Botticelli, from the Renaissance background of interest in the use of pictures as instructional, magical and mnemonic devices. These may be the threads from which their cryptic imagery is woven, though attempts to unravel the web have so far proved largely vain. At any rate, this is certainly the light in which the cards have been viewed in the modern revival of occultism. Modern magicians share many of the attitudes and preoccupations of the Renaissance humanists. They too believe in a profound wisdom of great antiquity, underlying different traditions and concealed from the common herd, and they have blended it from much the same ingredients – especially the Cabala, Pythagoreanism, Graeco-Egyptian gnosticism and the Hermetica, frequently spiced with oriental additions. To the secret doctrine which they discern behind these various systems, they take the Tarot as a master key.

2 THE UNIVERSAL KEY

Although the history of playing cards in Europe begins in the late fourteenth century, sustained interest in the Tarot as a coherent magical system and symbolic compendium of wisdom seems to go back only two hundred years. The Tarot cards were used for playing games and telling fortunes, but there is as yet no hard evidence of anyone attaching greater importance to them until 1781, when Antoine Court de Gébelin published the eighth and penultimate volume of his massive book on civilization, highly regarded in its day, *Le Monde Primitif Analysé et Comparé avec le Monde Moderne*. Court de Gébelin was a Protestant clergyman, born in 1725, who published the first volume of his great work in 1773. He was interested in occult and arcane matters, for three years later he became a Freemason and, not long before his death in 1784, he went for treatment by 'animal magnetism', as it was then called, to Mesmer, the pioneer of hypnotism.

Visiting friends one day, Court de Gébelin found them playing with a Tarot pack. He inspected the trump cards and within a quarter of an hour he had identified them, conclusively in his opinion, as being of ancient Egyptian origin. He was naturally excited by this discovery. It was astonishing but true, he said, that the Tarot had been in existence for no less than 3,757 years without anyone realizing its importance. Like Brother John of Brefeld, confronted with a pack of cards four centuries before, he thought that the trumps were symbolic pictures of the structure of the world. They contained the purest doctrine of the ancient Egyptian priests, who had deliberately disguised their knowledge in the form of a mere game, and so enabled it to survive the Christian defeat and extirpation of paganism. The pack had been brought in to Europe by the *bohémiens*, the gypsies, who were then generally believed to have emigrated originally from Egypt (hence our word 'gypsy', which is derived from 'Egyptian'). Court de Gébelin took the word Tarot itself to be Egyptian, derived from 'Tar', meaning road or way, and 'Ro', king or royal, so that the name meant the Royal Road. He also noticed that there were the same number of trumps, twenty-two, as there are letters in the Hebrew alphabet. This later became an essential factor in attempts to interpret them.

Court de Gébelin's theory was a product of the fascination with ancient Egypt which existed at the time. Egyptian hieroglyphics had not yet been deciphered, and would not be until the 1820s, and there was a widespread romantic feeling that they must contain all sorts of profound and captivating secrets. An 'Egyptian rite' of Freemasonry was founded by Cagliostro, the Sicilian adventurer and man of mystery who travelled all over Europe, posing as a powerful magician and alchemist, and selling love potions and elixirs of youth and beauty. Also much in vogue were the Knights Templar, the great medieval military order destroyed in the fourteenth century amid allegations of anti-Christian and obscene practices. It was said that after the Order's fall a group of ex-knights had preserved its secret teachings, which had been passed on under cover from each generation to the next until they had come to the surface again in Masonry. These teachings were rumoured to include the alchemistic technique of making gold from base metals, on the theory that only the possession of this secret could explain the Templars' colossal wealth.

There was a similar romantic interest in the mysterious Rosicrucians of the seventeenth century, and in the 1750s a new Order of the Gold and Rosy Cross was founded in secret. 'In 1767, this organization spawned a new rite of Rosicrucian freemasonry, too, influenced by the other masonic proliferations of the period. An

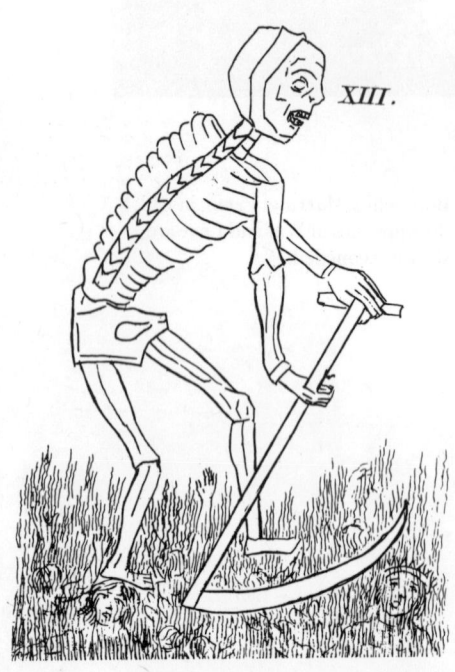

Pictures of Tarot trumps from the 1781 edition of *Le Monde Primitif* by Court de Gébelin, who suggested that the trumps were originally devised in ancient Egypt: ABOVE Death and OPPOSITE Temperance.

THE UNIVERSAL KEY 27

elaborate hierarchy of nine degrees was set up, the highest known as that of Magus. Members were organized in circles of nine, and swore oaths of obedience and secrecy. Their statutes and catechisms embodied a deal of unusually high-flown rubbish but seem to have attracted large numbers of members (one among whom was Mesmer).'[11] Also flourishing in France in the late eighteenth century were clandestine brotherhoods of Martinists, dedicated to the teachings of an obscure visionary and ceremonial magician named Martinez de Pasqually, who founded a pseudo-masonic society, the Order of Elect Cohens, and died in 1774.

The time was certainly ripe for Court de Gébelin to proclaim the ancient Egyptian origin and sublimely arcane and hieroglyphical significance of the Tarot, but the first person to make much use of the discovery was a humbler figure, a professional Parisian fortune-teller named Alliette. Describing himself as a cabalist and alchemist, Alliette made a good living by interpreting dreams and horoscopes, reading cards and palms, and selling magic charms. He claimed to be a pupil of the Count of Saint-Germain, another alluringly mysterious personage, supposed to be a great adept of magic and alchemy, who was over two thousand years old, had discovered the Elixir of Life and was possibly the Wandering Jew. Seizing gleefully on Court de Gébelin's theory of the Tarot (though he claimed to have anticipated it), Alliette added to it smatterings of the Cabala and Raymond Lull and some romantic notions of his own. 'He declared that the Tarot had been composed 171 years after the Flood, that seventeen magi had collaborated for four years to produce it, and that Hermes Trismegistus himself had conceived the plan of the book, which was therefore called *The Book of Thoth*. It had been written, he said, on leaves of gold in a temple three leagues from Memphis.'[12]

Hermes was the Greek equivalent of the Egyptian Thoth, god of wisdom and magic. Hermes Trismegistus, or Thrice-Great, was a mythical figure who had interested the Renaissance humanists. He was supposedly an ancient sage of surpassing wisdom, the builder of the pyramids, the author of the Hermetic texts and the founder of the art of alchemy.

Alliette wrote various books under the pseudonym of Etteilla, his own name spelled backwards, and designed sets of fortune-telling cards. Packs of this type had long been popular with card-makers and showed an assortment of future events – a journey by land, a sea voyage, a lawsuit, jealousy, a false friend, and so on. The Tarot symbols do not lend themselves readily to this kind of divination and are unlikely to have been invented primarily for telling fortunes.

Alliette published his own Tarot packs, partly for fortune-telling, but with a deeper significance. He claimed, as so many were to do after him, that he had restored the true, ancient symbolism of the cards by eliminating mistakes which had crept into them over the centuries. He altered the trumps' designs and changed their order where it suited him. For example, it offended him that the Juggler, a mere fairground trickster, should be dignified with the number one and stand apparently at the head of the trumps – the Fool was often put last or in twenty-first place at this period – so he placed the card lower, at number fifteen. Court de Gébelin had also been unfavourably impressed by the Juggler, and suggested that the Egyptian system must have run from the lowest numbers up to the highest, with the Juggler at the bottom, standing for life in this world as a perpetual game of chance. (When the Tarot cards are used for playing games, the Juggler does usually rank as the lowest trump.)

OPPOSITE Fortune-telling cards from one of the packs designed by the French cartomancer and astrologer Alliette, or 'Etteilla'; and BELOW a 16th-century conception of the mythical initiate Hermes Trismegistus, the supposed founder of alchemy.

A far more magisterial figure appeared on the Tarot scene in 1856, when Eliphas Lévi published *Le Dogme et Rituel de la Haute Magie*. This splendidly romantic work, vivid, verbose, vague, sometimes abstruse and sometimes patently absurd, was written with a verve, insight and evocative power which has kept it selling to this day and made its author a leading influence on the modern revival of magic. Lévi's real name was Alphonse Louis Constant. Born in Paris in 1810, the son of a shoemaker, he was trained for the Roman Catholic priesthood, but found he had no vocation. He busied himself with left-wing political journalism, hack writing and occultism. Dismissing Alliette with a contempt which he transmitted to later magicians (instead of revealing the secrets of the Tarot, he said, Alliette had revealed them), Lévi was the first writer to fit the Tarot systematically into the scheme of the Cabala. He connected the trumps with the twenty-two letters of the Hebrew alphabet, the four suits with the Tetragrammaton, the great name of God in four letters, and the cards from the Ten to the Ace with the ten aspects of God. That the Tarot and the Cabala are linked has been taken for granted by occultists ever since, though there is no independent evidence of the connection and the Tarot does not really fit as easily into the Cabala as is claimed.

Two famous figures of the modern occult revival: Giuseppe Balsamo, known as 'Count Cagliostro', and BELOW 'Éliphas Lévi', the French writer Alphonse Louis Constant, who first gave the Tarot the prominent place in occultism which it has retained ever since.

It was Lévi who first gave the Tarot the important place in occultism which it has since retained. In the introduction to his *Doctrine and Ritual* he describes it in terms reminiscent of both Court de Gébelin and the legendary Philosopher's Stone, the goal and summit of alchemy, as a key to wisdom which is well known and found everywhere, but unknown because no one understands its true significance: 'It is in public evidence without being known to the public; no one dreams of seeking it where it actually is, and elsewhere it is lost labour to look for it.' The Tarot, he goes on, is 'a monumental and extraordinary work, strong and simple as the architecture of the pyramids, and consequently enduring like those – a book which is the sum of all the sciences, which can resolve all problems by its infinite combinations, which speaks by evoking thought, is the inspirer and regulator of all possible conceptions, the masterpiece perhaps of the human mind, assuredly one of the finest things bequeathed to us by antiquity, an universal key...' Or again, in his *History of Magic*: 'The basis of absolute hieroglyphical science was an alphabet in which deities were represented by letters, letters represented ideas, ideas were convertible into numbers, and numbers were perfect signs.' This alphabet, the Book of Thoth, he believed was preserved in the Tarot and was originally Egyptian, though he took the Tarot cards themselves to be of Jewish origin.[13]

Lévi thought that the Martinists and Rosicrucians of the late eighteenth century had understood the true meaning of the Tarot. Some of the Renaissance humanists and the medieval alchemists had also possessed the secret, and so had the author of the Book of Revelation, which has twenty-two chapters. He derived the name Tarot from *rota*, the Latin for wheel or circle, which he connected in turn with the labarum, an early Christian emblem of Jesus.

Lévi died in 1875. Though he dealt enthusiastically with the Tarot in his books, he did not produce a Tarot manual. One of his pupils, Jean Baptist Pitois, who wrote under the name of Paul Christian, concocted a kind of cabalistic astrology involving the Tarot. Christian found what he thought was evidence of the Egyptian origin of the Tarot in a book on the Egyptian mysteries attributed to Iamblichus, a Neoplatonist writer of the fourth century A.D. The book describes how the initiate into the mysteries of Osiris was led through a long gallery which contained twenty-two pictures, eleven on each side. He was shown these pictures and instructed in their meaning. Christian believed that the pictures were the original twenty-two Tarot trumps, but unfortunately no trace of anything resembling them has ever been found in Egypt.

Pictures of Tarot cards from Court de Gébelin were reproduced in 1887 in *Les Mystères de l'Horoscope* by Ely Star, the pseudonym of Eugene Jacob, a quack doctor and seller of magical amulets, whose wife was a professional fortune-teller. In 1889 a set of 'rectified' Tarot trumps designed by Oswald Wirth was published in a limited edition of a hundred copies and Wirth's designs were used in the first handbook to the Tarot, published in the same year, *Le Tarot des Bohémiens* by Papus. This was translated into English and published in London in 1892, and is still on sale.

Wirth's designs and Papus's book emanated from the same lively circle of occultists in Paris in the '80s. Wirth was a Swiss practitioner of 'curative magnetism', or medical hypnosis. He was a Mason and a member of the French branch of the Theosphical Society, which had been founded by the redoubtable Madame Blavatsky in New York in 1875, to build a bridge between science and religion, and between the Eastern and Western magical traditions. Wirth became the secretary and disciple of the Marquis Stanislas de Guaita, a young French magician of curious reputation. He was said to own a familiar spirit, which he kept locked in a cupboard when not in use, and to be able to volatilize poisons and project both them and his own body through space. He lived in rooms hung in scarlet and was accused of constantly dressing up as a cardinal, though his friends said that the truth was merely that he had a favourite red dressing-gown. An aspiring poet and admirer of Baudelaire, Guaita experimented with morphine, cocaine and hashish, and took up occultism with passionate enthusiasm on reading Eliphas Lévi. He wrote commentaries on the Tarot trumps and Wirth's Tarot designs carried his imprimatur. Wirth later published a book of his own on the pack, *Le Tarot des Imagiers du Moyen Age*.

Papus, whose real name was Gérard Encausse, was a friend of Guaita's and a member of the Kabbalistic Order of the Rose-Cross, which Guaita founded in 1888. Another member was a wild-haired and exuberantly eccentric former bank clerk named Josephin Péladan, who split away in 1890 to found his own Rosicrucian Order, organize a series of successful Rosicrucian art exhibitions, and stage two lost plays of Aeschylus which he optimistically claimed to have discovered.

Guaita died in 1897, aged thirty-six. Gérard Encausse, or Papus, was four years younger. A doctor, apparently gifted with clairvoyant diagnostic powers, and a highly successful popularizer of occultism, he joined the Theosophical Society as a young man, but he was unhappy with its concentration on oriental religion. Like Guaita, he was far more interested in the Cabala and was impressed by Eliphas Lévi's books. He published his *Traité Élémentaire de Science Occulte* in 1888, his Tarot manual in 1889, *Traité Méthodique de Science Occulte* in 1891, and *Le Tarot Divinatoire* in 1909. He took over the leadership of one of the obscure Martinist groups and attracted a large membership, though he was not successful in grafting his society on to the stem of regular Freemasonry in France. By 1912 Encausse's group had links with the Order of the Temple of the Orient, or O.T.O., a German

occult organization preoccupied with sex magic, with which Aleister Crowley in England was also involved. Encausse travelled in Russia in the 1900s and became a friend of the Tsar. He served in the French army in the First World War and died in 1916.

'Materialism', Encausse thought, 'has given us all that we can expect from it.' It was time to look back to the ancient world for the basis of a synthesis which 'condenses in a few very simple laws the whole of acquired knowledge'. The same teaching, he believed, is concealed beneath the surface of the Bible, Homer, Virgil, the Koran and the Hindu scriptures. In the West it had been handed down from the initiates of the classical mystery religions to the Gnostics, and by way of the Arabs, the alchemists, the Knights Templar, Raymond Lull and the Rosicrucians to the Masons and Martinists. The key to the teaching is the gypsy Tarot, the Bible of Bibles, the book of Thoth Hermes Trismegistus, 'the book of the primitive Revelation of ancient civilizations', which is 'the most ancient book in the world'.

Meanwhile, interest in the Tarot had been growing in England, again among the spiritual heirs of Eliphas Lévi. Kenneth Mackenzie, author of *The Royal Masonic Cyclopaedia* (1877), held Lévi in earnest reverence and visited the Master in Paris in 1861. He intended to write a guide to the Tarot but never finished it, or if he did it was not published. He had become interested in Spiritualism after seeing a ghost, and liked to refer to himself grandly as 'Baphometus, Astrologer and Spiritualist' – Baphomet being the name of the mysterious and diabolical idol which the Knights Templar were accused of worshipping. Mackenzie was connected with the Societas Rosicruciana in Anglia, a fringe-masonic group familiarly known as the Soc. Ros., which was founded in 1866. Its principal interests were the Cabala, the Hermetica, unorthodox medicine and 'the curative effects of coloured light', spiritual enlightenment and the development of clairvoyant powers.

In 1888 a brief booklet on the Tarot, mainly concerned with fortune-telling, was published by Samuel Liddell Mathers. Mathers belonged to the Soc. Ros. and in the same year played an important part in the founding in London, largely by members of the Soc. Ros., of the Hermetic Order of the Golden Dawn. Though the Golden Dawn held together for only a few years, it has been the most influential of all modern magical groups and its offshoots are still flourishing. Its two most distinguished members, in their very different ways, were W.B. Yeats and Aleister Crowley. Others included Algernon Blackwood and Arthur Machen, the thriller writers; Annie Horniman, the founder of the Abbey Theatre, Dublin; and Allan Bennett, who became a Buddhist monk and had a good deal to do with the founding of the British Buddhist Society. The most dominant figure was Mathers, who during the Order's heyday in the 1890s was its Visible Head (it had several invisible heads as well). An eccentric, imperious and gifted authority on magic, and a keen armchair general, Mathers added 'MacGregor' to his name as a mark of his Jacobite sympathies and his supposed descent from the Scottish clan. He married Moina Bergson, sister of the French philosopher Henri Bergson, who resisted his brother-in-law's efforts to convert him to magic. Mathers, who used to repeat solemnly in moments of adversity, 'There is no part of me that is not of the gods', proved too dominant and authoritarian for a group of members of the Golden Dawn, who rebelled against him and expelled him in 1900, in an upheaval which splintered the Order into quarrelling factions. Mathers spent an afternoon

MacGregor Mathers, leader of the Order of the Golden Dawn, which has been a major influence on modern Tarot interpretation; and OPPOSITE Aleister Crowley, the most notorious magician of this century and at one time a pupil of Mathers: he designed a flamboyant Tarot pack of his own, bristling with erotic symbolism.

furiously rattling dried peas in a sieve while invoking the aid of the powers of darkness against the rebels, but could not prevent the split.[14]

The Golden Dawn gave the Tarot an important place in its teaching and has been a major influence on subsequent attempts to interpret the cards. It based its Tarot doctrines on Lévi, but significantly altered his connections between the trumps and the Hebrew letters, and carried far further than he had attempted the construction of a single coherent system embracing the Cabala, the Tarot, alchemy, astrology, numerology, divination, visionary experience and ritual magic. It functioned as an occult university, teaching these subjects, conducting examinations and conferring degrees.

The Order traced its spiritual ancestry back to the Rosicrucians, whose teachings were believed to have been handed down by word of mouth to a few wise men in Europe, generation after generation. Eliphas Lévi and Kenneth Mackenzie were regarded as two of the leading adepts of this succession. Going back beyond the Rosicrucians, the secret wisdom had its roots in the Cabala, from which it could be traced to Moses, traditionally the founder of the Cabala, who learned it in ancient Egypt.

Ancient Egypt was a satisfactory place to reach. Much of the Golden Dawn's teaching was gnostic and was influenced by the Hermetica, alchemy and other products of Graeco-Egyptian gnosticism and magic. And Egyptian mythology still had the double charm of antiquity and novelty: 'The pantheon of the land of magic, Thoth, Isis, Osiris, Horus, Hathor and Maat had not become, like Venus and Cupid and Apollo a currency worn thin by use, their numinosity long since faded.'[15] Mathers and his wife spent much of their time in Paris, where they founded an Ahathoor Temple, of which Papus and Ely Star became members, and celebrated 'Egyptian Masses' with recondite ceremonial in honour of the goddess Isis.

In 1891 A. E. Waite joined the Golden Dawn. He later devised what is now the best-known 'rectified' Tarot pack and wrote the standard introduction to the Tarot in English. Born in 1857, Waite died in the London blitz in 1940. Much fun has been made of him, especially by Aleister Crowley, who satirized him mercilessly as a pompous pedant and humbug, but in the Tarot field he showed a firmer grasp of reality than his predecessors and many of his successors. He wrote a sardonic and uncharacteristically lucid preface to the second English edition of Papus's *Tarot of the Bohemians* (which he elsewhere described as 'a tissue of errors', containing 'a limited quantity of fortune-telling rubbish'), in which he said: 'The chief point regarding the history of Tarot cards, whether used as pretexts for fortune-telling or as symbols for philosophical interpretation, is that such history does not exist.' But he went on to say that 'there are tangible symbolical reasons for believing that some part of them is exceedingly old in conception, though not in form...'

Waite was another believer in a secret tradition, handed down under cover for centuries, cloaked in symbols, hints and allusions. He wrote several massive books in which like a ponderous ferret he plunged into the rabbit-holes of the Cabala, alchemy, Rosicrucianism, Freemasonry, ceremonial magic and the Grail legends to flush out the secret tradition from its hiding places. In his book on the Grail he suggested that the four sacred objects of the Grail legends – the cup, the lance, the dish and the sword – reappear in the four Tarot suits of cups, batons, coins and swords. Jessie L. Weston adopted this suggestion in a brilliant book, *From Ritual to Romance* (1920), which was influenced by Frazer's *Golden Bough* and in turn

OPPOSITE The Hanged Man and three of the minor cards – the Two of Swords, the Seven of Batons and the Eight of Coins – from the best-known modern Tarot pack, devised by BELOW Arthur Edward Waite, a member of the Golden Dawn.

THE HANGED MAN.

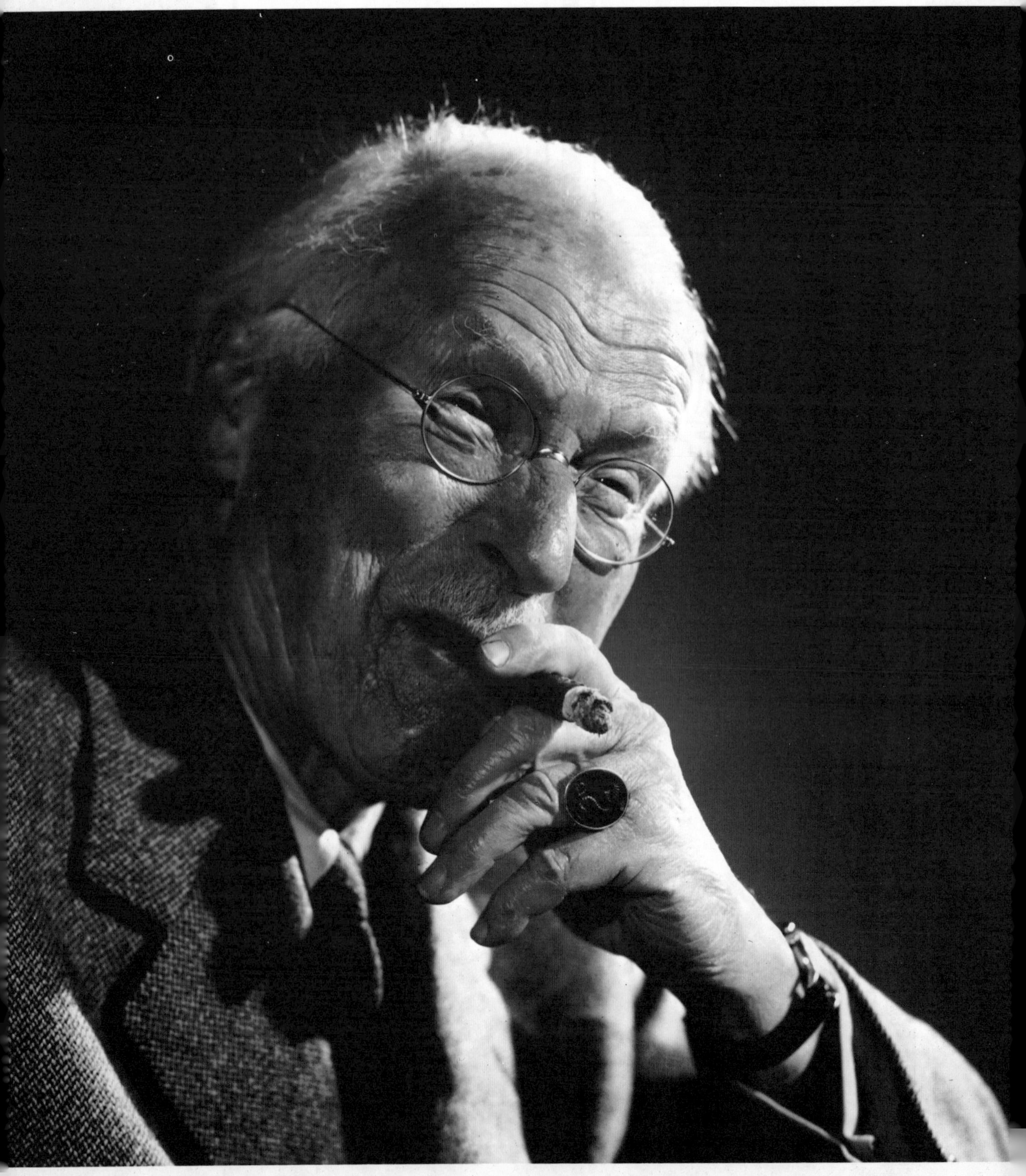

influenced T. S. Eliot's poem *The Waste Land*. She believed that the Grail legends conceal the rites and symbols of a secret cult, which had transformed primitive fertility ritual into an 'initiation into the secret of life, physical and spiritual'. She interpreted the lance and the cup as sexual emblems, 'primarily symbols of Human Life energy'. The theory fell on academically stony ground because of the lack of evidence for the existence of any such secret cult. However, the fact that the Grail legends were based on earlier Celtic traditions has led some authors along this track and Robert Graves has advanced the theory that the Tarot trumps are derived from the twenty-two letters of an ancient Celtic tree alphabet.[16]

Waite came to the Golden Dawn after flirting with Spiritualism and Theosophy. In 1903 he took control of the Order's temple in London, rewrote the rituals in a Christian spirit and set his face against the practice of magic. He attracted little support and closed down his version of the Golden Dawn in 1914. In 1910 he published *The Pictorial Key to the Tarot*, subtitled 'Being Fragments of a Secret Tradition under the Veil of Divination'. The book is impatient and contemptuous in tone, conceals far more than it conveys and on some points is deliberately misleading. It is illustrated by Waite's own 'rectified' pack, which was designed under his guidance by Pamela Colman Smith, who was also a member of the Golden Dawn and edited a magazine to which Yeats, Synge and Masefield contributed. Waite's hope that the designs would be regarded as 'very striking and beautiful' has not been realized, but the pack is the standard and the best-liked modern Tarot.

In his introductory chapter Waite commented sarcastically on various theories of the Tarot's origin and said that it would probably soon occur to someone with more zeal than sense to connect the trumps with the medieval Cathar heresy, which was suppressed by armed force when the Church organized a crusade against it in the south of France in the thirteenth century. The card called the Tower, for example, which shows a building split by lightning, cried out to be interpreted as 'the desired destruction of Papal Rome, the City on the seven hills, with the pontiff and his temporal power cast down from the spiritual edifice when it is riven by the wrath of God'. 'The possibilities', Waite said, 'are so numerous and persuasive that they almost deceive in their expression one of the elect who has invented them.'

Precisely this theory was put forward forty-five years later, though very cautiously and tentatively, by a distinguished historian, Sir Steven Runciman, and has gained its own following. Another, similar theory is that the Tarot may have been invented as a visual teaching aid by the heretical Waldensians, who lasted far longer as an organized group than the Cathars and in fact have survived to this day. They were founded by Peter Waldo in the late twelfth century and were persecuted by Rome. Most of them took refuge in the Alps, on the borders of Italy and France, where Catholic pressure against them continued into the eighteenth and nineteenth centuries.[17]

Aleister Crowley joined the Golden Dawn in 1898. Born in 1875, Crowley was brought up among the Plymouth Brethren, who unintentionally instilled in him a lifelong loathing of Christianity and the conviction that he was the Great Beast 666 of Revelation, whose mission was to destroy Christianity and replace it with the new religion of Crowleyanity. He was at first a devoted pupil of Mathers, but later fell out with him and summoned up the great demon Beelzebub and forty-nine attendant demons, whom he packed off to chastise the erring Mathers in Paris.

Carl Gustav Jung, the famous Swiss psycho-analyst, who was interested in alchemy, astrology and the occult: his ideas have influenced modern Tarot interpretation.

When Mathers died in the influenza epidemic of 1918, some suspected that Crowley had murdered him by black magic.

Crowley founded his own order of the Silver Star, achieved high rank in the O.T.O. under the splendiferous title of 'Supreme and Holy King of Ireland, Iona and all the Britains that are in the sanctuary of the Gnosis', or more briefly as Baphomet, and acquired a reputation in newspaper headlines as 'the Wickedest Man in the World'. He wrote his own guide to the Tarot, *The Book of Thoth*, which was published in a limited edition of two hundred copies in 1944. Though subtitled 'A Short Essay on the Tarot of the Egyptians', it takes up close to three hundred pages of print. Condemning other people's rectified Tarots as 'gross, senseless, pitifully grotesque' – no doubt with Waite's pack mainly in mind – Crowley produced his own designs, which were executed for him by Frieda Harris, the wife of a Liberal politician, Sir Percy Harris. She was with Crowley when he died in 1947 and presided over his cremation at Brighton.

Crowley's treatment of the Tarot was naturally influenced by what he thought were his own views of it during his previous incarnation on earth as Eliphas Lévi. He explained that Lévi had deliberately concealed the correct attribution of the trumps to the Hebrew letters, because he had been initiated into the Tarot by an occult order which had sworn him to secrecy. Crowley was more powerfully influenced, however, by the teaching of the Golden Dawn, which he had adapted into his own magical system. Sex was a crucial ingredient of Crowley's 'magick'. His interpretation of the Tarot and his redesigned Tarot cards bristle with erotic symbolism.

Crowley was not the first to see the cards in this light. On the contrary, sexual symbolism is seldom far beneath the surface of the most pious and outwardly respectable of the earlier books on the Tarot, including Waite's, which is riddled with innuendo. This does not mean that the earlier authors practised sexual magic, as Crowley did, but it does imply a less austere attitude to sex than is attributed to them by pure-minded admirers. To take only one example at this point, the trump called Justice shows a woman holding a sword in one hand and a pair of scales in the other. The symbol is a traditional one and seems quite obvious and straightforward. But in most Tarot interpretations the sword is a phallus and the scales are testicles. This explains Papus's otherwise mystifying description of the woman as the Mother, who is 'Nature performing the function of Eve'. Crowley simply called her the Woman Satisfied.

In the year of Crowley's death, the American occultist Paul Foster Case published *The Tarot: A Key to the Wisdom of the Ages*. Case, who was born in 1884, was principally influenced by the Golden Dawn and Waite, and his book is the fullest and most interesting account of the pack from this point of view. He claimed to be head of the Golden Dawn in the United States and Canada, with the title of Praemonstrator General, and later founded an organization called the Builders of the Adytum, which remained in existence after his death in 1954, with its headquarters in Los Angeles. Case produced yet another set of 'rectified' cards, drawn for him by Jessie Burns Parke. They are modelled closely on Waite's but with some variations in detail.

There are several other 'rectified' Tarots on sale, though none of them approaches the versions by Waite and Case in popularity. One is the 'Egyptian' pack

William Butler Yeats, here portrayed by Augustus John, took a deeper interest in the Tarot than any other leading writer of his time.

designed for Elbert Benjamine, an astrologer who wrote numerous books under the pseudonym Zain and founded the Church of Light in Los Angeles. Another was designed by Manly Palmer Hall, also the author of many books and the founder of the Philosophical Research Society, Los Angeles. Yet another has been produced by the Insight Institute.

P. D. Ouspensky included a brief survey of the Tarot, heavily influenced by Wirth, in his book *A New Model of the Universe*, published in London in 1931. Ouspensky was the leading disciple of the famous Russian mystic and teacher, Gurdjieff, and devoted most of his life to the exploration of Gurdjieff's ideas. His treatment of the Tarot includes interesting meditations on some of the trumps.

Tarot symbolism is used, though only to a very limited extent, in T. S. Eliot's *The Waste Land*, in a brief scene in which a clairvoyant and wise-woman, Madame Sosostris, reads the cards. The Hanged Man and the Wheel of Fortune are mentioned, and the card of 'the man with three staves' (the Three of Batons). Eliot explained in his notes to the poem that he knew little of the Tarot and had used it arbitrarily to suit his own convenience. He invented some cards which are not in the pack at all – the Drowned Phoenician Sailor, for instance, and the Lady of the Rocks. He associated the Three of Batons (in Waite's version, evidently) with the Fisher King of the Grail legends, the crippled ruler whose wound must be healed before the waste land can blossom. The Hanged Man reminded him of the hanged gods of Frazer's *Golden Bough* and also of the risen Christ seen by the disciples on the road to Emmaus. There is a much more extensive and knowledgeable literary treatment of the Tarot in *The Greater Trumps*, a novel by the mystical writer Charles Williams, who was a member of Waite's reconstituted Golden Dawn.

W. B. Yeats did not write a book on the Tarot, which is a pity, as he was far more interested in it than Eliot or any other writer of similar stature. Yeats was fascinated by magic, mythology and fairy-lore, and took a prominent part in the occult revival, which he described in a telling phrase as 'the revolt of the soul against intellect'. As a young art student in Dublin in the 1880s he was a member of a Hermetic Society, to which he proposed 'that whatever the great poets had affirmed in their finest moments was the nearest we could come to an authoritative religion, and that their mythology, their spirits of water and wind, were but literal truth'. He once met a young man who claimed to have inherited magical powers and invited him to a demonstration. 'He and a friend of his kill a black cock, and burn herbs in a big bowl, but nothing happens except that the friend repeats again and again, "O, my God", and when I ask him why he has said that, does not know that he has spoken; and I feel that there is something very evil in the room . . .'[18]

Yeats and his hermetic friends were seized with enthusiasm for oriental wisdom and turned themselves into the Dublin branch of the Theosophical Society. Yeats moved to London and in 1890 resigned from the Theosophical Society and joined the Golden Dawn. Kathleen Raine has said that 'his true education was a most serious, thorough and practical knowledge of magic and its literature, including alchemy, through the Golden Dawn, together with an introduction to the Platonic and Eastern traditions through the Theosophical Society'.[19] After the upheaval in the Golden Dawn in 1900, Yeats took command of the rebel faction, with the title of Imperator and clad presumably in 'the flame scarlet robe of Fire and Severity' proper to his office. He soon ceased to play any active role, though he remained a

The Judgment of Paris, painted in the early 16th century by Lucas Cranach the Elder: in this myth the Renaissance saw a symbol of opposites and their reconciliation. OVERLEAF A selection of cards from three minchiate packs, which have a far larger number of cards than what is now regarded as the standard Tarot pack.

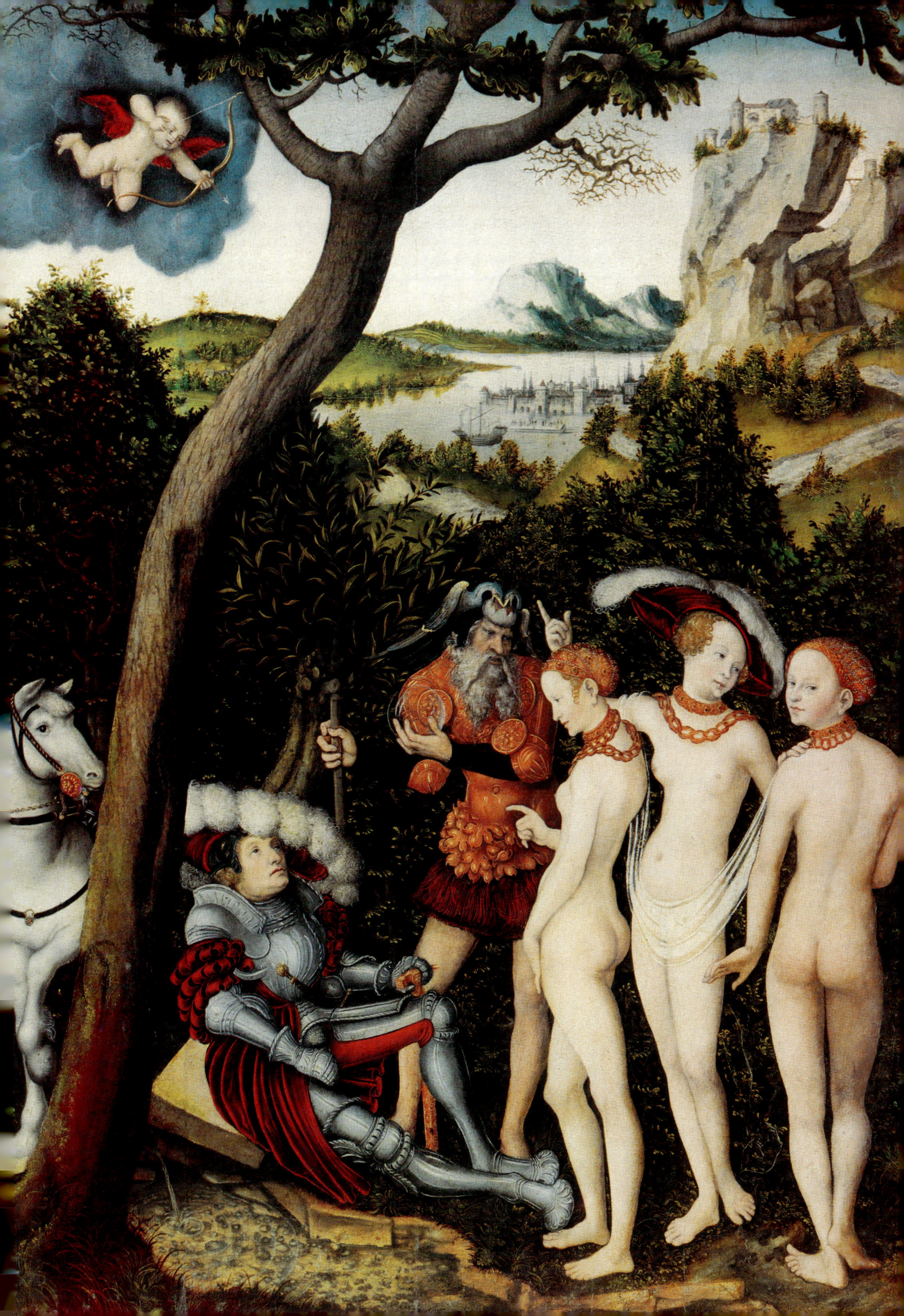

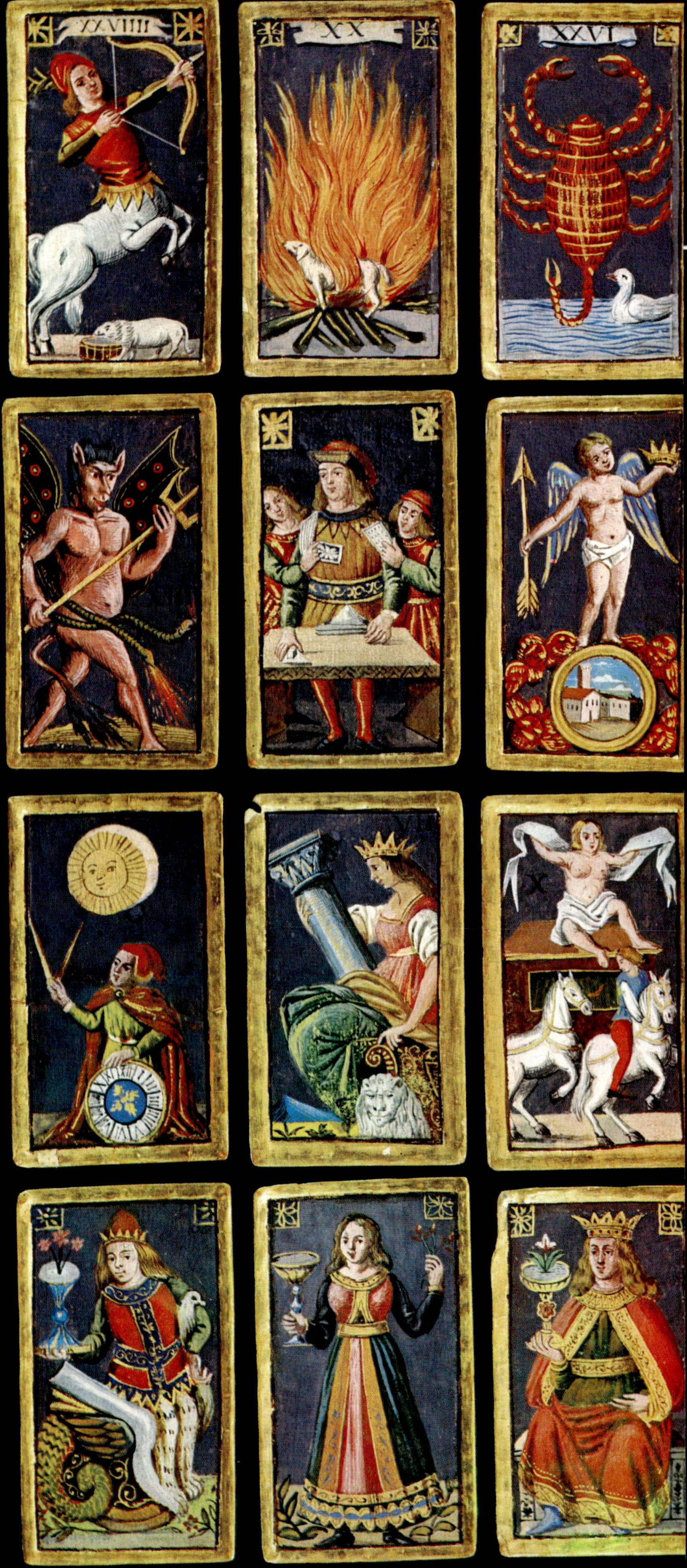
XXVIIII
XX
XXVI

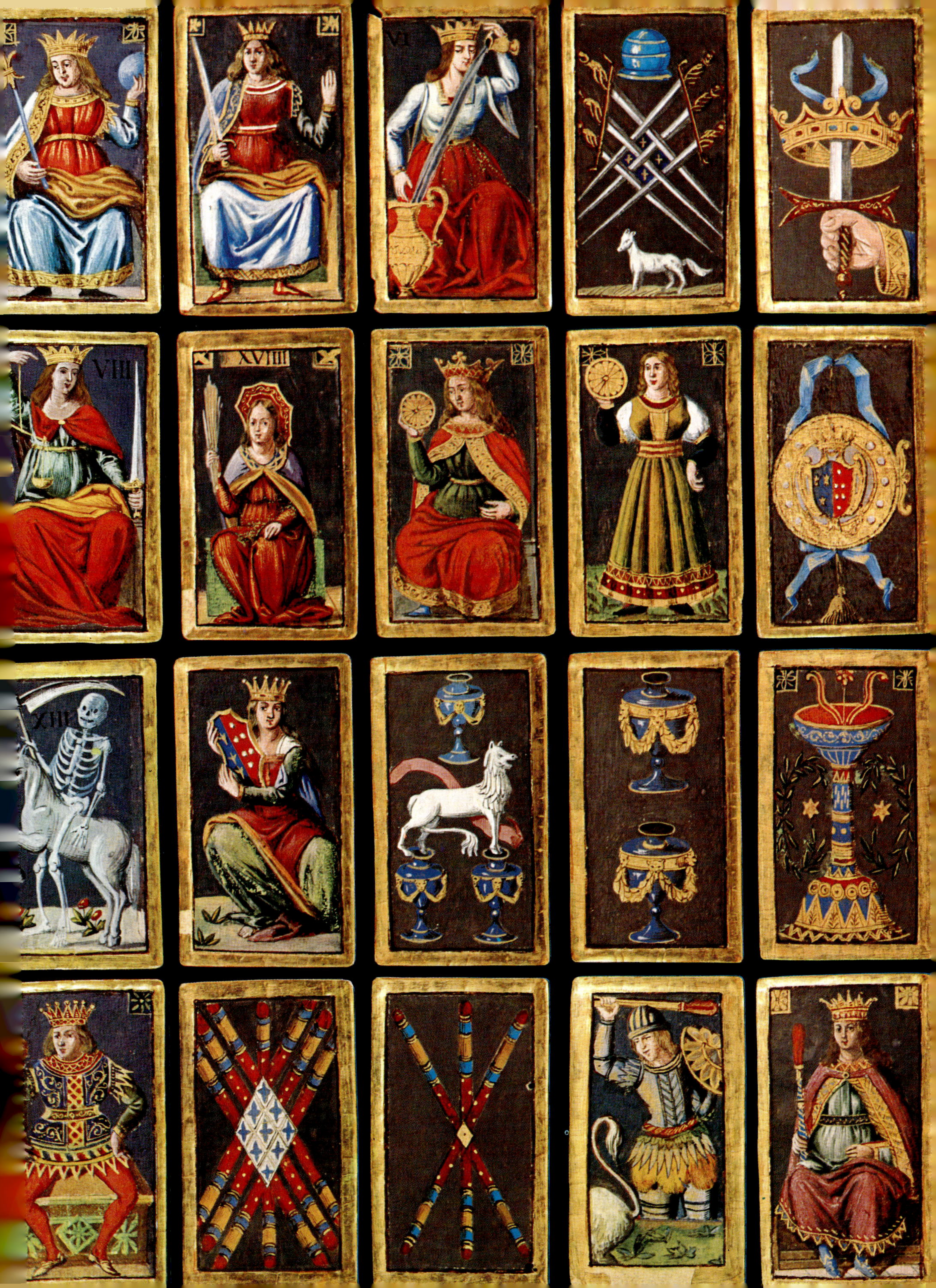
VIII
XVIIII

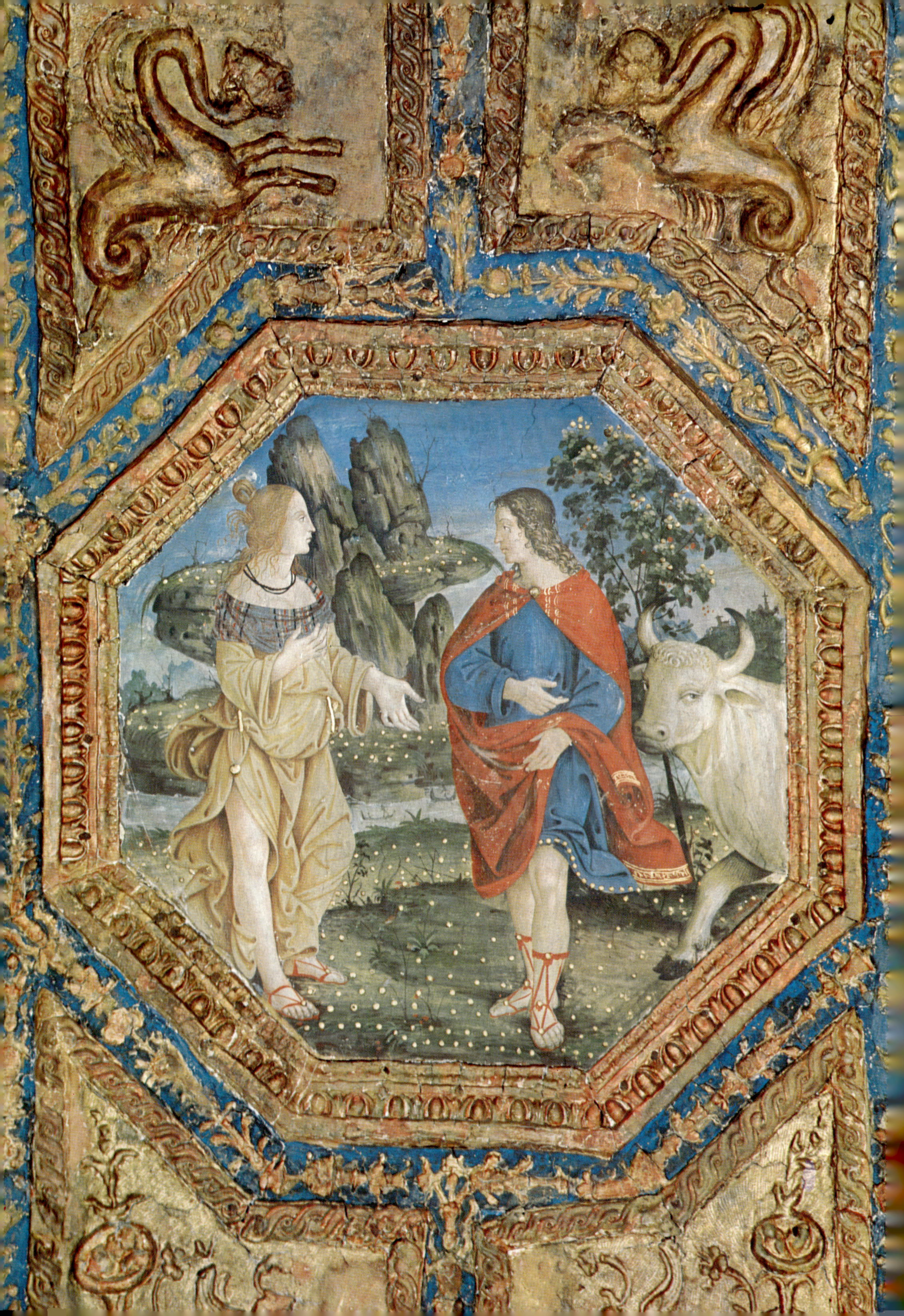

The bull, emblem of the Borgia Pope Alexander VI, identified with Apis, the sacred bull of ancient Egypt, in a painting by Pinturicchio: the Pope of the Tarot is frequently connected with Taurus, the sign of the bull.

member of one of the Golden Dawn's offshoots, the Stella Matutina or Order of the Morning Star, until about 1923.

Yeats first met MacGregor Mathers, who seemed to him 'a figure of romance', when they were both using the British Museum reading room. It was through Mathers that Yeats began experiments which convinced him that 'images well up before the mind's eye from a deeper source than conscious or subconscious memory'. For a time he invoked the moon just before going to bed, and after doing this for several nights he saw between sleeping and waking a vision of a galloping centaur and then of a beautiful woman, standing on a pedestal and shooting an arrow at a star. These visions recall the images of Ficino and Bruno, which expressed and contained the nature of a planet. Yeats found that sometimes, by thinking of a visual image, he could conjure up an appropriate vision in another person's mind. For example, he once used a symbol to 'send' another man to the Garden of Eden, which the latter saw as 'a walled garden on the top of a high mountain, and in the middle of it a tree with great birds in the branches, and fruit out of which, if you held a fruit to your ear, came the sound of fighting'.[20]

Yeats owned his own Tarot pack in his student days, and his concern with the Tarot was part of his interest in visual images as containers of inherent power, which affect a person's mind independently of his intentions. The use of Tarot cards to evoke visions and explore mysterious worlds was a technique of the Golden Dawn, and both the Golden Dawn and the Theosophical Society taught that human thoughts, desires, imaginings and fantasies have a separate reality on a plane of their own, the 'astral plane'. Yeats believed that by musing on certain symbols he came face to face with the *Anima Mundi*, 'the Soul of the World', a cosmic well of memories, as it were, which Yeats said was 'independent of embodied individual memories, though they constantly enrich it with their images and their thoughts'.[21]

Yeats and the occultists were not alone in speculation of this kind. William James, the philosopher and psychologist, who helped to found the American Society for Psychical Research in 1885, was impressed by the ability of a famous Spiritualist medium, Mrs Leonora Piper, to produce accurate accounts of past events which could not have been known to her normal conscious self. He suggested that she might be able in trance to tap 'some cosmic reservoir in which the memories of earth are stored'.[22]

Later, C. G. Jung put forward the theory of the 'collective unconscious'. Jung himself experienced visions, ghostly entities and other paranormal phenomena, and was interested in and influenced by gnosticism, alchemy, astrology, folklore and the occult revival in Europe. He believed that human brains have been shaped and affected by the experiences of mankind over millions of years, and he suggested that in a deeper level of the mind than the personal unconscious there is the collective unconscious, which contains certain very primitive 'images' or ways of thinking. These are the 'archetypes', which find expression in religion, mythology, philosophy, science, symbolism, dreams, visions and fantasies. Jungian theory has been one more influence on modern interpretations of the Tarot.

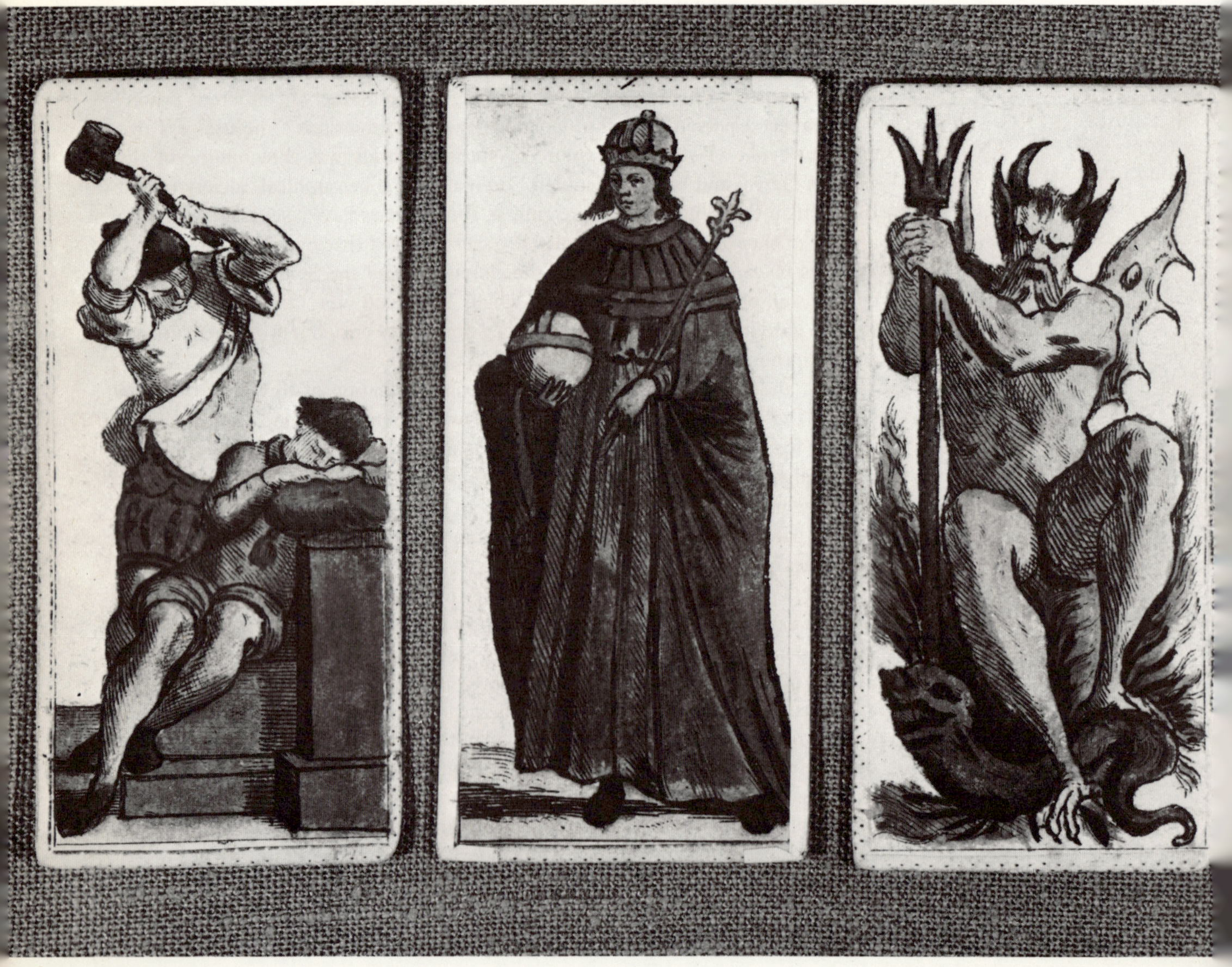

SECTION II

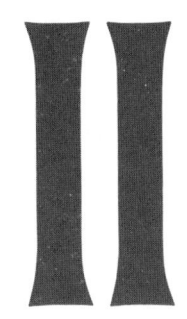

INTERPRETATION

All attempts to explain symbols are beset with pitfalls. Not only will the same symbol mean different things to different people but, almost by definition, a symbol can never be explained adequately in any case. It represents something else, and it is used very often precisely because the 'something else' cannot be stated fully in words. The meaning of a simple sign, like a red traffic light for 'stop', is clear enough, but more powerful symbols are meant to express what is otherwise inexpressible. Words can serve only as pointers to their meaning, not as substitutes for them.

Symbols frequently bring together in one image a wide range of connotations and can be interpreted simultaneously at different levels. This is true, for instance, of the sexual symbolism which lurks behind so many explanations of the Tarot. The general determination to discover erotic imagery in the cards is founded on one of the basic doctrines of the whole European tradition of magic, the belief that man is a microcosm, or 'little world', a miniature replica of the greater world outside him. It follows that whatever exists in man exists also in the greater world. Sexual desire is a cardinal factor in human behaviour and the spur to the creation of life, and so it is assumed to have a corresponding importance in the inner and mysterious workings of the cosmos, which the Tarot is believed to reveal. But physical desire can also be an image or parallel of something nobler: spiritual longing and aspiration. The use of erotic symbolism to convey spiritual truths has a long history and underlies many interpretations of the Tarot. The 'death' of the phallus when it collapses in orgasm, for example, and its subsequent 'resurrection' in renewed vigour and potency, is for many writers a symbol of human spiritual potential, a sign that there can be life beyond the grave, and at the same time a reference to the unending processes of exhaustion and renewal, death and new life, in the world of nature.

The Tarot trumps are generally explained as symbols of an inner reality concealed behind surface appearances, but within this broad context there are many different approaches. The cards are taken to stand for stages of human life and spiritual progress, beginning with the Fool or the Juggler and ending with the last of the trumps, the World. But alternatively they can be treated in the reverse order, so that the progress starts with the World and culminates in the Juggler or the Fool. Another approach, influenced by Jungian theory, splits the trumps into

From an Italian pack of the early 18th century: LEFT to RIGHT an execution curiously entitled the Hanged Man; the Female Pope; and the Devil.

two sets. The first set, from the Fool to the Wheel of Fortune, is concerned with responses to the outside world into which each human being is born, and with the development of a personality. Then comes a turning-point, appropriately located in the Wheel, at which the individual begins to look away from the world outside him and towards the world inside him, to search for wholeness and happiness not in his environment but in himself. The stages of this second part of his spiritual journey are shown by the second set of trumps, from Strength to the World. However, in practice interpretations on these lines do not seem very convincing.

Explanations of individual cards have drawn on an immense quantity of material – gnostic, cabalistic, alchemical, astrological, mythological, Christian, Theosophical, Jungian – and ingredients from different systems are blended together in the search for the truth thought to be hidden behind all traditions. Oswald Wirth, whose influence on Tarot interpretation has been considerable, said that 'a symbol can always be studied from an infinite number of points of view, and each thinker has the right to discover in the symbol a new meaning corresponding to the logic of his own conceptions. As a matter of fact symbols are precisely intended to awaken ideas sleeping in our consciousness. They arouse a thought by means of suggestion and thus cause the truth which lies hidden in the depths of our spirit to reveal itself.'[1]

Writers on the Tarot, on the whole, have accepted this claim in principle while denying it in practice. Broadly speaking, there are two ways to set about investigating what the Tarot means to you, as distinct from what it may have been intended to mean originally. One is to look at the cards and see what they suggest, allowing the mind to wander gently around them while ideas and associations come to the surface. This is recommended in practically all the textbooks, if only as an exercise in self-discovery, and it could lead to the construction of a system embracing the whole set of trumps. The other method is not to evolve a system from the cards but the other way round, to start with a system and fit the cards into it. The distinction between the two approaches is not as clear in practice as in theory, because exponents of the second method naturally allow their minds to wander round the cards too, but they will be more uncompromising in excluding associations which do not suit the preconceived pattern or more rigorous in forcing awkward ideas into it.

The second method always involves wrenching the symbolism and order of the trumps about, so as to make them fit into a set scheme, whether they want to or not; hence the numerous 'rectified' packs. When they have all been slotted or forced into place, the interpreter usually claims that he has now penetrated to the true and original meaning of the Tarot, which everyone else has been too blind to see. All the same, it is the second method which produces the most interesting results, and this is true whether you are mainly concerned with what the cards mean to you or with Tarot interpretation as part of the history of the modern revival of occultism.

1 THE CABALA

Although Christian, Jungian and other symbolic systems have affected modern interpretations, the set scheme which has had the greatest influence is based on the Cabala, and a short sketch of it is an essential preliminary to a detailed consideration of the Tarot trumps themselves. The Cabala is complicated, paradoxical and abstruse. Anything said about it in brief is bound to be oversimplified and even to talk of 'the' Cabala may be misleading if it suggests a single consistent structure, which the Cabala is not. It is a body of mystical speculations and teachings, elaborated by Jewish writers in the Middle Ages on the basis of older Jewish traditions and gnostic and Neoplatonic ideas. Renaissance humanists were interested in it and a Christian Cabala developed, from which modern occult varieties of Cabala are descended. It is the modern occult Cabala which is described here.

The Cabala explains how the world came into existence from God, how the world and man are organized, and how man can reach God. Its teaching is summarized in a symbol called the Tree of Life (see Diagram One, next page). This is an arrangement of ten circles in three columns or pillars. The circles stand for the *sefiroth*, or 'spheres', which are aspects of God. Like written Hebrew, the Tree reads from right to left as you look at it. The right-hand column is called the Pillar of Mercy and the spheres in it are classified as male, positive and active. The left-hand column is the Pillar of Judgment or Severity and its spheres are feminine, negative and passive. These two pillars represent two great opposites in God, the divine love which creates and upholds, and the divine wrath which punishes and destroys. The spheres of the Middle Pillar balance and reconcile those on either side. Reading from the top of the diagram downwards, the spheres are arranged in three triangles, with the tenth, Malkuth, left over at the bottom. Each triangle contains two opposing forces and a third factor, the common centre which holds them together. The universe, in other words, is based on deployments of two opposites with a third, uniting and transcending principle. This is equally true of man, and the Tree is sometimes given the form of a man's body, showing man as an image of the greater world outside him. The Tree is the framework or skeleton, as it were, of man, the universe and the divine.

The God of the Cabala is more It than He. It is *En Sof*, 'the Infinite', a vast, hidden and incomprehensible godhead. No qualities can be either ascribed or denied to it. You cannot say that it is good or evil, just or unjust, real or unreal, but neither can you say that it is not any of these things. It is called 'Nothing', since it has no qualities, but it is also everything, the One, the supreme unity of which all things are part.

In the Cabala the world does not come into existence by creation, as something made by a Maker, but by emanation, a flowing out of something from the godhead. The 'something' is described as a light or a ray and from it come further emanations or rays, until there are ten of them in all. These ten emanations are the sefiroth, the 'splendid lights', which are facets of the divine personality, types of the divine energy and stages in the process by which the unknown godhead makes itself manifest in the world. All phenomena can be classified in terms of them and all phenomena contain something of the divine.

The Tree of Life of the Cabala, showing the ten *sefiroth* or spheres.

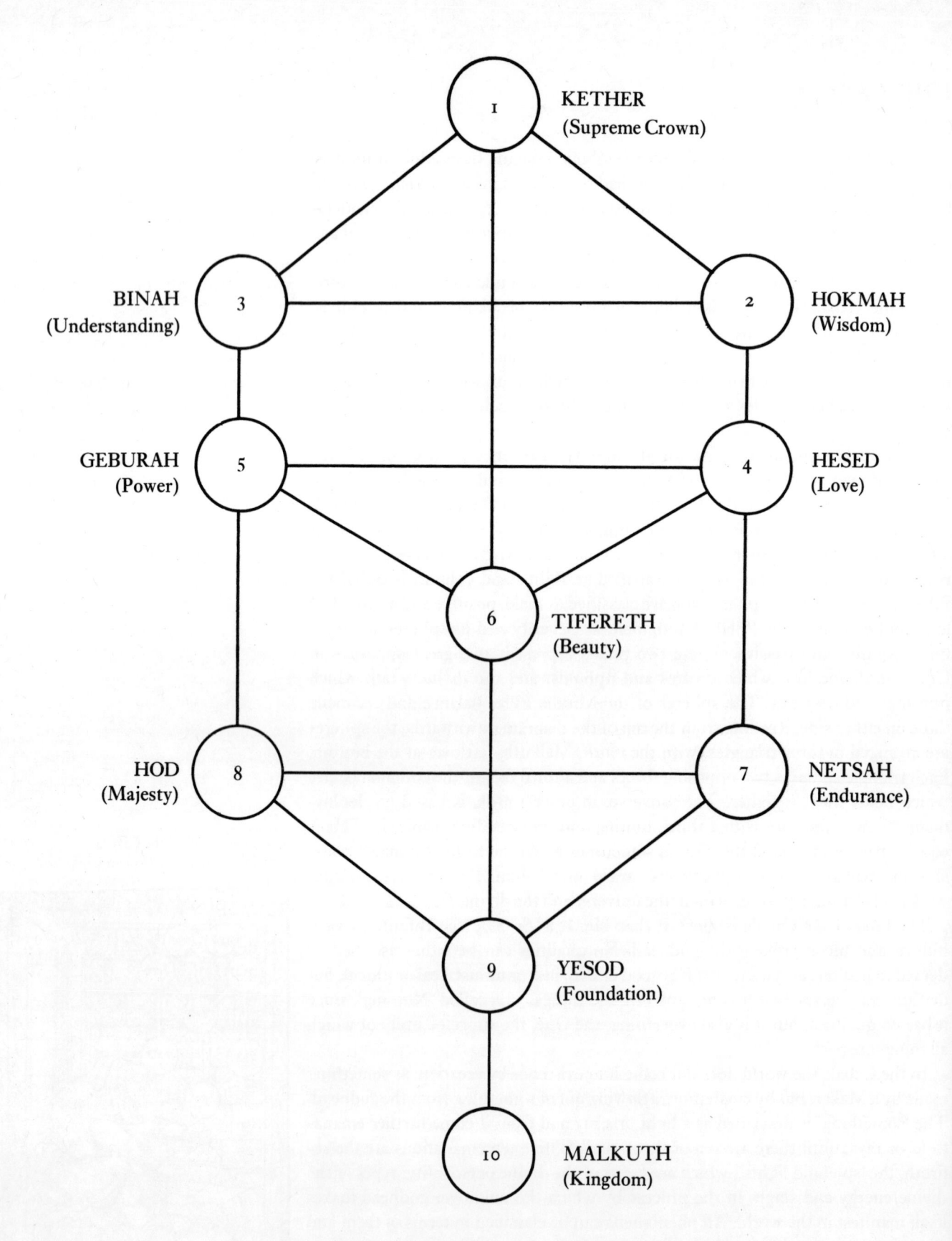

DIAGRAM ONE: THE TREE OF LIFE (See previous page.)

The sefiroth are also the steps of a winding stair of spiritual ascent. On the diagram of the Tree of Life twenty-two lines are drawn, which connect the sefiroth together and are called the Twenty-two Paths (see Diagram Two, page 54). To each line is allotted one of the letters of the Hebrew alphabet and one of the Tarot trumps, whose symbolism is taken as a key to the nature and experience of each path. Like the ladder arrangement of the 'Mantegna' cards, the Tree of Life runs in two directions. Reading from the top down, it shows the paths which lead from God to man. Reading from the bottom up, it shows the paths which man must negotiate to reach God, and reaching God can mean either the mystical goal of being absorbed into the unity of the divine or the magical goal of becoming the divine, of making oneself God.

The spheres of the highest triangle on the Tree are called the Supernals and are spoken of in awed and honorific language. They are aspects of God's abstract thought and are beyond comprehension by the human intellect alone. Between them and the lower sefiroth is the Abyss, the great gulf which separates the ideal from the actual, the infinite from the finite, divine consciousness from ordinary human consciousness. In terms of man the Supernals are the 'superconscious', a higher form of consciousness which in some ways resembles the Jungian collective unconscious.

Kether, the first emanation from the hidden godhead, is called 'the Inscrutable Height' or 'the Ancient One'. It is the sphere of God as the One, the Prime Mover, the Almighty and the Ancient of Days. Its symbols are the crown, for sovereignty, and the point for unity. 'In Kether', the Golden Dawn taught, 'is the Divine White Brilliance, the scintillation and coruscation of the Divine Glory – that Light which surpasseth the glory of the Sun and beside which the light of mortals is but darkness, and concerning which it is not fitting that we should speak more fully.'[2] The soul which can reach this sphere achieves union with God.

God contains two great opposing principles, active and passive, which are the Father and Mother of the universe, so to speak, Hokmah and Binah. These two spheres are the roots of all polarity, of positive and negative, male and female, mind and matter and all the opposites of life. Hokmah, called the Father of Fathers, is male and active, and the sphere in which the divine will to create is first manifested. It is the creative divine Word, the force behind everything positive and dynamic, the impulse which originates action.

The opposite sefira, Binah, is the Mother, the Throne, the Great Sea, the primeval chaotic waters of Genesis which were inert but contained in potential all the teeming life of the world. Hokmah acts and Binah is acted upon, Hokmah thrusts and Binah responds, Hokmah is God's active Wisdom, Binah his passive Understanding. Binah lies behind everything that is potential rather than actual, and stable rather than changing. Dion Fortune, who wrote the standard modern occult textbook on the Cabala, said that the Supernals demonstrate that 'everything rests upon the principle of the stimulation of the inert yet all-potential [Binah, female] by the dynamic principle [Hokmah, male], which draws its energy direct from the source of all energy [Kether, God]'. The sexual application is obvious, but the principle goes far beyond sex. 'In this concept lie tremendous keys of knowledge; it is one of the most important points in the mysteries.'[3]

In the Tree's second triangle, form is imposed on what is at this stage formless, substance is given to ideas. The two opposing principles, Hesed and Geburah, are lower reflections of Hokmah and Binah above them. They govern the interplay of creation and destruction on which all life is based. Hesed is the kindly loving divine force of construction and organization, which systematically builds things up. Geburah is the fierce and wrathful divine force which breaks them down, destroying all creatures and ideas when their day is done. They are held in equal balance by the sixth sefira, Tifereth, the reflection of Kether, which is the beauty and harmony of ordered nature and the vital energy of the life force, the drive which impels life to continue. Tifereth is said to be the highest sphere to which the human mind can attain in any normal state of consciousness: the higher levels can only be reached in supernormal states.

In the third triangle the same pattern of forces appears again lower down the scale. Netsah is the positive force of attraction and cohesion in the universe, which holds things together. It is the sphere of animal drives, the senses and passions, instinctive and unconsidered reactions, the natural as against the contrived. The opposite sefira, Hod, is the negative force behind flux and change, and is the sphere of mental faculties, intelligence, reason, considered reactions, the artificial and contrived. Cohesion and flux are held together in the sefira Yesod, 'the foundation of all active forces in God'. This is the sphere of the moon, whose constantly changing phases are part of a stable cycle, and which by old tradition governs the increase and decrease, growth and decay, of all things on earth. When the Tree is shown in the form of a human body, Yesod is the genitals. It is 'the spout for the waters from on high', the channel between divine vital energy and the earth or earthly man. In terms of human psychology it is the sphere of the unconscious mind.

Finally, at the foot of the Tree is the sefira Malkuth, which is the material world of earth and the physical body and brain of man, but which is also the whole manifest kingdom of God, the union of the sefiroth in the entire Tree. It is frequently called the Shekinah, the divine presence in the world, thought of as a feminine element in God, the divine Queen who is both Daughter and Bride. It is through Yesod, 'the spout', that the higher sefiroth flow into her. As the last of the sefiroth she is in exile, fallen into matter, with the implication that part of God is exiled from himself, and the great task of the Jewish Cabala was to reunite the Shekinah with her 'husband', to restore the wholeness of God. And as the last sefira she is the entrance to the divine, the sphere in which man begins his ascent of the Tree.

The idea of climbing the rungs of a spiritual ladder towards God came into occultism from other sources besides the Cabala. The sefiroth fit into the old classical and medieval picture of the universe as a set of spheres, arranged inside each other like the skins of an onion. The innermost sphere is that of the earth, corresponding to Malkuth in the Cabala. Outside it in turn are the spheres of the seven planets known in antiquity – the moon (Yesod), Mercury (Hod), Venus (Netsah), the sun (Tifereth), Mars (Geburah), Jupiter (Hesed) and Saturn (Binah). Outside these again is the sphere of the zodiac (Hokmah), and finally the sphere of God as Prime Mover (Kether).

It was long believed that each human soul came originally from God and descended to its incarnation on earth in a physical body by way of the planetary spheres, acquiring characteristics from each sphere in turn. After death it retraced its steps, rising up through the spheres and shedding characteristics in each of them until, if it was worthy, it returned to its source in the divine. It was also believed that this ascent could be made not only after death but, by mystical and magical techniques, during earthly life. In either case, however, the ascent would be difficult and dangerous. Hordes of demons lurked in the atmosphere between the earth and the moon, and each planetary sphere had its guardians who would try to turn the soul back. In gnostic texts of the early centuries after Christ, the Archons, the great spiritual powers which rule the planets, resent the soul's liberation from its imprisonment in matter on earth and oppose it. So do the 'gate-keepers' of the celestial palaces in the Jewish *Hekhaloth* texts, of the third century A.D. onwards, which describe the visionary experiences of mystics rising towards God's throne through the halls of heaven. To pass the Archons or gate-keepers the soul needed the correct passwords and certain magical diagrams and talismans. Similarly in modern occultism, the ascent of the paths is considered dangerous, and to be undertaken only with the proper equipment of knowledge and training. It is easy to stray from the right track and there are plenty of intelligences at large among the spheres which will try to trap the unwary.

The Tree with its paths is not only a ladder of spiritual descent and ascent, but a diagram of the world and everything in it. It is like a desk with thirty-two pigeon-holes, allotted to the ten sefiroth and the twenty-two paths and Tarot trumps, and all ideas and phenomena can be fitted into their appropriate slots in it. Elaborate systems of correspondences were worked out by Mathers and Crowley, which classify planets and signs of the zodiac, gods and goddesses, animals, plants, colours, precious stones, geometric figures and images in terms of the sefiroth and the paths.

These systems rest ultimately on the link between the Tarot and the Hebrew alphabet. The groundwork for them was found in the *Sefer Yetsirah*, the Book of Creation or Book of Formation, written in Hebrew by an unknown author some time between the third and sixth centuries A.D. The *Sefer Yetsirah* was translated into Latin and published in Paris in 1552. Eliphas Lévi praised it as 'a ladder of truths', and it was translated into French by Papus and into English by William Wynn Westcott, who was one of the founders of the Golden Dawn and Supreme Magus of the Societas Rosicruciana in Anglia. It is a short, gnostic, visionary and singularly obscure text, which mingles late classical number-lore with Jewish letter-mysticism.

The *Sefer Yetsirah* says that God 'engraved his name', or manifested his identity, in the universe through three means of expression – numbers, letters and sounds – 'in thirty-two wonderful paths of wisdom', which are the ten sefiroth and the twenty-two Hebrew letters. The sefiroth here are the numbers from one to ten, regarded as the essential numbers from which all other numbers are formed, and by extension as basic building-blocks of the construction of the universe (as they were in Pythagorean philosophy). The Hebrew letters are also regarded as structural components of the universe and the *Sefer Yetsirah* goes on to relate them to the heavens and the calendar, time and space and the world of man. Twelve of the letters are connected with the signs of the zodiac, the months of the year, twelve organs of the body and twelve human senses and activities. Seven other letters are assigned to the seven planets and days of the week, seven directions of

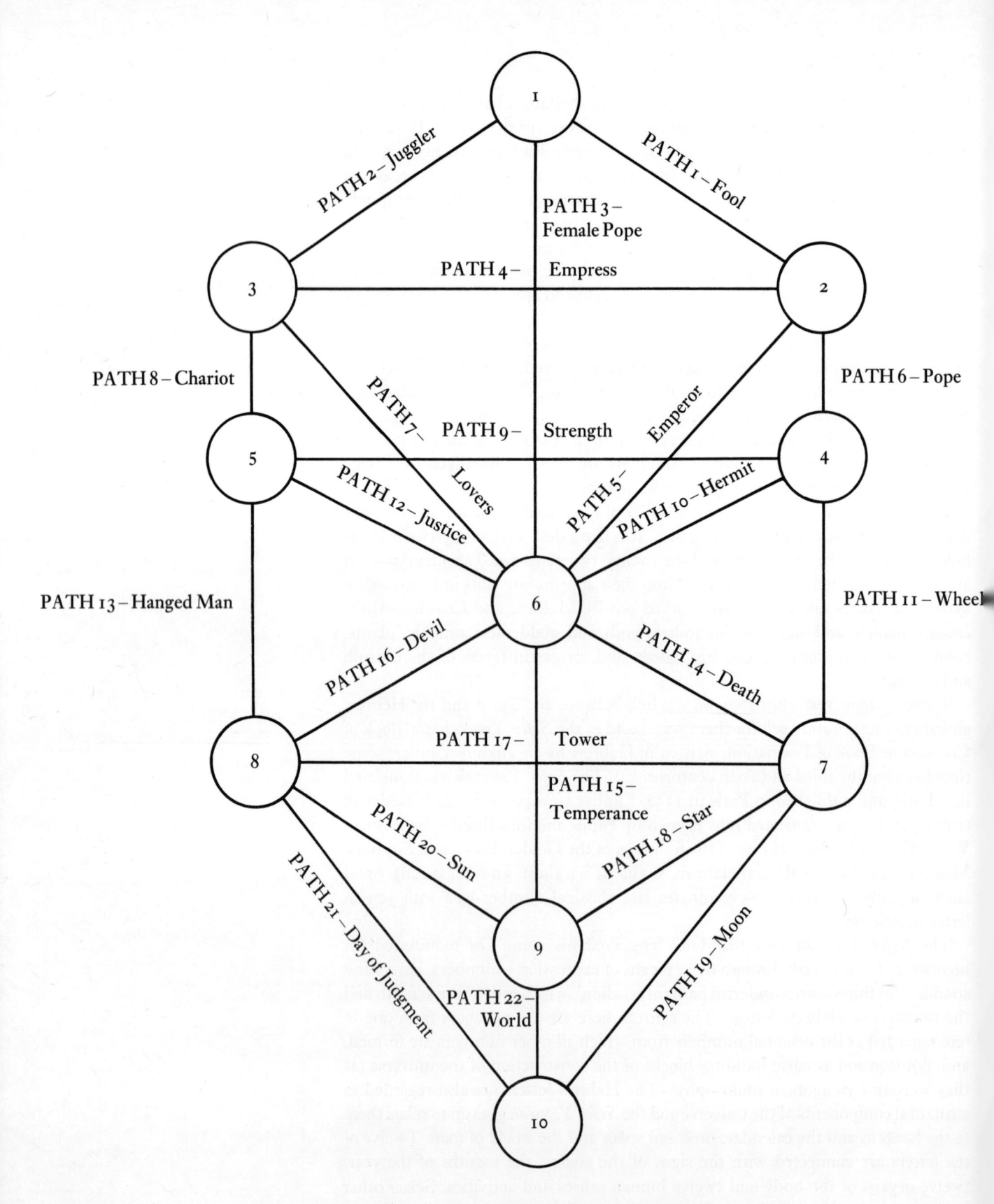

DIAGRAM TWO: THE TWENTY-TWO PATHS (See page 51).

space (east, west, north, south, above, below and the centre), and seven human conditions. The three remaining letters – *aleph, mem* and *shin* – are called 'mother letters' and are linked with three elements – air, water and fire; three divisions of the universe – heaven, earth and the atmosphere between them; three seasons of the year – spring, summer and winter; and three parts of the body – head, chest and belly. Everything in the world, in effect, is made of numbers and letters, and can be classified in terms of them.

Westcott thought that the *Sefer Yetsirah* 'sheds light on many mystic forms and ceremonies yet extant, notably upon Freemasonry, the Tarot, and the later Kabalah, and is a great aid to the comprehension of the Astro-Theosophic schemes of the Rosicrucians'. It was certainly a great aid to Tarot interpretation, though its author knew nothing of the Tarot pack, because it provided a pleasingly antique basis for a system of correspondences between the Hebrew letters and other phenomena which would illuminate the meaning of the Tarot trumps. Diagram Three (page 57) shows the astrological correspondences of the *Sefer Yetsirah*, as arranged by Westcott, though they have been altered by later authors. (The attributions are not entirely clear in the original text: planets in modern systems are connected with both the sefiroth and the twenty-two letters and trumps.) Diagram Three also shows the traditional symbolism of each letter – the object which its shape was supposed to represent – and each letter's number value.

The Hebrew letters did double duty as numbers, there being no separate numerical symbols like our Arabic numerals. This is of great importance in the Cabala and is the basis of techniques aimed at reaching a fuller experience and understanding of God, man and the world. Letters have innumerable combinations and permutations with each other, in all the words of a language, but these are made up of a comparatively small number of units which themselves form 'one body', as the *Sefer Yetsirah* says, the alphabet. Similarly, numbers stretch to infinity but all numbers are regarded as being made of a few basic units which obey orderly rules. So letters and numbers are taken to be the model and underlying pattern of the innumerable and apparently disorderly and disconnected phenomena of the universe, which under the surface are connected in the 'one body' of God.

Letter-mysticism is one of the oldest strands in the Cabala. In the ancient world writing seemed a mysterious and magical art and it was believed that the gods must have invented this marvellous method of capturing speech and giving it visible form. The fact that most people could not write, or read what was written, and that writing was generally the preserve of priests helped to give letters and alphabets a reputation as containers of secret wisdom and power. The Egyptians called the picture-writing which they carved on the walls of temples and tombs 'the speech of the gods', and the Greeks called the Egyptian letters hieroglyphics, 'sacred carvings'. Similarly in northern Europe, the letters used in the early centuries after Christ, the runes, were considered mysteriously powerful, magical and divine.

In Jewish and Christian traditions the Hebrew alphabet took precedence over all others because Hebrew was the native tongue of God. Not only was Hebrew the language in which the Almighty revealed himself and his law to Moses and the prophets, it was also the language which was used to make the world. God is described in Genesis creating the world by expressing commands in words. 'And

God said, Let there be light; and there was light.' When God spoke, evidently, the things which God named sprang instantly into existence. The letters of God's language were therefore intimately connected with the creation, and this belief has profoundly affected Jewish thought for centuries. The famous 'Master of the Name', Israel Baal-Shem Tov, who taught in Poland in the eighteenth century and acquired a reputation as a great saint and miracle-worker, believed that the words of the scriptures originally existed in an incoherent jumble of letters and took their present form when the events described in them occurred. 'For example, the written passage describing the creation of Adam automatically arranged itself into its present form as his creation took place. If any of the events which took place in the creation of Adam had been different, the written account would have been different as well.'[4]

The fact that writing captures something invisible and intangible, sound, and gives it visible and tangible form, carved on stone, stamped on clay tablets or penned on parchment, suggested that it was through the Hebrew letters that the hidden, invisible and intangible godhead made itself manifest in the world. Everything that occurs, on this view, is part of the language of God and the Hebrew letters are aspects of God and units of the divine nature and energy. A complete grasp of the letters and their combinations and relationships with each other, if such a thing were possible, would constitute a full understanding of God and the world. Once the twenty-two Hebrew letters had been identified with the twenty-two trumps of the Tarot pack, the same claim would be made for the Tarot.

In numerology, long before the Tarot was thought of, the number twenty-two had come to mean everything, totality, the whole world, all knowledge of God, all wisdom and truth, because of the Hebrew alphabet. This is why books by numerologically minded authors, intended to illuminate the mysteries of God and the world, are sometimes arranged in twenty-two parts. The Book of Revelation, as the Christian Cabalists noticed, has twenty-two chapters. St Augustine's *City of God* has twenty-two books. There are twenty-two chapters in each section of Lévi's *Doctrine and Ritual* and again in Crowley's 'Magick in Theory and Practice' (the third part of his major work, *Magick* or Book Four). The fact that there are twenty-two trumps in the Venetian and Marseilles Tarot packs may be a coincidence, especially as other early packs have a different number: or at least there is no definite evidence to the contrary.

DIAGRAM THREE: The Hebrew Alphabet (See pages 55–6.)

Hebrew Letters	Number Value	Traditional Symbolism	Elements	Planets	Zodiac Signs	Qualities, Senses
aleph	1	ox	Air			
beth	2	house		Moon		Wisdom
gimel	3	camel		Mars		Health
daleth	4	door		Sun		Fertility
he	5	window			Aries	Speech
vau	6	pin or hook			Taurus	Mind
zain	7	sword			Gemini	Movement
heth	8	fence			Cancer	Sight
teth	9	snake			Leo	Hearing
yod	10	hand			Virgo	Work
kaph	20	fist		Venus		Life
lamed	30	ox-goad			Libra	Sex
mem	40	water	Water			
nun	50	fish			Scorpio	Smell
samekh	60	prop			Sagittarius	Sleep
ayin	70	eye			Capricorn	Anger
pe	80	mouth		Mercury		Power
tzaddi	90	fish-hook			Aquarius	Taste
qoph	100	back of head			Pisces	Laughter
resh	200	head		Saturn		Peace
shin	300	tooth	Fire			
tau	400	T-cross		Jupiter		Beauty

DIAGRAM FOUR: Correspondences of the Paths and Trumps (See opposite page.)

Paths	Trumps	Hebrew Letters	Elements, Planets, Zodiac	Deities	Animals	Plants
1	0 Fool	aleph	Air	Zeus, Jupiter	man, eagle	aspen
2	1 Juggler	beth	Mercury	Thoth, Hermes	swallow, ibis, ape, cynocephalus	vervain, palm
3	2 Female Pope	gimel	Moon	Artemis, Diana, Hecate	dog	almond, moonwort
4	3 Empress	daleth	Venus	Hathor, Aphrodite, Venus	dove, swan, sparrow	myrtle, rose
5	4 Emperor	he	Aries	Athene, Minerva, Mars	owl, ram	tiger lily, geranium
6	5 Pope	vau	Taurus	Apis, Venus	bull	mallow
7	6 Lovers	zain	Gemini	Janus, Castor and Pollux	magpie	orchids, hybrids
8	7 Chariot	heth	Cancer	Khepera, Apollo	crab, turtle, sphinx	lotus
9	8 Strength	teth	Leo	Bastet, Sekhmet	lion	sunflower
10	9 Hermit	yod	Virgo	Adonis, Attis	anchorite, virgin, eagle	lily, narcissus, snowdrop
11	10 Wheel	kaph	Jupiter	Amon, Zeus, Jupiter	eagle	oak, fig, poplar
12	11 Justice	lamed	Libra	Maat, Vulcan	elephant	aloe
13	12 Hanged Man	mem	Water	Poseidon, Neptune	snake, scorpion	water plants
14	13 Death	nun	Scorpio	Seth, Mars	beetle, lobster, scorpion, wolf	cactus
15	14 Temperance	samekh	Sagittarius	Artemis, Diana	centaur, horse, dog	rush
16	15 Devil	ayin	Capricorn	Khem, Pan, Priapus	goat, ass	thistle
17	16 Tower	pe	Mars	Horus	bear, wolf	absinthe, rue
18	17 Star	tzaddi	Aquarius	Juno, Ganymede	eagle, peacock	coconut
19	18 Moon	qoph	Pisces	Khepera, Poseidon, Neptune	fish, dolphin, beetle	opium
20	19 Sun	resh	Sun	Re, Helios, Apollo	lion, sparrowhawk	sunflower, laurel, heliotrope
21	20 Judgment	shin	Fire	Hades, Pluto	lion	poppy, hibiscus, nettle
22	21 World	tau	Saturn	Sebek, Saturn	crocodile	ash, cypress, yew, hellebore

2 THE TWENTY-TWO TRUMPS

When a correspondence between the twenty-two paths, Hebrew letters and Tarot trumps has been accepted, analysis of each trump can begin. Or rather, it can once the placing of the Fool has been settled. Lévi and Papus put the Fool in twenty-first place, between the Day of Judgment and the World, and began the procession of the trumps with the Juggler. Other writers have put the Fool last, after the World. But the card does not fit easily into either of these positions, which do not seem right for the unnumbered or zero card in any case. Mathers and the Golden Dawn brought the Fool firmly to the head of the trumps. So did Crowley and so did Waite, though in his *Pictorial Key* he pretends otherwise. There are disadvantages in doing this – for one thing it puts the numbers of the trumps and Hebrew letters out of step – but on the whole it seems to work best. Diagram Four (opposite) shows the trumps and paths on this system, with some of the correspondences from Crowley's lists.

0 *The Fool*. Many writers on the Tarot regard the Fool as the most important and most profoundly mysterious card in the pack. It is the only one of the trumps to have survived in the modern pack of playing cards, where it is the Joker, the 'wild card' which is exempt from normal rules and can take the place and play the part of any of the others. The Fool is generally a man in jester's motley with cap and bells. He has a bundle slung over his shoulder on a stick and carries a staff. He is walking along in open country and in some packs is about to walk over a cliff because he is not looking where he is going. A peculiar animal, which may or may not be a dog, is following him closely and is either jumping up at him or biting his leg. He is sometimes shown chasing a butterfly which flutters in front of him, leading him over the cliff. In Oswald Wirth's design there is a fallen obelisk in the background and a crocodile lurks in the abyss, waiting to seize the Fool when he falls into it.

A few interpreters take the card at face value as a symbol of irrational folly and blindness. The Fool is humanity, wandering carelessly along the primrose path in pursuit of the butterfly of ephemeral values, at the mercy of gnawing animal drives and heedless of the yawning gulf into which he is about to tumble. His multi-coloured clothes are the muddled impulses which tug him this way and that, his poverty is spiritual, the bundle over his shoulder contains gimcrack notions, fads and fancies, the whole range of useless and dangerous gadgetry with which man is obsessed, from electric toothbrushes to ballistic missiles. Or the stick and bundle are phallic and represent the burden of fleshly desire which weighs him down, with the gnawing dog perhaps standing for remorse.

Most writers, however, have taken a very different view. In the long history of fools and fooling the key point about the fool is that, far from representing humanity at large, he is drastically unlike the majority of men because he is mad. And his madness links him not with the human but with the divine. In the ancient world the insane were regarded with awe because their madness showed that they were in the grip of a god or a spirit. There is similarly an old Christian tradition of the fool as someone closer to God than other men. The simpleton, at one remove from the complexities of everyday life with which he is helpless to cope, has a

OVERLEAF A complete set of Tarot trumps, of the Marseilles type, from a pack produced in Switzerland.
BELOW A woodcut showing a medieval conception of the Fool or Jester, who is the Fool of the Tarot and the Joker of the ordinary modern pack of playing cards.

XX
LEIUGEMENT
XVIIII
LE SOLEIL
XVIII
LALUNE
XVII
LETOILLE
XVI
LAMAISONDIEU
XV
LEDIABLE
TENPERANCE
XIIII
XIII
LEPENDU
XII
LAFORCE
XI
LE FOL

E BATELEUR.
JVNON.
III.
MPERATRICE.
IIII
LEMPEREUR.
V.
JVPITER.
VI.
LAMOUREUX.
LE CHARIOT.
IVSTICE.
VIII
LERMITE.
VIIII
X.
XXI
LE MONDE

better set of values and a clearer perception of God than ordinary mortals, who are entangled in the complexities and unable to see beyond them. The word 'silly' originally meant 'blessed'. There is an old saying that children and fools cannot lie, and if a fool and his money are soon parted, perhaps it is the fool who holds money at its true worth.

St Paul told the Corinthians that 'the unspiritual man does not receive the gifts of the Spirit of God, for they are folly to him, and he is not able to understand them because they are spiritually discerned.... If any one among you thinks that he is wise in this age, let him become a fool that he may become wise. For the wisdom of this world is folly with God.' St Paul's 'gifts of the Spirit' included, besides the gift of faith, what are now called psychic abilities – clairvoyance, the ability to foresee the future, healing power and speaking in tongues. The older positioning of the Fool in twenty-first place had the advantage of connecting the card with the Hebrew letter *shin*, which in the Cabala is the letter of the Holy Spirit. The *Sefer Yetsirah* linked *shin* with fire, and the shape of the letter suggested the tongues of fire which rested on the apostles on the Day of Pentecost, when they became possessed by the Holy Spirit and spoke in tongues. Some of the astonished onlookers muttered that the Christians must be drunk, but St Peter quoted to them from the Old Testament prophet Joel: 'And in the last days it shall be, God declares, that I will pour out my spirit on all flesh, and your sons and your daughters shall prophesy, and your young men shall see visions, and your old men shall dream dreams....'[5]

Eliphas Lévi took up this theme in connecting the Fool of the Tarot with prophesy and divination, clairvoyance, precognitive dreams, premonitions and mysterious intimations of truth. Other authors have identified the Fool as the dreamer and visionary, in closer communion with God than is given to most men. His attention is concentrated on the things of the spirit and he is consequently blind to the trivial concerns of everyday life. The bundle he carries contains his past experiences, which he values at nothing. The biting dog can now become a symbol of longing for God – 'dog' spelled backwards is God – and the crocodile, even more strangely, can stand for the divine which the Fool is approaching.

Alternatively, when the Fool is placed at the head of the trumps and they are interpreted as successive stages of human life and progress, he represents the child in the womb, about to fall over the cliff into earthly life in being born. He is simple, pure and innocent, ignorant of the trials and pitfalls that await him. The butterfly is now a symbol of the soul or the psyche, as it was in classical pagan art, fluttering towards life in a physical body. In Christian art a butterfly is an emblem of resurrection. It sometimes appears in paintings of the Virgin and Child, usually perched on the Child's hand. The three stages of its life-cycle, as caterpillar, chrysalis and butterfly, stand for life, death and rebirth. Some interpreters take the Fool's butterfly as a symbol of reincarnation and say that his bundle holds the few belongings which he brings with him from previous lives.

In the Golden Dawn system the Fool is placed on the first path, leading from Kether, which is the sphere of God as Prime Mover, to Hokmah, 'the Father of Fathers'. Conversely, if the ladder of the trumps is read from the bottom upwards, his is the last path which the soul must tread on its way to the godhead. He is marked zero for the No-thing, the indefinable and limitless source of all things,

OPPOSITE Versions of the Fool from three packs. LEFT Alliette; RIGHT, TOP Waite; BOTTOM Italian, 1943. BELOW The Holy Spirit descending upon the Apostles at Pentecost in the form of a dove: the Fool is identified with the divine Spirit by many modern writers.

THE TWENTY-TWO TRUMPS 63

the figure o of the womb which gave birth to the world. His Hebrew letter is now *aleph*, which in the *Sefer Yetsirah* corresponds to air. The eagle is lord of the air, the aspen quivers to every breath of breeze, and the word 'fool' itself is derived from Latin *follis*, 'wind-bag'. Air is invisible, intangible, void, and yet also the breath without which the body cannot live. The connection with spirit is retained, because 'spirit' comes from the Latin *spiritus*, 'breath', and is the vital and divine ingredient breathed into Adam by God in Genesis to bring him to life. The descent of the Holy Spirit upon the apostles at Pentecost was accompanied by the sound of a rushing wind. The Fool is the divine Spirit about to descend into the abyss at the beginning of time. He is also the perfected spirit of man approaching the godhead, drawn to it as the butterfly is drawn towards the light. If he is mad, he is a holy madman. He is as free, as insubstantial, as all-pervading as the air. 'The wind blows where it wills, and you hear the sound of it, but you do not know whence it comes or whither it goes; so it is with every one who is born of the Spirit.'[6]

Seen in this light, the Fool is bisexual or neuter, to show that the ultimate unity combines and transcends male and female, active and passive, and all opposites. Waite's Fool is of youthful and epicene appearance. His stick and bundle are masculine but instead of a staff he holds a rose, a female symbol. The Fool corresponds to the Egyptian god Nu, or Nun, in the creation myth of Heliopolis, the primeval waste of waters which was the source of all things, the self-created father of all the gods: 'the great god Nu, who gave birth to himself, and who made his names to come into being and to form the company of the gods'.[7]

The Fool also corresponds to the Greek and Roman supreme gods, Zeus and Jupiter, but especially to Zeus as sky god, sometimes identified with air. In the *Clouds* of Aristophanes, for instance, Socrates begins a prayer to Zeus: 'O Lord and Master, measureless Air, who sustainest the Earth aloft . . .' A fragment of Euripides identifies Zeus with *aither*, the upper air of heaven where the gods live. The Golden Dawn gave the Fool the title of Spirit of Aither (or Ether, in terms of nineteenth-century physics, an all-pervading substance or medium, the one omnipresent reality, of which it was believed that everything might ultimately be found to consist).

As a symbol of the perfected human spirit, the Fool is a child. 'Truly, I say to you,' Jesus told his disciples, 'unless you turn and become like children, you will never enter the Kingdom of heaven.'[8] But conversely, the Fool is also a foetus or child as a symbol of divine potential, the Babe in the Egg, as Crowley called him, connected with the Egyptian god Horus the child, whom the Greeks named Harpocrates. Pictures of the infant Horus on the lap of his mother, Isis, influenced the Christian iconography of the Virgin and Child, and the Egyptians celebrated the birth of Horus on what later became the birthday of Christ, 25 December. The young god was shown with a plumed sun-disk on his head, and in some Tarots the Fool has a plumed hat, as in Waite's pack, where his costume is covered with sun-wheels and there is a huge blazing sun in the sky behind him. The feather in ancient Egyptian religion was the emblem of divine order and truth.

The child Horus was nursed by Isis in the swamps of the Nile Delta, where she hid from his wicked uncle, Seth, who intended to kill him. One of Seth's forms

Dionysus and the Maenads, his female worshippers, on a Greek vase of the 5th century B.C. Dionysus as the Liberator is connected with the Fool by some modern interpreters.

was the crocodile, and the legend of St George and the Dragon is partly descended from pictures of Horus fighting Seth as a crocodile. Horus eventually vanquished Seth and succeeded to the throne of his murdered father, Osiris. He was lord of the sky and the sun, and each pharaoh of Egypt was Horus in his lifetime and Osiris after his death. Horus the child, or the Fool, is the heir to the throne who will master the forces of evil and succeed the dead king (the fallen obelisk in Wirth's card), to become ruler and father himself.

Similarly, the Fool has been connected with the Greek god Dionysus, who as a child was attacked by his wicked uncles, the Titans, the old gods. They made friends with the little boy by bringing him toys, and when they had won his confidence they tore him to pieces and devoured him. But he was reborn, to triumph as the god of ecstasy and joy, of wine and sap and sperm and fruitfulness, who was mad and who sent his worshippers mad. He was Lusios, the Liberator, whose great gift to mortals was to set them free of their everyday, conventional, fettered selves in his orgiastic rituals, to drive them into a frenzy in which they became insane and divine. 'Salvation, whatever salvation may mean,' Crowley said of the Tarot Fool, 'is not to be obtained on any *reasonable* terms. Reason is an impasse, reason is damnation; only madness, divine madness, offers an issue.'[9]

The wandering fools and buffoons of the Middle Ages, who amused audiences with horseplay, pratfalls, mockery and obscenity, also took the spectators for a moment out of their ordinary humdrum lives and selves into a realm of topsy-turvy inspired lunacy. The fool's connection with lustful and life-creating vigour is shown in his hood, with its cock's comb, ass's ears and dangling bells, and his phallic bauble or slap-stick, a short staff topped with a comic head and a blown-up bladder with which he belaboured his victims. The fool of the old mumming dances capers about obscenely and makes grotesquely indecent advances to the spectators, and in some of them he is killed and then revives again. The Green Man, a figure dressed in leaves and branches who led springtime processions in various parts of Europe and was sometimes connected with St George, has been linked with the Fool of the Tarot. He is the principle of new life and new beginning, who comes for the salvation of nature and mankind from darkness and dearth, the child of spring who succeeds the dead king of winter.

From this point of view, the Fool is a young male child, and the shape of his hat in some modern Tarot packs seems to have been influenced by the theories of Hargrave Jennings, an obscure nineteenth-century author of highly eccentric books. Jennings was obsessed by sexual symbolism and delighted in seeing genital emblems in the most improbable places. He insisted, for instance, that the Order of the Garter was founded in honour of the sanitary napkin and that its original motto was *yoni soit qui mal y pense*. He also maintained that the medieval jester's hood was derived from the Phrygian cap of the god Mithras, which he thought preserved the original form from which all helmets and defensive headgear are descended. 'It is always masculine in its meaning. It marks the "needle" of the obelisk, the crown or tip of the *phallus*, whether "human" or representative. It has its origin in the rite of circumcision...'[10]

The Fool has also been linked with Parsifal, the naïve simpleton of the Arthurian legends. Like Horus, he is the child whose father is dead and who is brought up by his mother in seclusion, ignorant of the ways of the world. But he grows up to triumph over all obstacles and to achieve the Holy Grail. Wagner's treatment of this theme in his opera *Parsifal* convinced Crowley and the O.T.O. that the great composer was also a great adept of magic.

The crocodile which waits in the abyss to seize the Fool or the 'child' when he is born suggests the animal drives and desires which he will inherit with his body, the ravening beast in human beings or what Plato called the 'old Titan nature' of man. But it is a cardinal principle of modern magic that the animal nature of man is a vital instrument of his spiritual progress. The crocodile, though evil, is not necessarily as negative an element in the card as it may seem. There is a rather similar scene in one of the 'mind games' devised as 'guides to inner space' by R. E. L. Masters and Jean Houston at the New York Foundation for Mind Research. In this game the player, who is in a state of trance or semi-trance, imagines himself or herself standing at the edge of a deep gorge which fills with water until it becomes a lake. From the lake a monster rears up, 'a horrible-looking sea serpent, monstrous and menacing, opening its long jaws to reveal yellow teeth like daggers'. The player is frightened but reaches out to the creature and this gesture of welcome and love brings the realization that the monster is really a beautiful young princess or prince, who has been bewitched but now turns back into human form. The player is told by the 'guide', who controls the vision, that the transformed monster 'may be a very valuable ally for you in the future, a strong beneficent force within you...'[11]

The Wild Man, from a Latin codex: the Tarot Fool has been connected with the Wild Man or Green Man, who led springtime processions in many parts of Europe.

1 *The Juggler*. The repositioning of the Fool has made interpretation of the Juggler more difficult. In many ways the Juggler is better suited to his older place as the first of the trumps, and the shape made by his body and arms resembles the first Hebrew letter, *aleph*. In the Golden Dawn system, however, the Juggler belongs to the Tree's second path, connecting Kether and Binah, and corresponding to the second letter, *beth*. Following Eliphas Lévi's lead, the Golden Dawn named him the Magus of Power. He is usually called the Magician or Magus in modern packs and is given a dignified and earnestly spiritual look. In the older packs, however, the Juggler is a travelling huckster or con-man, standing in the open behind a table on which are various small articles. He is apparently either selling these articles or about to gull his audience with a piece of profitable sleight-of-hand, probably some variant of Find the Lady or the shell game. The one thing he is certainly not doing is juggling, but the card's French name, *Le Bateleur*, is a general term for a juggler, conjurer, showman or trickster. He holds up a small rod in one hand and his other hand points to the table. In the Tarot of Marseilles he wears a large floppy-brimmed hat, shaped roughly like a figure 8 lying on its side. Plants are growing in the ground behind him and under the table.

The card is linked with Mercury, Hermes and Thoth, gods of intelligence and magic. Mercury was among other things the patron of thieves and businessmen, which suits the Juggler's character as a huckster, and it has been suggested that the Tarot design may be descended from earlier pictures of Mercury. The floppy hat might be a debased version of the god's double-winged cap and the rod might originally have been his flute or the caduceus – the staff with two snakes twined round it which he carried as the herald of the gods. The position of the arms and hands is roughly the same as in the figure of Mercury in Botticelli's *Primavera* and in the famous statue of the god by Giovanni Bologna, in Florence. But there are plenty of ancient, medieval and Renaissance pictures of Mercury which do not recall the Tarot card, including the one in the 'Mantegna' pack, which shows the god with winged cap and boots, holding the caduceus and playing the flute.

If the Fool is the Nothing which, so to speak, precedes the Beginning, the Juggler is the Beginning itself. The card's number is one, the first of all numbers, and *beth* is the first letter of the first word of the Bible, *bereshith*, 'in the beginning'. If the Fool is the child in the womb, the Juggler is the child born in an individual body and growing to manhood. The figure 1 resembles an erect phallus and the figure 8 lying on its side in this connection stands for the testicles and so for creative potential. 'In the beginning God created the heavens and the earth', and the Juggler points with one hand to the sky and with the other to the ground.

The card is generally seen as a symbol of the creative power, will and intelligence of God and man, of dominance, individuality and action. The Juggler's gesture is the key factor in most interpretations. It is taken to demonstrate the magical principle of 'as above, so below', that as God is in heaven, so man is on earth. Man is made in the image of God, as Genesis says, and so Papus connected the Juggler with Adam. Man is a replica of the Almighty in miniature and the ruler of things here below. At the top of the card is the heaven of God, at the bottom is the earth with its products, the world of nature. In the centre, joining the two, is man. Mercury was the messenger of the gods, the link between heaven and earth, the divine and the human. The 'above' and 'below' of the gesture can be interpreted as

The card of Mercury from the 'Mantegna' pack, and RIGHT the Juggler from an Italian pack. OPPOSITE LEFT another version of the Juggler, and RIGHT Waite's representation of the Juggler, renamed the Magician and given a more spiritual look.

positive and negative, spirit and matter, good and evil, God and the Devil. 'Man with one hand seeks for God in heaven,' Papus said, 'with the other he plunges below, to call up the demon to himself, and thus unites the divine and the diabolic in humanity.'[12]

The conclusion can be drawn, though not everyone would draw it, that man, made in the image of God, potentially is God: that God is man raised to his highest power. In this case, the main significance of the connection with Mercury and his Greek equivalent, Hermes, is that Hermes gave his name to the Hermetica, the 'hermetic' art of alchemy and Hermetic systems of occultism in which man attempts to raise himself to his highest power and so become God.

The card is numbered one for God as the One and for the single-mindedness of the human being who in the ascent of the Tree has reached this inscrutable height. The figure 1 suggests 'I', the ego, the conscious, thinking, active, self-serving factor in both the divine and the human personality. Lévi quoted the God of the Old Testament's ringing declaration of himself, 'I am that I am', in connection with this card, which he referred to the master magician who is 'invested with a species of relative omnipotence and can operate superhumanly – that is, after a manner which transcends the normal possibility of men'.[13]

The Juggler's hand is raised to show the transmission from on high of the vital energy of the godhead – the Divine White Brilliance of Kether. He is the gigantic active and creative potential of God and man. The analogy between mental and sexual potency is constantly drawn in occultism, religious symbolism and language: the words 'genius' and 'genital' come from the same root. In Wirth's design and most modern packs the Juggler's rod is a magic wand with a phallic tip, and the wand is interpreted as both a phallic symbol and an emblem of will-power. In Waite's version of the card the plants and flowers on the ground have become far more numerous and luxuriant, and others have been added at the top of the design, as a sign of fruitful creative power. Adam was a gardener, and a fertile garden can be a symbol of the unconscious mind and of woman: the Juggler's path leads up from the sefira Binah, called the Mother and also the Great Sea, and linked with the primeval waters of chaos and the depths of the mind.

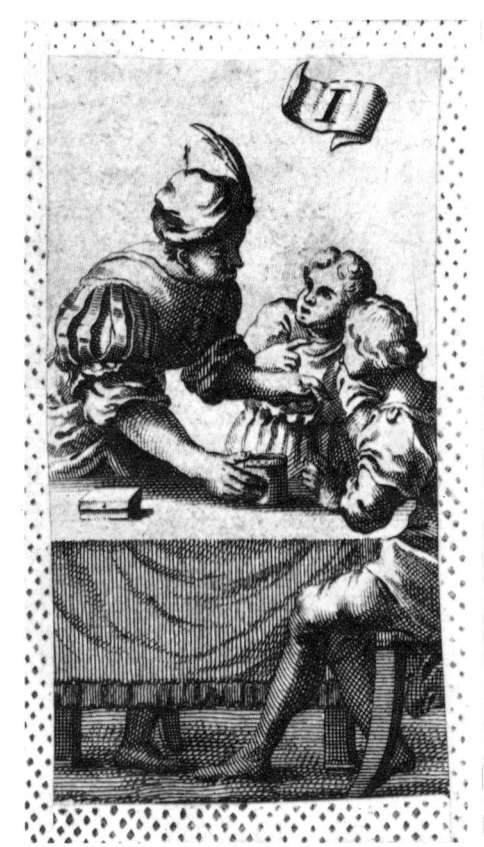

In modern packs the articles on the Juggler's table are usually symbols of the Tarot suits, to show that he dominates all things. The shape of the floppy hat, the lemniscate or horizontal figure 8, is the mathematical symbol for infinity and is also understood as an emblem of eternal life, like an endless cord. Eight in numerology stands for new life, a new beginning. Baptismal fonts in churches are often octagonal and in Christian symbolism eight is the number of resurrection. In terms of erotic symbolism the erect phallus has been 'resurrected' after its 'death'

in orgasm and is here permanently or infinitely erect, raised to its highest power. In Waite's card the lemniscate above the Juggler's head is echoed by his belt, which is in the shape of a snake devouring its own tail. This old gnostic and alchemical emblem, called the ouroboros, has been explained as a symbol of time and continuity, or of the union of opposites. Or it has been seen as 'symbolic of self-fecundation, or the primitive idea of a self-sufficient Nature – a Nature, that is, which . . . continually returns, within a cyclic pattern, to its own beginning'.[14] The godhead is self-fecundating, in the sense that it contains all opposites and has no partner, and the adept who has ascended the Tree is self-sufficient and has returned to his own beginning, his source in the divine.

In the list of correspondences the swallow stands for spring and the beginning of a new cycle. In Renaissance art it is sometimes a symbol of Christ's incarnation in a human body. Vervain is a plant with a reputation for magical power in folklore. The palm means both fertility and conquest. In Christian art martyrs are shown holding palm branches as a sign of their triumph over death. Jesus is often depicted bearing a palm branch as a token of victory and the tree is associated with his triumphal entry into Jerusalem, when palms were strewn beneath his feet.

The ibis belonged to Thoth in Egypt and so did the ape, especially the cynocephalus or dog-headed baboon, which stood for intelligence, cunning and the magical power of speech. It was Thoth who provided Isis with the words of the spell which she used to restore the murdered Osiris to life so that he could father Horus on her, which again brings in the theme of resurrection and new life. The ape also has an evil connotation, for in Christian imagery it is linked with Satan, who is 'the ape of God'. It therefore 'unites the divine and the diabolic', in Papus's phrase, and the ape is to man as man is to God. It is the 'below' of which man is the 'above', but is itself 'above' the other animals in its likeness to man. C. G. Jung made an interesting comment on the cynocephalus as an appropriate symbol for 'that part of the psyche which transcends the conscious level'. It is a familiar notion now that there are levels of the mind 'below' the conscious level, but less so that there may be layers 'above' as well. But Jung said: 'In my experience the conscious mind can only claim a relatively central position and must put up with the fact that the unconscious psyche transcends and as it were surrounds it on all sides.'[15] He might almost have been writing with the Juggler in mind, as the conscious ego in a central position between 'above' and 'below', superconscious and unconscious.

Mercury, the metal, in alchemical symbolism, stood for the spirit or vital energy of the divine concealed in matter, just as the Juggler following the Fool is the human spirit incarnated in flesh. Mercury had a double nature in alchemy. It was believed to combine opposites and was frequently portrayed as a hermaphrodite, self-fecundating and self-sufficient. The Juggler's gesture and the twin snakes of the caduceus also suggest the blending of opposites, and so do the two kinds of ibis, the black and the white. But because the Juggler unites the divine and the diabolic, and is shown in the old packs as a trickster, there are sinister possibilities in the card. The Juggler has all the confident strength, determination and self-centredness of youth setting out to master the world, using his body and his will and intelligence as weapons. He can be egotistical, brutal and ruthless, abusing his powers for his own selfish ends. The magician can be a black magician. Evil, as well as good, has its roots in the divine.

Thoth, the Egyptian god of wisdom and magic, shown in the form of an ape.

2 *The Female Pope*. The Female Pope is a very oddly named card. It presumably represents the mythical Pope Joan, whose story was told in the thirteenth century by a French author, Stephen of Bourbon, and repeated with variations by later writers. According to one version, she was an English girl who fell in love with a monk and dressed as a man to be with him without arousing suspicion. After his death she went to Rome, still disguised as a man, and became a priest. She rose rapidly in the Church, was appointed Cardinal, and in 855 was elected Pope as John VIII. Unfortunately, she was pregnant and died embarrassingly in childbirth on the steps of St Peter's. Authors intent on finding traces of the Cathar heresy in the Tarot have pointed out that in the Cathar Church, unlike the Roman Catholic one, women could rise to the highest positions. But the myth of Pope Joan was widely accepted as true at the time when the earliest Tarots were produced, and it also fits in quite easily with modern interpretations of the card.

The Female Pope is usually called the High Priestess in modern packs. She is the feminine counterpart of the Juggler, passive and withdrawn where he is active and outgoing, subordinate where he is dominant, sitting quietly still where he is standing up and waving his arms about, the virgin Eve to his youthful Adam. In human terms the Juggler is the adolescent male and the Female Pope the nubile female. In legend she is the virgin who tames the unicorn, which lays its single phallic horn in her lap. In universal terms, the Golden Dawn taught, 'She is the great feminine force controlling the very source of life, gathering into herself all the energizing forces and holding them in solution until the time of release.'[16]

The legendary unicorn, tamed by a virgin, from a medieval MS.

The old packs show a robed woman, crowned with the papal tiara, seated and holding an open book. In Wirth's card her tiara is topped by a crescent moon and behind her are two pillars with a curtain or veil stretched between them. Her book is now closed, though she is marking her place in it with her finger, and she holds the two papal keys of heaven and hell. More recent designs usually follow Wirth, with some changes. She holds a scroll instead of a book, the keys have been left out, a cross hangs at her breast and her crown has become the horned headdress of the Egyptian goddess Isis.

The pillars are the two great hollow columns of bronze, named Jachin and Boaz, which stood at the threshold of the Temple in Jerusalem. They have an important place in Freemasonry and stand at the entrance to some Masonic temples, or on either side of the chair in which the Master of the lodge sits. Masons interpret Jachin to mean 'to establish' and Boaz 'in strength', and the two together to signify 'stability'. They are connected with the presence of God in the pillar of fire and cloud which led the Israelites out of captivity in Egypt and towards the Promised Land. The fire lighted the Israelites on their way and the cloud smothered the pursuing Egyptians in darkness.[17]

Like the horns of the headdress, the pillars stand for the balance of opposites of which reality is made – fire and cloud, light and darkness, positive and negative, and the rest. They are the two outer columns of the Tree of Life – the pillars of Mercy and Severity – and the opposites of the other, fatal tree which grew in Eden, the tree of the knowledge of good and evil. The Female Pope's number is two, which means duality, opposites, and female as opposed to male. She is the feminine side of the divine, and in some old packs is named Juno, the consort of the Roman supreme god, Jupiter. The pillars are an emblem of woman and the curtain between them is both the unbroken hymen of virginity and the veil which covered the entrance to the Holy of Holies in the Temple, the secret dwelling-place of God himself.

Another important symbolic feature of Masonic temples is the Blazing Star, set in the ceiling or the centre of the floor. Placed close to it is the letter G (equivalent to *gimel*, the She-Pope's Hebrew letter), for the Glory of God. The Golden Dawn called the Female Pope the Priestess of the Silver Star and recognized in her a symbol of the Shekinah, the glory of the presence of God. Shekinah means 'indwelling' and in the Cabala is the female element or principle in God which is also his presence in the world, in his chosen people and in the soul of man. The Shekinah is the radiance of glory through which the hidden godhead can be known to men and with which the mystic can unite himself.

The Shekinah is the Middle Pillar of the Tree of Life, known in her highest aspect as the Supernal Mother or *Anima Mundi*, 'the Soul of the World', a part of which exists in each human being. In Jungian theory the *anima* is the female archetype, or psychological ingredient, existing in the collective unconscious and in each man's individual unconscious. If the godhead joins male and female in the ultimate unity, then to be like God man must unite the masculine and feminine elements of his nature. In Jungian terms, he must unite himself to his *anima*. In terms of sexual symbolism, he must penetrate and 'know' his own virgin feminine component, to enter the Temple where the godhead is concealed.

As in many other mystical traditions, the Cabala frequently uses erotic imagery in speaking of the soul's dealings with the divine. The 'outer garment' of the

The Female Pope, most unusually, presented as a male in an 18th-century Belgian pack, and RIGHT a more orthodox French version.

Shekinah is the Torah, 'the law', the holy scriptures in which God is outwardly displayed. There is a famous passage in the *Zohar*, the principal work of the medieval Cabala, in which the Torah and the mystic are likened to a beautiful girl and her lover. 'For the Torah resembles a beautiful and stately damsel, who is hidden in a secluded chamber of her palace and who has a secret lover, unknown to all others . . . She opens the door of her hidden chamber ever so little, and for a moment reveals her face to her lover, but hides it again forthwith . . . He alone sees it and he is drawn to her with his heart and soul and his whole being . . . When he comes to her, she begins from behind a curtain to speak words in keeping with his understanding, until very slowly insight comes to him . . .' Gradually she yields to him and reveals 'all her hidden secrets and all her hidden ways. Such a man is then termed perfect, a "master", that is to say "a bridegroom of the Torah" . . .'[18]

In modern packs Tora is written on the Female Pope's scroll, referring simultaneously to the Torah, the Tarot and *rota*, 'wheel' in Latin, the wheel being one of the symbols of Isis. The scroll is also the 'Volume of the Sacred Law' in Masonry, the book of divine Providence on which rests the ladder that leads to heaven. One of the teachings of the mysteries of Isis was that behind all the vicissitudes of life, behind apparent chance and luck, there is Providence, the divine plan which leads men to salvation. The two pillars are relevant here again, because the Golden Dawn connected them with the entrance to the Hall of Truth in the afterworld of ancient Egyptian belief. The soul went to the Hall of Truth to be judged after death, and if it passed the test was granted immortality among the gods.

The worship of Isis spread beyond Egypt to become one of the major mystery religions of the Roman world. She was a great mother goddess, who had many aspects, forms and symbols. She was 'the one of the many names' or 'the one with ten thousand names' or 'the one who is all'. She was the ideal and complete woman and the prototype of the human woman. 'Her whole being is impenetrable,' it has been said of her, 'but behind her many faces and names there is one and the same divine Unknown.'[19]

The central myth of the mystery religion of Isis was the story of how her husband, the good king Osiris, was murdered by his evil brother, Seth. Isis sorrowfully searched everywhere for his body, and when she found it she used her magic to bring the dead man back to life, and conceived Horus by him. The resurrected Osiris became a god and the myth of his death and restoration to life was believed to have provided a pattern which human beings could follow. Just as Isis had brought Osiris back to life, so her mysteries promised immortal life after death to those who were initiated into them. The ceremonies of initiation included a mock death and resurrection (which is similarly part of the usual initiation ritual of occult groups and secret societies, including initiation as a Master Mason). There was probably also a 'sacred marriage' or sexual union of the initiate with a woman representing the goddess, which again brings in the theme of penetrating the woman, the divine Unknown, to gain salvation.

Anubis, the dog-headed god, was the faithful servant of Isis, and it was Anubis who led the soul after death to the Hall of Truth to be judged. The star of Isis was Sirius, the dog-star, whose rising marked the Egyptian New Year's Day and brought with it the outpouring of the resurrected Osiris in the annual Nile flood which renewed the fertility of the land. Coming at the height of the blazing heat of summer, the Nile flood was regarded as the miraculous achievement of Isis.

In the Golden Dawn system the Female Pope's path lies on the Middle Pillar of the Tree of Life, connecting Kether with Tifereth. Tifereth is the 'son' of Kether in the sense of being directly descended from Kether on the Tree. It is the sphere of the sun, and in the Christian Cabala of Christ as the Son of God and the spiritual Sun, the light of the world. In relation to Egyptian mythology the Female Pope is Isis who will become the mother of Horus, the sun god. From a Christian point of view she is the Virgin Mary, one of whose emblems is the closed gate and whose silver star is the Star of Bethlehem which announced the birth of Jesus. In cabalistic language she is the radiance of the Shekinah, and one of the principal symbols of the Shekinah is the moon, the silver star which pours out heavenly light into darkness.

Conversely, looking up the Tree from Tifereth to Kether, the She-Pope is the door of perfection, the gate of the heavenly Paradise, the portal of escape from spiritual captivity in Egypt and entry to the Promised Land. She is the Shekinah as mystic bride, Isis through union with whom Osiris became a god. Christian mystics have spoken of 'becoming Mary and bearing God from within'. The cross at her breast is the symbol of the Crucifixion, when 'the veil of the Temple was

Isis nursing Horus, the son she conceived by Osiris after his death; and BELOW the Female Pope as Isis enthroned, from Waite's pack.

rent', and stands for the union of the sexes and the union of Christ and his Church, which was described in erotic language by Christian writers as being consummated on the cross. It is the sign of the sacrifice of God on the altar of the world and his subsequent resurrection, which brought to all who believed in him the promise of eternal life.

The Female Pope is also *gnosis*, the intuitive knowledge of God, not brought by reason but by inspiration and insight, and intuition is by common consent a feminine gift. She is the Church or the mystic as the Bride of Christ, which makes the story of Pope Joan more relevant than it might seem at first. Seated between her pillars, she is a symbol of the Cabala, and of initiation into wisdom. She is the virgin of the unconscious mind, concealed by a veil, as it were, but full of fruitful potential if the veil is pierced.

The almond in the correspondences is another emblem of the Virgin Mary and also means priesthood, because in the Old Testament the rod of Aaron blossomed and brought forth almonds. In Jewish custom only the High Priest was allowed to pass the veil and enter the Holy of Holies in the Temple. But the almond has both a life-giving and a life-denying significance, because it is one of the earliest trees to blossom and so is peculiarly at risk to damage by frost. In human terms, if the young girl's potential is not realized she becomes the frosted spinster of the popular stereotype – acid, envious, frustrated and destructive. Similarly, the Greek Artemis and the Roman Diana correspond to the Female Pope as virgin goddesses of the moon, but there was another classical moon goddess of chilling and evil repute. This was Hecate, with whom Isis was identified as lady of enchantments and mistress of magic. Hecate was goddess of witchcraft, ghosts, crossroads, nightmares, blood and terror, and her animal was the dog, the eater of corpses.

Like the Juggler, the feminine side of the divine or the female archetype contains an evil potential – barrenness, hatred and death. Writers hunting for Celtic influences in the Tarot have galloped enthusiastically off on the trail of Morgan le Fay, the great enchantress and witch-queen of the Arthurian legends. There are sinister figures in her ancestry, the trio of lustful and murderous Irish goddesses of war and fertility known collectively as the Morrigan, who took the form of ravens to feast on the bodies of dead men on battlefields. The sheelagh-na-gigs, the peculiar Celtic fertility figures found carved in some old churches, have also been pressed into service, and may in fact be connected with the Celtic tradition of the divine hag.

More to the point, however, is the fact that initiations always include an experience of terror. Initiation into the mysteries of Isis was through a mock death, and so through an approach too close for comfort to the clutches of Persephone, the queen of the dead, who was identified as an aspect of Isis herself. To penetrate the divine Unknown is an experience both potentially rewarding and hideously dangerous. At actual physical death in Egyptian religion the soul faced the terrifying possibility of failing the judgment test, or in Christian belief of being condemned to the horrors of hell. This is why the Female Pope in Wirth's card holds the twin keys of heaven and hell. She stands for an equal balance of opposites, of good and evil, fruitfulness and sterility, life and death. The balance may tilt the wrong way.

3 *The Empress*. In the next card, however, promise is sweetly fulfilled and the maiden becomes a mother. The Empress is interpreted by all writers on the Tarot as a symbol of fertility and in modern packs she is invariably pregnant. Her Hebrew letter is *daleth*, 'door', and she is the entry to Venus's bower and the door through which life comes into the world. She is Mother Earth, Mother Eve, nature pregnant with teeming life, the smiling and gracious goddess who gives birth and nourishment to all living things. Her path on the Tree joins Hokmah with Binah, the Father of Fathers with the Mother or Throne, linking the active and passive or male and female principles in the divine. The sefiroth below the abyss are the product of this union, and the card demonstrates, in Dion Fortune's words, that 'everything rests upon the principle of the stimulation of the inert yet all-potential by the dynamic principle'. Or as Crowley put it: 'The doctrine implied is that the fundamental formula of the Universe is Love.'[20]

The card's number is three, standing for the reconciliation of opposites that produces a new unity. The obvious example in human terms is the union of man and woman which creates a child. In terms of the divine the Empress's pregnancy represents the evolution of the godhead from infinite to finite in the creation of the universe. Just as in a child a spark of life is mysteriously contained in flesh, so in the universe at large divine life is mysteriously infused into matter.

The Empress corresponds to pagan goddesses of nature, fertility and love. She has been linked with Ishtar, the great Babylonian goddess, known to the Greeks as Astarte, and with the many-breasted Artemis of Ephesus. The modern witches see their own great goddess in her. The Golden Dawn connected her with Isis as divine mother and queen. As queen, the hieroglyphic symbol of Isis was the throne and she is often shown in Egyptian art with it perched rather oddly on her head. As giver of corn Isis was identified with the Greek Demeter and the Roman Ceres, and as the beautiful goddess of love with Aphrodite and Venus. The cow-headed Egyptian goddess of love and fertility, Hathor, is also included in the correspondences as a form of Isis. There was a myth that Horus killed Isis and cut off her head, but Thoth restored her to life and gave her the head of a cow. Hathor, in other words, is Isis on a lower plane, in the world of nature and matter.

The Empress can also be connected with the Virgin Mary because in the conception and birth of Christ the divine became finite in being incarnated in a human body. And Mary was not only the mother of Christ but also, in her role as a symbol of the Church, his sister and his bride. The Tarot card may originally have been based on or influenced by medieval pictures of the coronation of Mary as queen of heaven, dressed in royal robes and crowned and throned like a Byzantine empress. Christ the King stands beside her in a scene which was carved above the doorways of many cathedrals and churches. The eagle, among its many roles in Christian symbolism, was an emblem of the majesty of Christ. The eagle on the shield which the Empress holds in some old Tarot packs stands for imperial power, but it may also have been meant to suggest Mary's relationship with Christ.

Despite the reservations of theologians, for many Christians the Mother of God took the place of the great goddesses of the ancient world. Like them she had a triple sovereignty as queen of heaven, the earth, and the underworld or hell. Like Venus she was crowned with stars, like Isis she rode on the crescent moon.

The coronation of the Virgin Mary, a theme which may have influenced the symbolism of the Empress card in the Tarot.

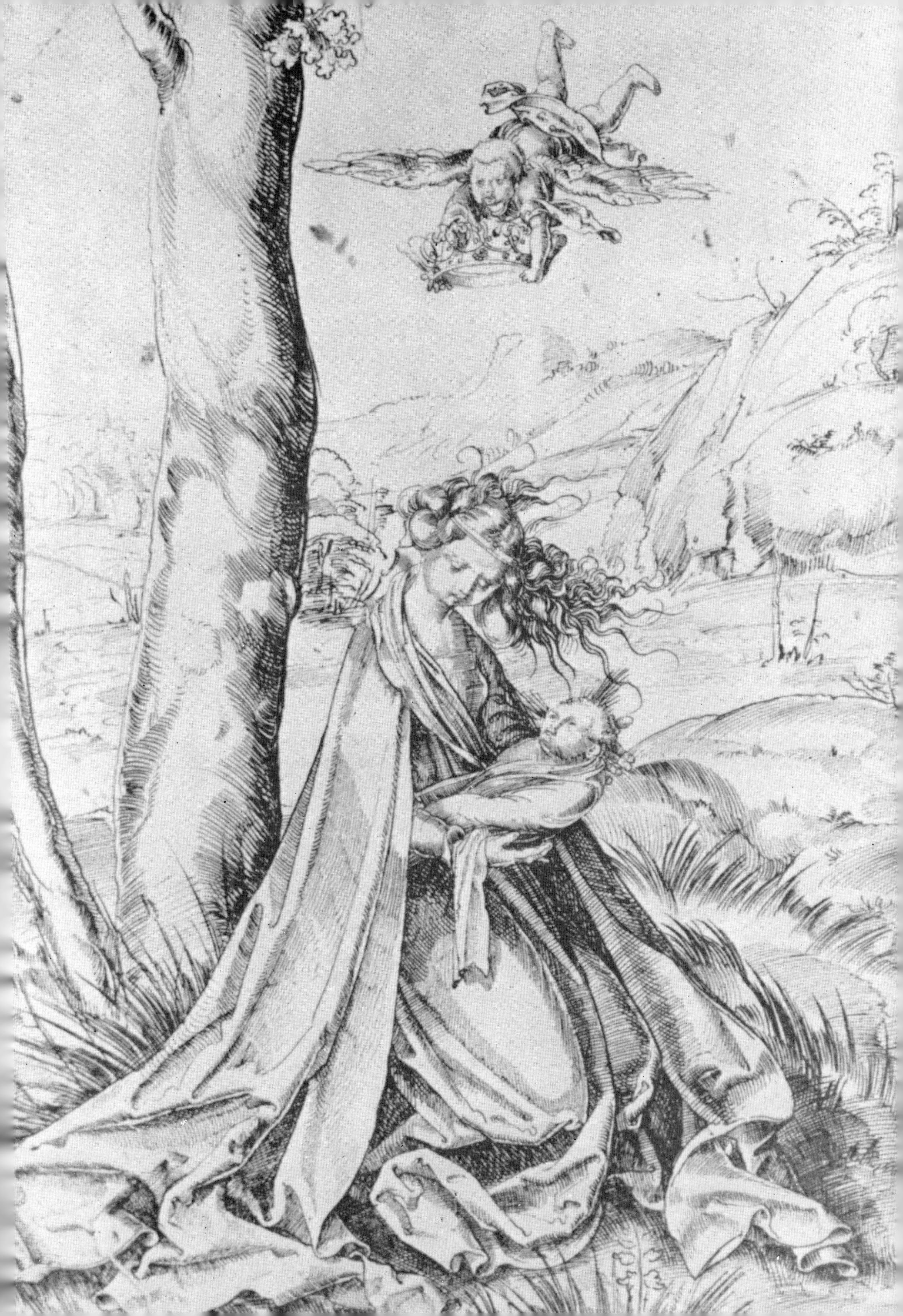

Figures of the throned Minerva, the Roman goddess of wisdom, were identified in the Middle Ages as images of Mary. Like the pagan goddesses she was connected with plants and flowers and fertility. She was often linked with springtime festivals and was identified with the May Queen, May Bride or Queen of Spring, who brought new life after winter.

The dove and the sparrow of the correspondences belong to Venus as amorous birds, and the swan with its phallic neck joined to its cteic body stands for satisfied desire. The myrtle was sacred to Venus and so was the rose, which was also an attribute of Isis and one of the principal emblems of the Virgin Mary, the Mystic Rose and 'the rose without a thorn'. The rose is a symbol of woman, and in Christian legend the rose which grew in Eden had no thorns. But when Adam and Eve fell from grace they were expelled from the beautiful garden into the everyday world of human experience. And so the rose acquired the thorns of sin, but it kept its beauty and its fragrance as reminders of the lost paradise.

One of Mary's titles is *hortus conclusus*, 'the enclosed garden', from the Song of Solomon: 'A garden enclosed is my sister, my spouse; a spring shut up, a fountain sealed.' A garden suggested Eden, the earthly paradise, and Venus also owned a garden (and in fact was originally a goddess of gardens), which was not a haven of virginal seclusion but a bower of sensual delight, the earthly paradise of love. There were complaints in the early fifteenth century that the two gardens were being confused and there was a tendency in the Renaissance period for Mary and Venus to be blended into one. The Venus of the *Primavera*, for instance, has very much the look of a Madonna.

'Whether it is the rose-garden of sexual union or that of the heart's desire in some other symbolic form, the garden represents the lost paradise, which is the lost unity of things. It is idle to say there is no such garden. Everyone recognizes the same nostalgia. . . . Paradise is neither a moment nor a place; it is a condition.

A Roman relief of Demeter, the Greek corn goddess and presiding deity of the Eleusinian mysteries. OPPOSITE LEFT the Empress, renamed La Grande Mère in a pack issued during the French Revolution when titles were in disfavour, and RIGHT the Empress enthroned as the Earth Mother in Waite's design.

So when the lover calls to his or her beloved to come into the garden, it is, in the final implication, a summons to overcome the human condition.'[21]

In Waite's pack the Empress is enthroned in a cornfield. She wears a crown of twelve stars and the device on her heart-shaped shield is the astrological symbol of Venus. In the background are trees, a river and a waterfall. An ear of corn is an attribute of both the Virgin Mary and the goddess Demeter, whose mysteries at Eleusis were believed to hold the key to immortal life. Water falling into a pool is a symbol of the union of male and female. The river recalls the Nile flood bringing life to the parched soil. The twelve stars stand for the zodiac and so for the course of the year, for the infinite becoming finite in periods of time.

The starry crown is also a reference to 'the woman clothed with the sun' of the twelfth chapter of Revelation, 'with the moon under her feet, and on her head a crown of twelve stars; she was with child and she cried out in her pangs of birth, in anguish for delivery'. (In some modern packs the Empress has a crescent moon at her feet.) Later Christian writers took the woman clothed with the sun to be Mary as queen of heaven. The Golden Dawn understood her as a symbol of the highest triangle on the Tree, the three Supernals taken together as the superconscious, the shining light of the higher self.

Waite's card anticipated many of the theories which Jung later evolved about the *anima*, the female archetype or constellation of ideas and images which he thought had been built up over thousands of years of man's experience of woman. The *anima* is often symbolically connected with both earth and water. She is pictured as timeless and profoundly wise, but her knowledge is not intellectually acquired. It is an ancient, enigmatic, intuitive wisdom. Each man's first and formative experience of the *anima* is with his mother. Her true function in the mind, according to Jung, is creativity.

4 *The Emperor*. The Emperor is the Empress's consort. When the trumps are treated as stages of human life, the Emperor and Empress represent the adult male and female, the Juggler and the Female Pope who have now grown up to become parents. When the trumps are treated as stages of the divine life, the Emperor stands for the dynamic principle, or 'the great energizing forces' which penetrate and organize everything passive and potential. Once divine life has been infused into matter, the next stage is the arrangement of matter into finite forms. Or similarly, when a child has been born, he must be trained and affectionately but firmly organized into an individual person, which in the Cabala is classified as a paternal activity.

The old packs frequently show the Emperor in profile, and this is taken to indicate that he is the outward and visible aspect of a power whose other side is concealed. The Emperor is God as father and maker. In him the divine creative potential of the Juggler becomes actual and works in the universe to generate life and mould form. His path crosses the abyss between the ideal and the actual to link Hokmah, the active paternal principle with Tifereth, the divine Son. In some of the old packs he roughly resembles the astrological symbol of Jupiter (♃), the Roman supreme deity, father of gods and men. In most modern designs his arms and head make a triangle and his legs are crossed, so that he forms the symbol for sulphur (🜍), which the alchemists believed to be the fiery, active, male force in nature.

The Emperor's number is four, which stands for solidity, system, the earth and the form and construction of things. He suggests temporal power, patriarchal authority, government, administration, the imposition of order on chaos, the rule of law in nature and society. He also suggests war, conquest, discipline, and the suppression of hostility and rebellion. In modern packs the arms of his throne end in rams' heads. The ram stands for Aries, the first sign of the zodiac, which marks the beginning of an organized structure, the division of time into finite periods. In astrological tradition Aries is governed by Mars, the principle of vigorous and fiery energy which, if not held on the leash, causes violence, war and destruction. As consort of the Empress, the Emperor has another link with Mars because in mythology Mars was the lover of Venus. Their child was Harmony, the ordered and regular arrangement of things.

The Emperor in Wirth's pack is seated on a cube, which is a symbol of solidity. He holds an orb as a sign of his royal dominion over the earth, and a sceptre topped by a fleur-de-lis, the heraldic lily, often called *fleur de luce* or 'flower of light', which is an emblem of royalty and fire. Harold Bayley, an author whose eccentric perambulations along various symbolic paths have influenced many modern occultists, contrived to find the origin of the word 'sceptre' in Sanskrit *se pitar*, 'Fire Father'. In Waite's pack, where the Emperor is shown full-face, the upright sceptre of male vigour and dominance is crowned by an ankh, the ancient Egyptian symbol of life. He is the masculine potency of Osiris, restored to life by the magic of Isis and fathering on her the child Horus. The barren mountains in the background refer to the earlier condition of Osiris, lying dead.

The sefirah Hokmah is called the Wisdom of God and the owl is the bird of Athene and Minerva, the martial Greek and Roman goddesses of wisdom. Psychologically, the Emperor has been interpreted as the organizing, defining and classifying power of reason, with the implication that reason, like Mars, is destruc-

From four packs, the Emperor depicted as a figure of authority, order and temporal power. TOP LEFT the 'Mantegna' version, orb in hand, and RIGHT from the 'Charles VI' pack, holding an orb and a sceptre topped by a fleur-de-lis. BOTTOM LEFT The Emperor from Waite's pack, and RIGHT a French 18th-century version renamed Le Grand Père.

tive if not held sufficiently in check. From a Jungian point of view the Emperor is the *animus*, the male counterpart of the *anima*, as father, ruler and warrior, enterprising, dominating, opinionated and aggressive. The modern witches see him as one of the Tarot symbols of their horned god, the consort of their great goddess, supposed to have been worshipped with her since prehistoric times.

82   INTERPRETATION

5 *The Pope*. The Pope is nowadays usually called the Hierophant or 'revealer of sacred things', which was the title of the chief priest of the Eleusinian mysteries. In some of the old packs he was replaced by Jupiter. He is generally treated as the twin and counterpart of the Emperor. God the Father is known through his acts, in the Emperor, and through the teachings of his prophets and priests, in the Pope. Where the Emperor wields temporal power, the Pope has spiritual authority. He stands for accepted and traditional teaching, established religion, orthodox theology, conventional moral codes. He is the 'father' of his people as their guide and confessor. In some packs he wears gloves to show that he keeps his hands clean.

The stock interpretations, however, conceal something deeper. According to the first chapter of Genesis, when God had made all his other creations, or when he had given all other things their finite individual forms, he said: 'Let us make man in our image, after our likeness.' And he made man, male and female, and said to them: 'Be fruitful and multiply, and fill the earth and subdue it.' The Pope is God making man in his image and man made in that image. This is hinted at in Waite's pack by the fifteen trefoils of the Pope's tiara. Each trefoil has three points, so that the total number of points is forty-five, and forty-five, for reasons explained later, is the number of man as the image of God. The papacy in medieval Christendom was the highest office to which a man could aspire and the occupant of Peter's chair was the Vicar of Christ on earth.

In modern packs the Pope's right hand is raised in the blessing called 'the sign of esotericism', with the thumb and the first two fingers pointing upwards and the last two fingers folded onto the palm. This indicates a distinction between 'above' and 'below', God and man, and the Pope is the pontiff or 'bridge-builder' who links them. It is a sign of the Trinity or the three Supernals above, and man made in two sexes in the world below. The card corresponds to Taurus and the symbol of Taurus (♉) unites the symbols of the sun and the moon, the 'above' from which light shines and the 'below' which reflects the light. Taurus is ruled by Venus in astrology and Venus is the principle of 'be fruitful and multiply', or out of two make three.

The symbol of Taurus also recalls the myth of Isis (the moon) hovering above the dead Osiris (the sun) to revive him. Occultists have drawn a parallel between this myth and the Eleusinian mysteries. According to early Christian writers, before celebrating the mysteries the hierophant made himself impotent by drinking hemlock (equivalent to Osiris lying dead). Later there was a 'sacred marriage' between the hierophant and a priestess (the union of Isis and Osiris). The supreme revelation was the showing to the initiates of 'a green ear of corn reaped in silence', followed by the proclamation of the birth of a child to the goddess (Horus the child, or Harpocrates, was among other things god of silence).

In this light the Tarot Pope is Osiris who was born a man and became a god and whose myth sets an example which other men can follow. The Golden Dawn connected the card with the Masters, the great superhuman adepts or god-men of Theosophical theory, believed to watch over the welfare and progress of humanity. In terms of alchemy the card corresponds to the process called 'projection' in which the Philosopher's Stone, the perfect substance, was mixed with a base metal to turn it into gold.

The Pope's tiara is phallic and the triple-barred papal cross in his left hand,

The card of the Pope has been given various names in different packs. FAR LEFT, TOP As Bacchus, the Roman equivalent of Dionysus, in a Belgian pack of the 18th century, and BOTTOM as the Hierophant in Waite's pack. NEAR LEFT The Pope was also called Jupiter, the subject of this sketch by Dürer. BELOW In the 'Charles VI' pack the Pope is shown with two attendants, often nowadays interpreted as the opposites.

which can be interpreted as an emblem of the Trinity or of the Supernals, is also regarded as a symbol of the resurrected Osiris. The keys of heaven and hell at the foot of his throne stand for the knowledge of good and evil, or for the superconscious and the unconscious. The pillars behind him mean obedience and disobedience, law and liberty, the choice which confronted Adam and Eve in Eden. The two figures kneeling before him are interpreted as the two sexes, or as thought and desire, or as the good and the wicked, the saved and the damned, the sheep and the goats.

The Pope's number is five and in modern Tarots he is arranged to form a pentagram or five-pointed star, which is a symbol of spirit united with and dominating matter. Five is made of 1 + 4, the one for spirit, the divine ingredient breathed by God into Adam, and the four for the elements of fire, air, earth and water, of which in classical and medieval theory all material things were made. The pentagram is also a symbol of man, because a man with his arms and legs stretched out forms a five-pointed star.

Taurus is the sign of the bull and Apis was the sacred bull of Memphis in Egypt, revered as an incarnation of divine procreative power. When each Apis bull died, he was identified with Osiris and named Oserapis. If this association with the Pope seems curious, it is nothing new. In the Egyptian scenes painted in the Vatican in the 1490s by Pinturicchio for Alexander VI, the Borgia pope, the Apis bull is identified with the heraldic bull of the Borgia family, and so by implication the Pope himself is identified with Osiris. (The painting of the enthroned Isis in this series, incidentally, resembles the Female Pope of the Tarot.) The mallow is included in the correspondences as a reference to the creation of Eve from Adam's rib. It gets its name from its emollient or softening properties, and to emolliate means 'to soften' or 'to render effeminate'. Popes, of course, are celibate, and there is possibly a Crowleyan pun here on 'infallibility'.

The Egyptian god Osiris in the afterworld: modern interpretations link Osiris with the Pope. OPPOSITE The bull, emblem of Pope Alexander VI, painted by Pinturicchio.

Taken in descending order, the trumps from the Juggler to the Pope recall the gnostic accounts of the creation of the universe. It was believed that in the beginning the One became Two by thinking, so that there was a Mind and a Thought. The Juggler can be equated with the divine Mind, the Female Pope with the Thought in its original purity, and the Empress with the Thought after it had been impregnated by the Mind to become the mother of all the lower powers. Among these lower powers was the Demiurge or Cosmocrator, the maker of the visible world. He was the creator of things material (the Emperor) and also of things spiritual in the sense of conventional religion and morality (the Pope).

Gnostics frequently identified the Demiurge with the God of the Old Testament. He was regarded as an evil power, the maker and ruler of matter and the flesh in which the divine spark of the spirit is held prisoner. In the Golden Dawn system the Emperor's path on the Tree is a continuation of the path of the Devil, and the title which the Golden Dawn gave him, Sun of the Morning, suggests a punning reference to the Devil as Lucifer, 'son of the morning'. The Emperor is connected with sulphur, which is associated with the Devil and the flames of hell, and it is interesting that in most Tarot packs only the left side of the Emperor's face is visible, for the left is by long tradition the side of evil. Hargrave Jennings, intent on demonstrating that the fleur-de-lis of the French royal arms was based on the louse, concocted a link between the fleur-de-lis, *fleur de luce*, Lucifer, lice, other small insects, and Satan as Lord of the Flies.

The Pope also has some sinister undertones. Gnostics maintained that the evil Demiurge invented conventional religion and morality to keep men enslaved to him by inducing them to worship him and obey his laws. Eliphas Lévi pointed out that when the hand is raised in the Pope's 'sign of esotericism' it casts a shadow shaped like the head and horns of the Devil. Without going as far as this, writers interpreting the Pope as the card of established religion usually imply that the seeker after truth must look much deeper.

86 INTERPRETATION

6 *The Lovers*. This card, called the Lovers or Love, varies even more in design from one pack to another than most of the other trumps. Some of the old cards show a young couple apparently being joined in marriage by an older figure. Cupid, who may or may not be blindfolded, is hovering in a cloud above their heads and aiming an arrow at them from his bow. The shapes of the arrow and the bow suggest sexual union. In other old packs a young man is standing between two women who seem to be trying to lure him in different directions, with Cupid again hovering above the scene, much as he does in the *Primavera*. It has been suggested that this type of card was based on the myth of the Judgment of Paris, but this seems unlikely, as it was essential to Renaissance interpretations of the myth that there be three female figures, not two.

The old cards have been explained along the obvious lines as symbols of love, marriage and choice. The young man between two women has to choose between

ABOVE LEFT Waite's drastically 'rectified' card of the Lovers, showing them as Adam and Eve in Eden before the Fall, and ABOVE RIGHT the Lovers of the 'Charles VI' pack. OPPOSITE From a German woodcut, the serpent of Eden, persuading Eve to eat the fatal apple.

vice on his left and virtue on his right, and there is usually little doubt of what his decision will be, because Cupid is aiming the arrow of desire nearer to vice than to virtue. According to various authors, the young man is torn between his conscience and his passions, or between the sacred and the profane, or between his attachment to his mother and his desire for a mistress, or more broadly between security and independence, between the safe familiar world of home and a longing to strike out into the cold world outside.

Behind all this is the story of Adam and Eve, the forbidden fruit and the serpent. In the Pope man is made in the image of God, in the Lovers he is shown in two sexes, an original unity now split into two and enmeshed in duality. Like Adam in Eden, like all human beings, the young man in the card has to choose between obedience and disobedience, and like Adam he will fall. In the Bible it was the Fall which brought death into the world as the consequence of Adam's choice. And so the card is interpreted as a symbol of love and inevitable death, both in the sense of the 'little death' of love, the collapse of the phallus after orgasm, and in the wider sense of 'the way of all flesh'.

The Golden Dawn, however, completely redesigned the card to show Perseus rescuing Andromeda from the monster – 'the Dragon of fear and the waters of stagnation' – to which she had been offered as bride and prey in the classical legend. The card's Hebrew letter is *zain*, 'sword', and this version of it was meant to show 'the impact of inspiration on intuition, resulting in illumination and liberation – the sword striking off the fetters of habit and materialism'.[22]

This design was presumably too close to the bone for Waite. It could readily be interpreted in terms of the old gnostic belief in the evilness of the God of the Old Testament. The serpent of Genesis, on this hypothesis, was not the Devil in disguise, as in orthodox Christian tradition, but a saviour who came to open the eyes of Adam and Eve to the evil nature of the Demiurge's creation and to free them from his fetters. Perseus is the serpent or angel of inspiration from on high and the dragon of fear and stagnation is the Demiurge, who wishes to keep the soul imprisoned in matter and materialism.

Waite redesigned the card again, to show Adam and Eve innocently naked in Eden. Behind Adam is the Tree of Life, which has twelve fruits on it, standing for the signs of the zodiac and so for the twelve basic types of human character in astrology. Behind Eve is the fatal tree of knowledge. It bears five fruits for the five senses and the serpent is coiled round it. Taking the place of Cupid or Perseus in the sky is a gigantic winged angel. Waite said that his card represented the pure love of Adam and Eve before the Fall, before they ate the forbidden fruit and 'knew that they were naked' and their love became carnal and gross, but that the Fall was also implied in it. Adam is looking at Eve, and Eve at the angel, which suggests that the conscious intellect (Adam) cannot approach the higher realms of the superconscious (the angel) directly but only through the unconscious (Eve).

In Genesis, the serpent tells Eve that if she and Adam eat the fruit their eyes will be opened and they will be like God. The serpent is an old symbol of wisdom, immortality and sex, and behind most Tarot interpretations is the belief that the serpent was right. Through eating the fruit the first man and woman discovered sex and became like God in being able to reproduce themselves and so create new life. On the spiritual level, what they discovered was the possibility of regaining the original unity. In erotic terms the lost unity is recovered through the ecstatic mingling of the sexes in which a child is conceived, but this is a paradigm of something far greater, the union of the warring, contending forces in human personality which creates the 'new life' of the higher self. This view of the story in Genesis turns the conventional interpretation of it upside down. Obedience to God's command would have been fatal, for Adam and Eve would have remained a pair of barren opposites. Disobedience brought physical death but the possibility of spiritual life. The story itself is a myth, of course, but a myth of profound meaning.

The card is consequently explained as a symbol of both analysis and synthesis, of the separating out of opposite factors which are brought into equal balance with each other so as to be reconciled in a harmonious unity. 'Love', Eliphas Lévi said, 'is one of the mythological images of the great secret and the great agent, because it at once expresses an action and a passion, a void and a plenitude, a shaft and a

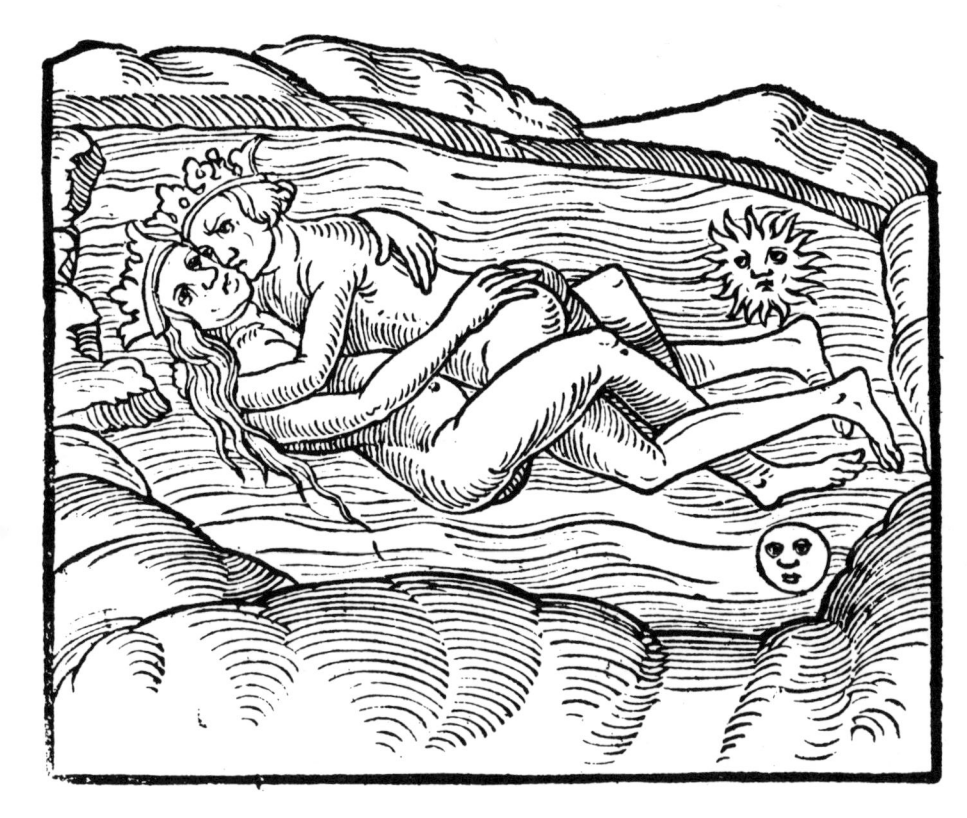

The alchemical 'royal marriage' of opposites, from a 16th-century German woodcut.

wound.'[23] This is shown in Adam and Eve, in Gemini which is the sign of the twins, and in the twin gods Castor and Pollux, the two-faced Janus, god of entrances and exits, the magpie and all hybrids, where two factors are joined into one. To cross the abyss to reach the highest triangle on the Tree, man must balance and reconcile the warring opposites in himself.

Similarly in psychoanalysis, Jung said, the problem of opposites is 'the dissociation of the personality brought about by the conflict of incompatible tendencies, resulting as a rule from an inharmonious disposition. The repression of one of the opposites leads only to a prolongation and extension of the conflict, in other words, to a neurosis. The therapist therefore confronts the opposites with one another and aims at uniting them permanently.'[24] It was this which Jung discerned behind the mysterious 'royal marriage' of which the alchemists spoke in riddles, the union of the king and the queen or the sun and the moon.

Crowley explained that in the passage of the abyss the adept has a choice, which is implied in the Lovers, between obedience and disobedience to a higher law. To attain the supreme heights he must destroy himself as an individual and submerge himself in the life of the universe as a whole, which means in the divine. If he accepts self-annihilation he will be 'reborn' on the path of the Empress. If he refuses and clings to his individuality, he remains in the abyss as a Black Brother, isolated in the hard shell of his own egotism. 'Such a being is gradually disintegrated from lack of nourishment and the slow but certain action of the attraction of the rest of the universe, despite his now desperate efforts to insulate and protect himself, and to aggrandize himself by predatory practices. He may indeed prosper for a while, but in the end he must perish...'[25] Crowley thought that MacGregor Mathers had succumbed to this fate. Others believed that it overtook Crowley himself.

7 *The Chariot*. In the ascent of the Tree, the path of the Chariot is the first which crosses the abyss and the card is always treated as a symbol of triumph, the victory of the soul which has conquered on one plane and now rises higher. It may originally have been based on the old Roman custom of the triumph awarded to a successful general, which was revived for their own glorification by Renaissance strongmen in Italy. In 1326, for example, Castruccio Castracane rode into his city of Lucca as a Roman victor in a chariot, with the prisoners he had taken on campaign being driven before him through the streets. When Alfonso the Great of Aragon, who had a similar taste for classical antiquities, made his state entry into conquered Naples in 1443, he was enthroned on a triumphal car drawn by four white horses, with a canopy of cloth of gold above his head.[26]

There was also a well-known medieval and Renaissance type of Mars in fury, riding in a horse-drawn chariot. Both Petrarch and Chaucer describe the god of war in this way and the imagery goes back to a twelfth-century text intended to bring out the hidden meanings of classical myths, *Liber Imaginum Deorum* by an obscure author named Albricus.[27] Painters showed Mars in a chariot, helmeted and wielding a whip or a sword. The Mars of the 'Mantegna' cards follows this pattern. In the Chariot of the 'Charles VI' pack the warrior brandishes a battle-axe. In later packs he is more often holding a sceptre.

The Chariot was one of the cards which Eliphas Lévi 'rectified', and Wirth and Waite based their designs on his. Among other alterations, he changed the horses pulling the triumphal car into two sphinxes, one black and one white. Lévi interpreted the card as a symbol of 'magical power in all its fullness' and his two sphinxes stood for the opposites yoked together to draw the chariot. He said that the angel with a flaming sword who guarded the gate of Eden after the expulsion of Adam and Eve from the garden had the form of a sphinx with a human head on the body of a bull, like the winged man-headed bulls of ancient Mesopotamian art. The charioteer in Lévi's card is both the angel who guards paradise and man who regains it.

ABOVE God is seated in a fiery chariot in William Blake's painting of the Lord passing judgment on Adam. OPPOSITE Three cards in which the Charioteer bears different weapons: LEFT TO RIGHT a sceptre; a sword held by the Mars of the 'Mantegna' pack; and a battle-axe carried by the warrior in the 'Charles VI' pack.

The charioteer is not driving the triumphal car but being drawn along in it. The card marks the release from earthly bondage of the adept's true and higher self, in an emotional and spiritual rapture which sets him free to soar beyond the normal limits of human consciousness into a communion with the divine. In Crowley's design the charioteer is a mailed knight who bears the Holy Grail in the form of a circular dish. The card corresponds to the process called 'exaltation' in alchemy, the achievement of a peak of mystical ecstasy in which the alchemist himself became the Philosopher's Stone, the summit of all earthly aspiration, the perfect substance which metaphorically turned everything it touched into gold. The remaining trumps, following the Chariot, show stages in the discovery and development of the true self, roughly in parallel with the alchemical processes which led up to the making of the Stone.

Just as the Chariot stands for a triumphal rise above the mortal condition in the ascent of the Tree, so conversely in the descent it refers to the myth of the Fall and its consequences. When God discovered that Adam had eaten the forbidden fruit, he said, 'Behold the man has become like one of us...' To prevent Adam and Eve from eating the fruit of the Tree of Life and becoming immortal, he drove them out of Eden and set the angel with the flaming sword to guard it. And then, 'Adam knew Eve his wife, and she conceived...' The charioteer is man 'become like one of us', the progenitor of a child in his image as God had made man in the divine image. This theme is continued in the interpretation of the following cards.

Lévi placed on the front of the triumphal car the Indian symbol of the lingam and the yoni combined in the joining of the sexes, surmounted by a winged globe. In some of the older packs the letters V.T. can be seen on the front of the chariot. If read from right to left they can be taken to spell out the Hebrew letter *tav*, the T-cross which again stands for union of the sexes or the opposites. But another consequence of the Fall was death and the Chariot is also an emblem of death and punishment. Its path lies on the left-hand pillar of the Tree, the punishing side of the divine, and joins Binah with Geburah, the sefira of fierce destructive force, corresponding to Mars. Conversely again, reading up the Tree, the card stands for the conquest of death.

Interpretations of the Chariot have been influenced by Merkabah mysticism, which was an earlier variety of Jewish mysticism than the Cabala. Its object of aspiration was the Chariot or Throne of God, seen in the vision described in the first chapter of Ezekiel. It was the Merkabah which was reached by the ascent (or descent, some said) through the *hekhaloth*, the heavenly halls, and it stood in the seventh of them. The Chariot's number in the Tarot is seven and one of the titles of the sefira Binah is the Throne. The being seen by Ezekiel on the chariot-throne was 'a likeness as it were of a human form', guarded by the four sphinx-like 'living creatures' (shown in Crowley's version of the card). The Chariot is placed on the Pillar of Severity, and the experience of the Merkabah mystics was of the awesome and fearful power of the Almighty, rather than of divine love and mercy. There was a tendency to identify the figure on the throne as the Demiurge, the creator of the visible world, not as the evil being which he was in gnostic theory, but as an aspect of the ultimate godhead.

God made the world in six days, according to Genesis, and rested on the seventh, and one of the victories which the Chariot celebrates is this achievement of the Creator or Demiurge, shown triumphant in the chariot of the world he made. The crescent moons on the charioteer's shoulders are also connected with the number seven. Each phase of the moon's cycle is complete in seven days, and in numerology seven governs the underlying rhythms of the universe. The four pillars which support the canopy of the chariot are the four elements of which the world is made, or in modern occultism the four conditions in which energy can exist – electricity (fire), the gaseous state (air), the liquid state (water) and the solid state (earth). Each pillar is divided into two equal parts, which represent 'above' and 'below', as do the star-spangled canopy itself and the cubical body of the chariot below it. The two sphinxes or horses stand for spirit and matter, soul and body, intellect and emotion. Plato in the *Phaedrus* spoke of the lover's soul as a charioteer driving two winged horses, the noble steed of reason and the ignoble one of passionate desire.

The crab and the turtle of the correspondences, at home both on land and in the water, again suggest the union of 'above' and 'below', as does the sphinx, which combines a human head with an animal body. Jung regarded the sphinx as a symbol of the Terrible Mother, the female principle in its destroying and hideous aspect, which fits in well with the Chariot's path on the Tree. The sphinx also stands for the enigma, the mystery, the riddle which the charioteer has solved. The lotus, like the rose, is a symbol of woman and paradise. Cancer is the sign of the sun at the summer solstice and the god Apollo, the ideal type of male beauty in Greek art, was often pictured riding in the chariot of the sun. The Egyptian god Khepera was also connected with the sun. He had the head of a scarab or dung-beetle, which rolls its eggs laboriously along in a ball of dung and so became an emblem of the life-giving ball of the sun rolling up from the darkness of the underworld into the morning sky. Sir Wallis Budge, whose books on Egyptian religion and magic have had considerable influence on occultists, said that Khepera stood for 'matter which contains within itself the germ of life which is about to spring into a new existence'.[28]

The Virgin Mary in the walled garden of paradise – 'A garden enclosed is my sister, my spouse': *The Little Paradise-Garden* by an anonymous painter, early 15th century. OVERLEAF LEFT The Lovers and RIGHT the Chariot from a 15th-century pack designed by Bonifacio Bembo.

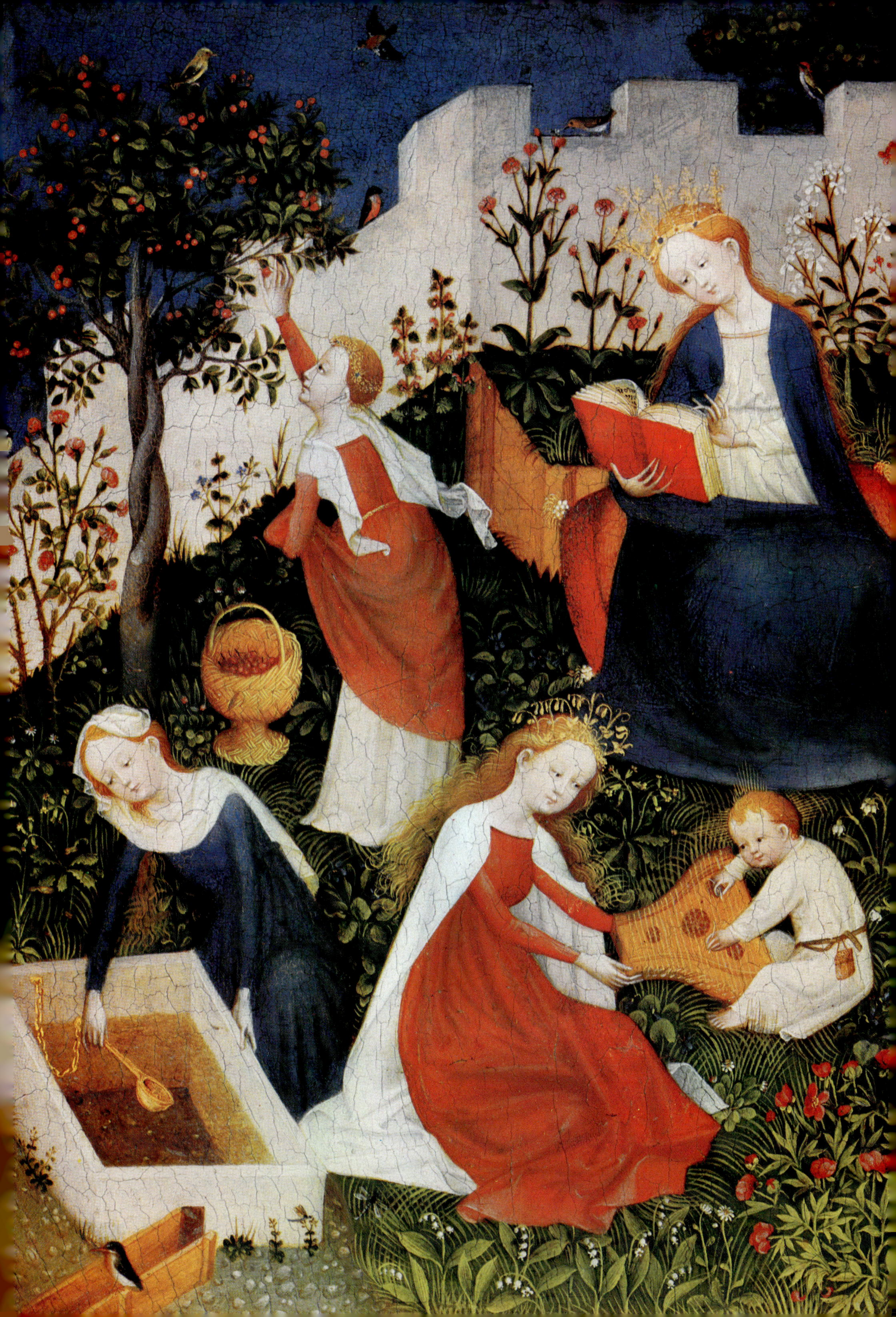

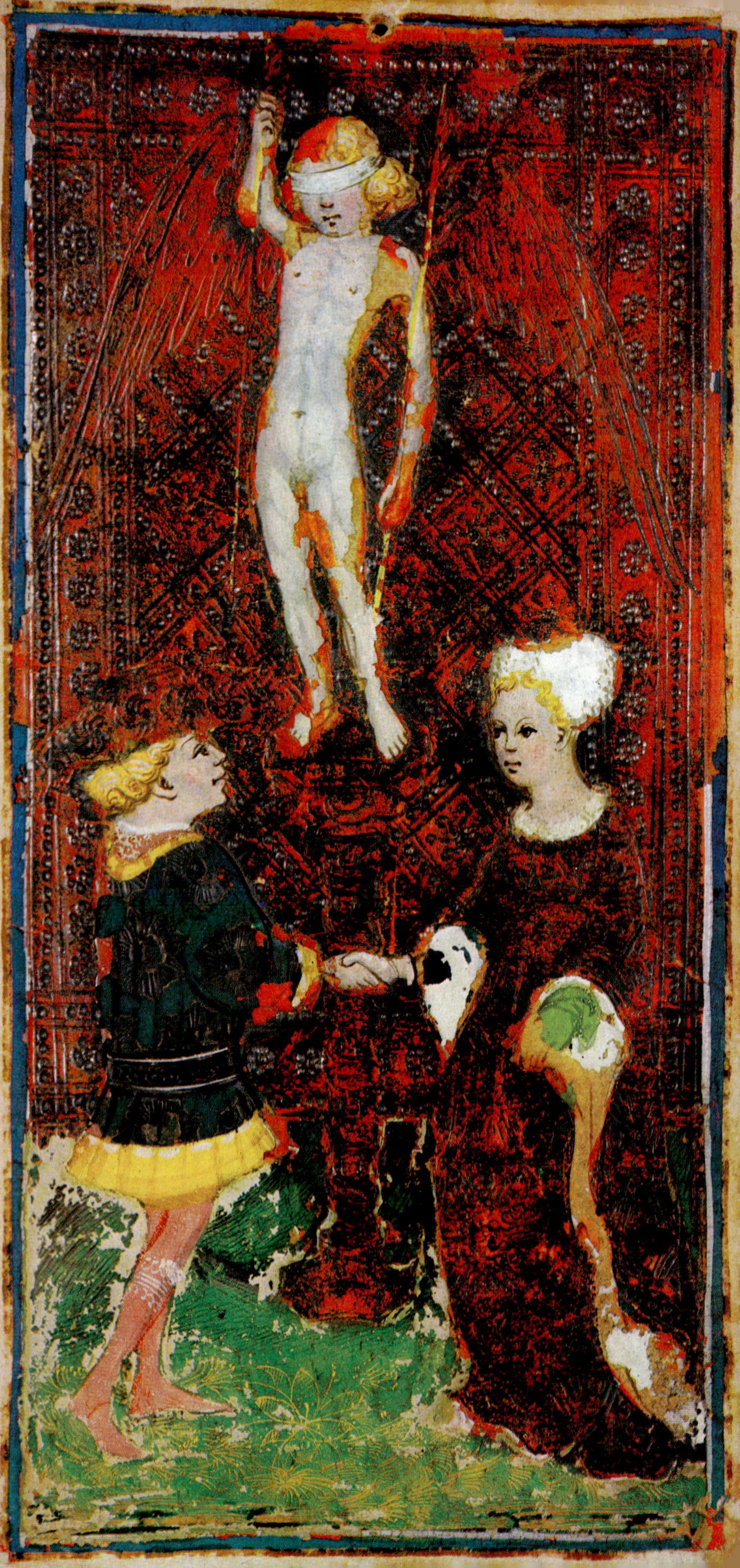

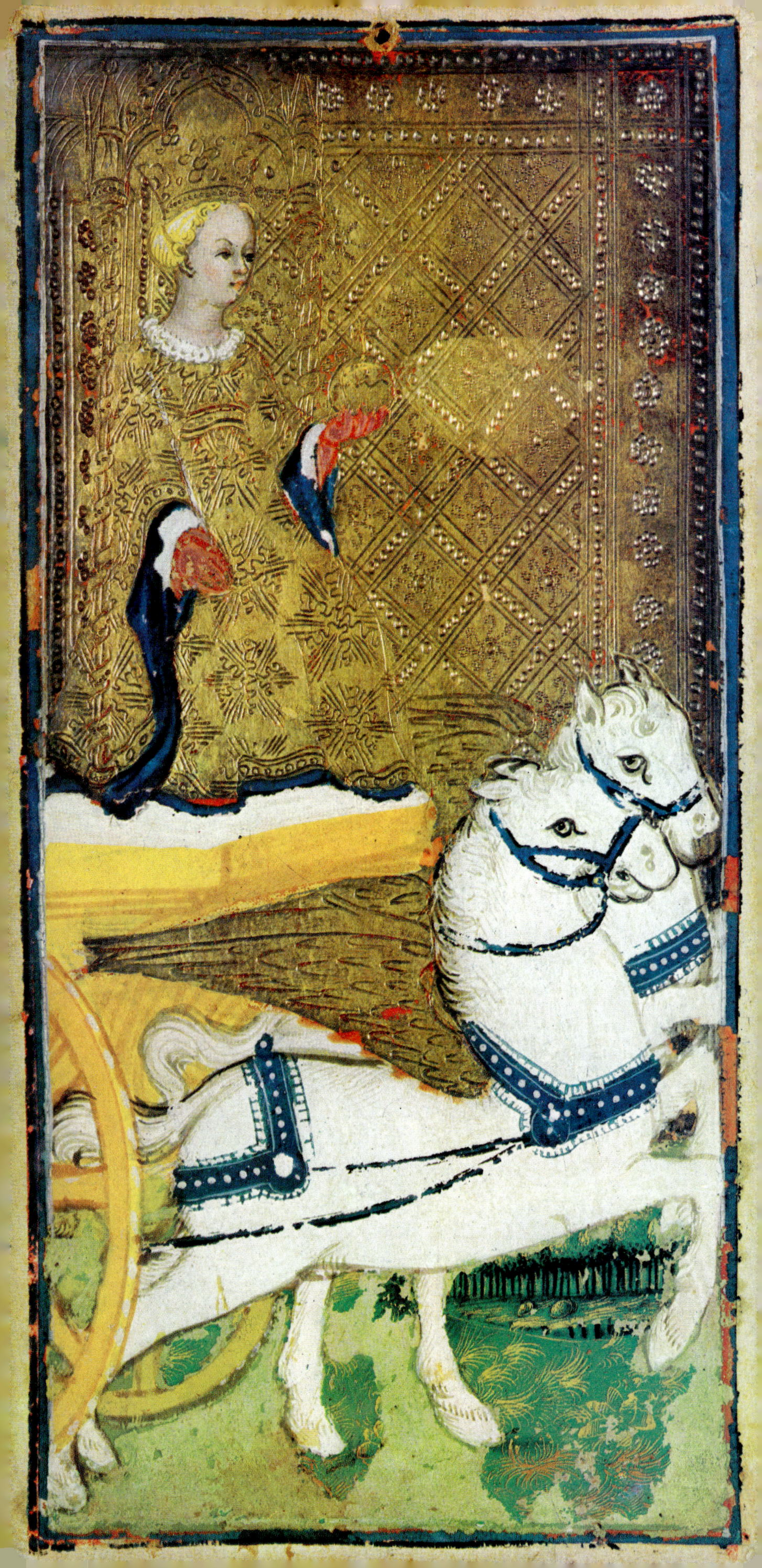

1

THE MAGICIAN

8 *Strength*. There is considerable disagreement about which trump should follow the Chariot. In the old packs Justice is the eighth trump and Strength the eleventh, but the Golden Dawn changed them round, partly because Strength goes better with the lion of the sign of Leo and Justice with Libra, the sign of the scales. Waite also put Strength in the eighth place and so did Crowley, though he retained the card's traditional number, eleven. It is a revealing fact, not only about the Tarot but about the interpretation of symbolism in general, that with a little ingenuity either card can be fitted quite neatly into either slot.

Strength or Force was originally a picture of Fortitude, one of the four cardinal virtues of prudence, fortitude, justice and temperance which the medieval world of ideas inherited from Plato, Cicero and other classical writers. The three Christian virtues of faith, hope and charity were added to make a set of seven. All seven are included in the 'Mantegna' cards and the minchiate packs, but the standard Tarot, puzzlingly, has only three – though there have been many attempts to find the missing classical virtue of prudence among the other trumps. Abstract nouns in Greek and Latin are frequently feminine in gender, not neuter, which facilitated the personification of abstract ideas as goddesses or demi-goddesses. The virtues appeared in medieval and Renaissance art as female figures, often wearing armour and crowns to show their success in battle against the vices. Fortitude might be a she-warrior with a lion on her shield, or a woman holding or breaking a pillar (as in the 'Charles VI' pack). Or she might be a woman subduing a lion, which is her most common form in the Tarot.

The Tarot card has been described as the feminine equivalent of St George defeating the dragon. The woman taming the king of beasts is a sign of victory over brutishness and evil. The conquest of the lion stands for the subjugation of the passions, the instincts, pride, ignorance or temptation. According to some authors, the woman is Virgo, following Leo in the zodiac and damping down the fierce heat of summer. Or she is 'Venus repressing the fire of Vulcan', the lame smith who was the husband of Venus in mythology. The lion can be identified with the Jungian concept of 'the shadow', the dark and primitive, instinctive and dangerous part of each human being, which is feared and repressed. It is the Mr Hyde who lives inside each Dr Jekyll. In the ascent of the Tree the brutal, instinctive driving forces of man's nature are tamed to the service of his higher, spiritual impulses. (Both sides of his nature are yoked together to draw him in triumph in the Chariot.)

The card is a symbol of discipline. The woman is not killing the lion, but quietly and firmly mastering it. She is apparently opening its jaws. Wirth took this to mean that the savage urges and instincts of the animal in human nature should not be despised and shut away but released, controlled and put to use. Similarly the Golden Dawn taught 'a dangerous secret', not to be openly divulged, about the evil side of human personality: 'The evil persona can be rendered as a great and strong, yet trained, animal whereupon the man rideth . . .' In Crowley's version of the card, which he called Lust, the woman is riding on the Great Beast of Revelation, the apotheosis of evil, anarchy and destruction. Above them is the astrological symbol of Leo (♌), turned upside down. The woman's unnatural dominance of the lion suggested to Crowley the discipline of submission to the abnormal and perverse. 'Nature is outraged by Magick; man is bestialized and woman defiled.' He kept the number eleven for the card because the eleventh degree ritual of the O.T.O. involved abnormal sexual intercourse. Some other writers on the Tarot have renamed

A modern version of the Magician, from the 007 pack, designed for one of the 'James Bond' films.

the card the Enchantress, which suggests an allusion to Circe, the great enchantress in the *Odyssey* who turned men into animals.[29]

Strength's path on the Tree joins Hesed and Geburah, linking the opposites of love and hate, mercy and cruelty, the constructive and destructive forces in the universe, the woman and the lion. Following the Chariot and continuing with the myth in Genesis, the woman is Eve taming Adam in the embrace in which she conceived a child. Eight is the number of new life and the woman's hat is the same shape as the Juggler's, a symbol of fecundity. Preceding the Chariot on the way up the Tree, the card corresponds to the alchemical process called 'fermentation', in which the alchemist worked himself into a frenzy of seething emotional excitement that culminated in 'exaltation', the making of the Stone. The alchemists, describing mystical and psychological processes in terms of metal-working operations in their workshops, said that all too often in practice the 'ferment' died away with no lasting result. The Stone was only achieved if 'the heat of the furnace' could be raised to a sufficient pitch of intensity, or in other words if the alchemist's own fervour was sustained and carried to the highest peak of rapture.

Waite had both alchemy and erotic symbolism in mind in designing his version of the card. The lion is red for the fiery, active, male principle of sulphur (which is red in its natural, unrefined state). The woman is closing the lion's mouth instead of opening it, which is another piece of sexual innuendo. Fortitude means endurance, and Waite explained the change by saying that 'Fortitude, in one of its most exalted aspects, is connected with the Divine Mystery of Union.'[30]

The motif of ferment and torrid heat and excitement underlies the card's correspondences. The sun is in Leo in high summer. The terrible lion-headed goddess Sekhmet of Memphis, lady of slaughter and frightfulness, personified the withering, death-dealing heat of the desert sun. Her twin, Bastet, was the cat-headed or lion-headed goddess of Bubastis. Her connection with sex and fertility comes out in Herodotus's account of her annual festival, during which her women worshippers exposed themselves and shouted bawdy jokes. She stood for the sun's other aspect of life-giving warmth.

ABOVE, NEAR RIGHT The Hermit of the 'Charles VI' pack, holding up a lantern, and FAR RIGHT the solitary hunchback of the 007 pack. OPPOSITE, LEFT TO RIGHT The lion appears three times in the 'Mantegna' card of Strength; Waite's version, in which the woman is closing the lion's mouth; and an unusual Strength card from the 007 pack showing a circus strong man.

9 *The Hermit*. This card is also known as the Old Man, the Hunchback or the Capuchin. It may originally have been meant to represent Time, but ever since Court de Gébelin the Hermit has been interpreted as the wise man in search of truth. He is an old man wrapped in a heavy cloak and carrying a staff and a lantern. Solitary and withdrawn, treading the lonely path of his pilgrimage, he is at the same time a light and a beacon to others. Lévi, identifying him as the missing cardinal virtue of prudence, said that his lantern is the light of reason and knowledge, his cloak is the protective mantle of self-possession, and his phallic staff shows that he has the help of the secret and everlasting forces of nature. The staff has alternatively been explained as the weapon which chastises error or as the sign of faith in the Supreme Being, referring to Psalm 23: 'thy rod and thy staff, they comfort me'.

Wirth gave his hermit an immensely long beard and a snake, coiled at the foot of the staff, a symbol of virile power held in reserve. Papus said that the Hermit is the young man seen earlier in the card of the Lovers, who has chosen the right path and through experience has become a sage. Other authors have connected him with legendary wise men, including Hermes Trismegistus, King Solomon and Christian Rosenkreuz, the mythical founder of the Rosicrucians, whose body was supposed to have been discovered perfectly preserved when his tomb was opened a hundred and twenty years after his burial. The Hermit has also been identified with the Jungian archetype of the wise old man – the father, king, sage or teacher possessed of profound and inscrutable learning.

The Hermit's path connects Hesed, the fatherly loving-kindness of God, with Tifereth, the sphere of Christ or the sun, and Waite said that the card blends the ideas of the Ancient of Days and the Light of the World. A hermit is an obvious symbol of withdrawal, isolation, austerity, purity and concentration on spiritual things. The Hermit in one French pack of the early eighteenth century is an almost exact copy of a German woodcut of 1550, showing St Jude, the saint invoked for help in desperate situations.[31] In modern interpretations, however, the Hermit is also a phallic symbol and an emblem of masturbation, standing for the fertility of self-reliance. His Hebrew letter, *yod*, has phallic connotations and is the first letter of the name of God (Yahweh or Jehovah). At this stage in the ascent of the Tree the true self has reached puberty, as it were, the seeker for truth has found the Master in himself. Adonis and Attis are included in the correspondences as dying and rising gods, like the phallus itself. Taken in either ascending or descending order, the Chariot, Strength and the Hermit are symbols of life, death and life regained.

Nine is the number of initiation and is also a number of completeness because it is the last of the basic numbers from one to nine, of which all higher numbers are composed. The Hermit is complete in himself, self-possessed and self-sufficient, corresponding to the sign of Virgo and to the anchorite, the virgin and all solitary beings. His plants have white flowers, emblems of purity and detachment. The lily is a symbol of virginity and the narcissus stands for self-love and self-absorption, from the Greek story of Narcissus who fell in love with his own reflection in a pool.

10 *The Wheel of Fortune.* The Wheel of Fortune varies considerably in detail from one pack to another and also has a great variety of possible interpretations. The symbol itself is another classical emblem which survived into the Middle Ages, largely through the influence of one of the most famous books of late paganism, the *De Consolatione Philosophiae* of Boethius, written in the sixth century A.D. The image of the blind and fickle goddess turning the wheel to which men are fastened, so that their fortunes rise and fall with it, became a favourite medieval symbol of the vanity and emptiness of all worldly ambitions. It taught the lesson that power, wealth and pleasure crumble to dust and that men's only lasting hope is in God. A French abbot in the twelfth century installed in his monastery a wheel of Fortune that was turned by machinery, 'that his monks might ever have before them the spectacle of human vicissitudes'.[32]

A typical medieval picture of the wheel shows Fortune turning it with a lever. As it turns, human figures which are moving backwards, to show that they have no control of their destinies, rise towards the summit where a crowned king is perched. On the other side more human figures are sinking, looking wistfully back to the top, and at the bottom one is falling off the wheel altogether. In the Tarot the wheel is usually turning by itself and the figures on it are often animal instead of human. The crowned monkey which squats on top of the wheel in some of the old designs looks like a sardonic comment on the folly of human pretensions.

Fortune's wheel is a symbol of fate carrying men to the zenith of their lives and then inexorably on to defeat and death, and the Tarot card is interpreted in this way by some writers. But a wheel can have many other connotations. It is a very old symbol of the sun, either by itself or as part of the sun's chariot. As a useful artefact it can stand for power and progress, a move into new territory, the advance of civilization. In various ancient traditions God is represented fashioning the world and man on a potter's wheel. The rolling wheels of Ezekiel's vision, whose rims were full of eyes, are symbols of divine activity and intelligence. In Christian art a wheel is sometimes an emblem of God's power in scenes of the expulsion of Adam and Eve from paradise, and a wheel and a sword are attributes of the angel who guarded the gate of Eden.

The wheel also appears in alchemical texts as a symbol of spiritual ascent and descent. It could be understood as a reference to Christ's descent into a mortal human body and the promise of immortality which he brought to mankind, on the authority of one of the sermons of St Bernard, the great theologian and preacher of the twelfth century: 'By his descent he established for us a joyful and wholesome ascent.'[33]

As a circle, a wheel stands for wholeness, for diversity contained within a unity. The axle which stays still while the wheel revolves is a sign of stability at the heart of change. The turning rim is the ever-rolling stream of time, year succeeding year in a cyclical progression. The sun, moon and planets, long believed to control human destinies, appear to revolve in the wheel of the zodiac. The seasons go round in the wheel of the year, the tides ebb and flow, day follows night and night follows day. There is nothing new under the sun and all things return.

And yet, though each point on the wheel's rim recurs, the wheel moves forward. Life proceeds through the symmetry and equal momentum of opposite factors – expansion and contraction, growth and decay, birth and death. We live by alternately breathing in and breathing out. For every action there is an equal and

OPPOSITE LEFT The Capuchin or Hermit from one of the packs designed by Alliette and RIGHT from an 18th-century French pack.

opposite reaction. In the most influential of her books, *The Secret Doctrine*, Madame Blavatsky identified the 'law of periodicity', of flux and reflux, as a fundamental principle in the universe.

The Theosophists connected this fundamental law with the Indian doctrine of karma, which teaches that there is no such thing as chance and that everything which happens is determined by cause and effect. It is also the principle of 'as a man sows, so shall he reap.' Our good or evil fortune in life is not the outcome of luck or accident but is what we have deserved by our own actions in earlier lives. Karma is bound up with belief in reincarnation and the image of the sorrowful weary wheel of earthly existence, the round of successive reincarnations in which the consequences of previous lives are worked out. Only the soul that has reached the highest level of spiritual evolution can escape from the wheel altogether and leave the human sphere for the divine.

All these symbolic connotations of the wheel have influenced interpretations of the Tarot card. Papus, who thought it an emblem of karma, said that the Chariot, the Wheel and the card of Death correspond to the Hindu trinity of Brahma the Creator, Vishnu the Preserver, and Shiva the Destroyer. In Wirth's and Waite's designs the wheel stands for the law of periodicity and the symmetrical alternation of flux and reflux, cause and effect, action and reaction, which keeps the world in being. It is a symbol of the order and regularity of things, of unity behind diversity and stability amidst change.

On the rim of the wheel in Waite's card are the letters ROTA interspersed with the Hebrew letters of the Tetragrammaton, the great name of God in four letters (*yod he vau he*, spoken as Jehovah or Yahweh). If the letters on the rim are given their Hebrew number values they add up to 697, and $6+9+7=22$, which is the number of all things as parts of a connected whole. The name of God in the wheel shows that all events occur within the order of Providence, the systematic divine plan for the world. The card's number is ten, which can again stand for all things, the entire universe, and in numerological theory ten is constituted by four (because $1+2+3+4=10$). Hence the four winged figures at the corners of Waite's design. They stand for the 'living creatures' of Ezekiel's vision, the four Christian gospels and the four elements, and are related to the four letters of the divine name.

The sphinx with a sword at the top of the wheel in most modern designs is another symbol of diversity contained in a unity. It also stands for escape from the wheel and recalls the angel at the gate of Eden and the riddle which is solved in the Chariot. On the ascending side of the wheel is Anubis, who in Egyptian belief led the soul to judgment in the Hall of Truth after death. On the descending side is the evil Seth. On one side the soul is rising to a higher level, on the other it is sinking into bondage on the material plane. Anubis and Seth recall a famous passage in Blake's *Marriage of Heaven and Hell:* 'Without Contraries is no progression. Attraction and Repulsion, Reason and Energy, Love and Hate, are necessary to Human existence. From these contraries spring what the religious call Good and Evil. Good is the passive that obeys Reason. Evil is the active springing from Energy.'

In the ascent of the Tree the Wheel marks the birth of the true self at the still centre of a man's own being, the self in which his diversity becomes a unity. The card can be connected with birth not only as the wheel of reincarnation but because a wheel is an emblem of woman, and the card's Hebrew letter, *kaph*, transliterated

LEFT TO RIGHT A humorous woodcut in which the Wheel of Fortune is ridden by asses and guided by a hand from above; a minchiate card in which an ass perches on top of the wheel; and the blind Lady of Fortune from a pack by Alliette.

into Greek, is the initial letter of *kteis*. Hargrave Jennings identified the wheel-shaped Round Table of the Arthurian legends and the rose windows of churches as female symbols, and the menstrual cycle on which all human life depends is an example of the law of periodicity. The Roman goddess Fortuna, to whom the wheel belonged, was originally a deity of fertility and the life of women, and a wheel was also one of the symbols of Isis.

Descending the Tree, the Wheel's path is a lower continuation of the Pope's. Where earlier God made man in his image, here mankind reproduces itself. The children born to Adam and Eve after their expulsion from Eden were Cain and Abel, the first agriculturalist and the first pastoralist, the first to begin the march of civilization. They were also the first murderer and the first victim, the human prototypes of evil as 'the active springing from Energy' and good as 'the passive that obeys Reason'.

The Egyptian god Amon was worshipped at Thebes as the power which kept the world in being and was identified with the sun god, Re. In Hebrew letters his name adds to 91, and 9 + 1 = 10, which is the Wheel's number. Zeus and Jupiter, to whom the eagle and the oak belong, are also included in the correspondences as supreme gods and preservers of universal order. The planet Jupiter in astrology governs the circulation of the blood and circular motion in general. Some authors identify the figure at the top of the wheel as Osiris, the preserver of life. The fig is an emblem of woman. The poplar is phallic and also stands for the symmetry of opposites, because the two sides of its leaf are different shades of green.

Yet another interpretation identifies the Wheel as the missing virtue of prudence. The three figures on the wheel are the three divisions of the virtue as analysed by Cicero and medieval theologians: memory, intelligence and foresight, which together provide a grasp of the past, present and future. They also illustrate Cicero's definition of prudence as the knowledge of what is good, what is bad, and what is neither good nor bad.

11 *Justice*. Many of the ideas associated with the Wheel recur in interpretations of Justice, another of the classical virtues, which appears in the Tarot in the traditional form as a seated woman holding a sword and scales. The card has been linked with the judgment after death of Egyptian belief, when the soul was weighed in the balance against the feather of Maat, the principle of order and truth. To pass the test the dead man's conscience had to weigh exactly the same as the feather, so that the scales were level, and this has influenced explanations of the card as a symbol of equilibrium. The motif of the weighing of the soul descended into Christian art and in some medieval scenes of the Last Judgment the dead are shown being weighed in scales. It also occurs in oriental art.

Another connection is with the law of karma. In Indian belief, after each period of life on earth the soul is judged in the afterworld. Depending on its actions in life, it is then sent to be rewarded or punished in a paradise or a hell, after which it is reborn once more on the wheel, to trudge through another existence on earth. The Tarot card has also been linked with the Roman Catholic doctrine of Purgatory, where souls too good for hell but not good enough for heaven are purged of their sins by punishment after death.

What the traditional figure of Justice immediately suggests is the principle of 'as a man sows, so shall he reap', and in Raphael's painting of the virtue, in the Vatican, she has the motto *Ius suumcuique tribuit*, 'Justice gives each his due.' Some writers interpret the Tarot card in terms of the Indian concept of dharma, the orderliness and essential rightness of the universe, moral law and the call of duty. To some it stands for conscience and discrimination. More often it is explained as a symbol of justice in the old Greek sense of an equal balance of opposite factors. Ebb and flow, cause and effect, good and evil, which go round in the Wheel, are here displayed in a stable equilibrium.

The card is also considered a symbol of copulation as a balance and harmony of opposites. The woman in Waite's design wears a mantle which is green, the colour

THE TWENTY-TWO TRUMPS 105

The judgment after death of ancient Egyptian belief, when the conscience is weighed in the Hall of Truth, from the Papyrus of Ani, and OPPOSITE, LEFT to RIGHT Justice as one of the classical virtues, in an early 18th-century Italian pack; a minchiate version of Justice with sword and scales; and a design for the subject by Dürer.

of Venus, over a robe which is red, for Mars. Her crown has three turrets and a four-sided jewel, and $3+4=7$, which in the Cabala is the number of Venus. In some ways the woman resembles the Female Pope. Justice's number is 11 and $1+1=2$, which is the Female Pope's number.

In the Golden Dawn system Justice's path leads up from Tifereth, the central sefira on the Tree, round which the other spheres form a symmetrical and balanced arrangement, to Geburah, the sefira of punishment and destruction. On this path the adept is in a state of passive equilibrium in which he matches each idea with its contrary and does not prefer any course of action to its opposite. He is undergoing a 'purgatory' or spiritual cleansing of his being through the cancelling out of warring opposites. The purgative drug bitter aloes is made from Justice's plant. In astrological tradition Libra, the sign of the scales, governs the kidneys, which are excretory organs and so suggest the same theme of purging and the elimination of waste material.

In Christian numerology eleven is the number of martyrdom. It also means 'a new beginning' because it is the first of a higher series of numbers, above ten. The card marks the conception of the true self, shown in the impregnation of female (the woman) by male (the sword and scales). The adept is in the womb, as it were, or in the forge of Vulcan, which is the belly of Venus, passive and inert, waiting to be born. The true self has been 'sown' in Justice and will be 'reaped' in the Wheel.

Libra is ruled by Venus in astrology and is connected with ideas of relatedness, partnership, communication and communion. The elephant is a symbol of massive strength and sexual energy. According to Indian tradition, the first elephant was named Airavata, 'the possessor of moisture', because he emerged from the sea. He was also known as 'lust-garmented' and 'ever in rut'. In the East white elephants are associated with rain-clouds and fertility, and there is a legend that the Buddha was fathered by a supernatural white elephant. The popular Hindu elephant god, Ganesha, was regarded by his followers as the sustainer of the universe.

The Hanged Man turned the wrong way up, after the mistaken design by Court de Gébelin.

12 *The Hanged Man.* The Hanged Man is one of the strangest and most fascinating cards in the pack. It shows a man suspended upside down from a gibbet made of two tree-trunks and a crossbar. He is usually hanging by one leg, with the other twisted behind it to form a cross. His hands are behind his back and the upper part of his body forms a triangle with one point downwards. Sometimes he is holding two money-bags, or coins are spilling out of his pockets. The oddest thing of all is his expression. Far from looking tortured or even uncomfortable, he is generally relaxed and contented.

So peculiar is the card that Court de Gébelin thought it had erroneously been printed upside down and was originally meant to be a symbol of prudence – a man standing on one foot while cautiously deciding where to put the other. This theory had been anticipated. In a French pack of the early eighteenth century the Hanged Man has been turned the other way up and renamed Prudence, and is shown balancing on one leg. Similarly in some Belgian packs of the eighteenth century he is standing insecurely on tiptoe. In the Sicilian Tarot he is hanged by the neck.

In the 'Charles VI' pack, however, and most of the others the Hanged Man is dangling head downwards. This is frequently taken to mean that the conventional values and standards of society are topsy-turvy: truth is the reverse of what most people think it is. Or according to one school of thought, the Hanged Man is accumulating 'orgone energy' on the lines of Wilhelm Reich's mysterious theories, drawing life-energy from the bright blue sky. Or he is upside down as a sign of self-abasement and submission to the will of God. But another explanation of his curious posture and serene expression is that he is an erotic symbol, an emblem of passion spent. He is the male who has satisfied the women of the Justice card. The old and persistent belief that a man loses some of his allotted store of vital energy in orgasm is one ingredient of the theme of sacrifice, affliction and martyrdom associated with the card.

The implication is also that, having 'died', the victim is capable of rising again. The Hanged Man, Waite said, hints at 'a great awakening that is possible' and that 'after the sacred Mystery of Death there is a glorious Mystery of Resurrection.' In Waite's version of the card the gibbet is shaped like the letter T, which is a symbol of the union of the sexes. But this is also a reference to the story of Moses fastening a bronze serpent to a pole as a cure for snake-bite when the Israelites were crossing the desert towards the Promised Land. According to tradition, the pole was a T-cross, foreshadowing the Crucifixion. 'And as Moses lifted up the serpent in the wilderness, so must the Son of man be lifted up, that whoever believes in him may have eternal life.'[34]

The Hanged Man has reminded many authors (including T.S. Eliot) of the theme of the dying and rising god as expounded in Frazer's *Golden Bough*, the god whose death and resurrection each year was the guarantee of the annual rebirth of the crops, and by analogy the guarantee of life after death for men. Osiris was one of these gods and was depicted lying dead but with his phallus erect and plants growing from his body. The same complex of ideas gathered round Christ and there are medieval pictures of the Saviour crucified on a tree whose branches are laden with flowers and fruit. In Waite's version of the Hanged Man, similarly, leaves are sprouting from the gibbet. Another god who has been linked with the card is Attis, whose cult spread from Asia Minor to Greece and Rome. According to one version of his myth, Attis castrated himself under a pine tree and bled to death. During the festival of his death and rebirth in spring an effigy of the young god was tied to a pine tree, which his eunuch-priests spattered with their blood. It was then buried, with sorrow and fasting. Frazer suggested that in earlier times the figure hanging and dying on the tree was not a dummy but a human being representing the god.

In pagan northern Europe men and animals were hanged on trees or gallows, and sometimes stabbed with a spear, as sacrifices to Odin. He was not a dying and rising god but the lord of war, magic, poetry, inspiration and the dead. In the poem *Havamal* or 'Utterance of the High One', Odin describes how he himself was hanged on the world-tree to win mastery of the magic runes.

> I know that I hung on the windy tree
> For nine whole nights,
> Wounded with the spear, dedicated to Odin,
> Myself to myself.

Odin hung on the tree to gain secret knowledge and power, not to rescue men from sin and death, like Jesus crucified on the world-tree of the cross and pierced with the lance. But the Hanged Man has been connected with both Odin and Christ as examples of a god being sacrificed to himself to recover something hidden or lost.

It is doubtful whether the card originally had anything to do with dying and rising gods, human sacrifice, Odin or Christ, but these associations have attracted modern interpreters. The Golden Dawn linked the Hanged Man with Osiris and Christ. Crowley identified him with Christ, though in a different spirit, as an image of the Slain God, a beautiful, immemorial but moribund formula which had been put out of date by the new religion of Crowleyanity. More recently, Arland Ussher has described the Hanged Man as the Crucified God, 'who opened a new Era by accepting the human tragedy, an acceptance which meant a complete somersault or reversal of posture'.[35]

Alternative names for the card in the old packs are the Thief and the Traitor, and the old popular interpretation of the Hanged Man identified him not with Jesus but with Judas, the arch-traitor, and the money-bags or falling coins with the thirty pieces of silver. Eliphas Lévi connected the card with Prometheus, expiating by torture the crime of stealing fire from heaven and bestowing it on men. Oswald Wirth thought that the mythological figure nearest to the Hanged Man was Perseus, flying through the air to save Andromeda from the dragon of evil. Both of them had in mind the theme of something 'higher' coming to the rescue of something 'lower', which was taken up by the Golden Dawn.

In the Golden Dawn system the card's Hebrew letter is *mem*, which the *Sefer Yetsirah* links with water, in which things are reflected upside down. Water is the blood of the soil, the carrier of life and fertility. It is *fons et origo*, 'the fount and origin', from the old belief that all things originally derived from water. Water also suggests the 'depths' of the mind, as do the snake and the scorpion of the correspondences, whose lairs are in dark and secret places. In the process of the Hanged Man the adept is drowned in the floodtides of his inner being. He sacrifices himself to recover something hidden or lost in his own depths.

The Hanged Man is the wrong way up on his gibbet to show that at this stage of the quest the seeker for truth must stand himself spiritually and psychologically on

In a Belgian Tarot of 1740, the Hanged Man balances on tiptoe.

his head, so to speak. Before his true self can be 'conceived' in Justice and 'born' in the Wheel, his old and false self, with its whole structure of attitudes, standards, habits and ways of thinking must be destroyed. In a reversal of values this structure is overturned and fragmented to release the fertile waters of the depths, which carry the seed of new life. And this submergence of the 'higher' in the 'lower', this descent into one's own hell, is the salvation of the lower, animal nature, which is transformed and transmuted by it.

The paths of the Hanged Man and Justice both lead to Geburah, the sphere of destruction, and stand for the killing and purging of the old self before the creation of the new. The Hanged Man's path is a lower continuation of the path of the Chariot and is itself continued lower still by the path of the Day of Judgment. All three cards are connected with ideas of death and rebirth, of passing from a lower state to a higher. The card opposite the Hanged Man on the Tree is the Wheel, which stands for rebirth where the Hanged Man is a symbol of death.

The Golden Dawn taught, in Israel Regardie's words, that 'we are, in essence, gods of great power and spirituality who died to the land of our birth in the Garden of Hesperides, and mystically dying descended into hell. And moreover . . . that like Osiris, Christ and Mithra, and many another type of god-man, we too may rise from the tomb and become aware of our true divine natures.'[36] This is the background to Waite's version of the Hanged Man. The figure's shape – an inverted triangle below a cross – shows the descent of higher into lower. It is the same shape as the Emperor, but turned upside down, implying the submergence of order in chaos. The triangle and the cross also stand for three and four, and $3 \times 4 = 12$, which is the Hanged Man's number. The legs form a fylfot cross or swastika, a symbol of the sun, fire and vitality. Round the head is a halo of radiant light. The Latin word for light, *lux*, if turned into Roman numerals adds up to 65, which is also the total of the Hebrew word *Adonai*, 'Lord'. The halo is the radiance of the descending higher principle which will transform the lower nature. It is also the Light of the World, the light shining in darkness, Christ the Lord who came down into a human body to redeem fallen and brutish man.

Alchemy has been an important influence on interpretations of the Hanged Man. Lévi described him as 'the great and unique athanor, which all can use, which is ready to each man's hand, which all possess without knowing it'.[37] The athanor was the alchemist's furnace. Some modern occultists take it as a cover-name for the phallus, but generally it means the fierce heat of the alchemist's own transforming fervour. The first main stage in the making of the Stone culminated in the *nigredo* or blackening, when the material in the alchemist's vessel was 'killed' by heating it and driving off vapour, which was regarded as its 'spirit' or spark of life. Then the vapour was allowed to condense and saturate the 'dead' material, so 'resurrecting' it in a new and improved form. Here again is the theme of the higher redeeming the lower.

Jung commented on the dangers of the psychological process implied, the plunge into the mind's own depths. 'By descending into the unconscious, the conscious mind puts itself in a perilous position, for it is apparently extinguishing itself. It is in the situation of the primitive hero who is devoured by the dragon.' The conscious mind has 'volunteered to die in order to beget a new and fruitful life in that region of the psyche which has hitherto lain fallow in darkest unconsciousness, and

Head-downwards, the Hanged Man of the 'Charles VI' pack clutches his money-bags: popular tradition associates him with Judas Iscariot.

under the shadow of death... The dread and resistance which every natural human being experiences when it comes to delving too deeply into himself is, at bottom, the fear of the journey to Hades.' To make this journey, Jung thought, was to run the risk of psychological disintegration and possibly schizophrenia.[38]

In Wirth's design and in some of the older packs the tree-trunks supporting the Hanged Man's gibbet show the stumps of twelve lopped branches, six on each side. These are associated with the signs of the zodiac. The sun has run its course through the signs, the Twelve Labours of Hercules are at an end, the adept has completed one stage of his progress and hangs motionless like the stopped pendulum of a clock. The gibbet as a whole is shaped like the Hebrew letter *tau*, which belongs to the last of the trumps, the World, so that the victim is sacrificed on the symbol of the ordinary world of everyday experience from which he began his spiritual ascent. The coins dropping from his pockets have been explained as showing that he has abandoned all title to this world's wealth, or in the opposite sense as symbols of the spiritual riches to be gained by self-sacrifice.

BELOW Part of Master Bertram's 14th-century painting from the Grabow altar, with the same design as the one used by Giuseppe Maria Mitelli in his 17th-century version of the Hanged Man.
BELOW RIGHT Christ crucified on the Flowering Tree.

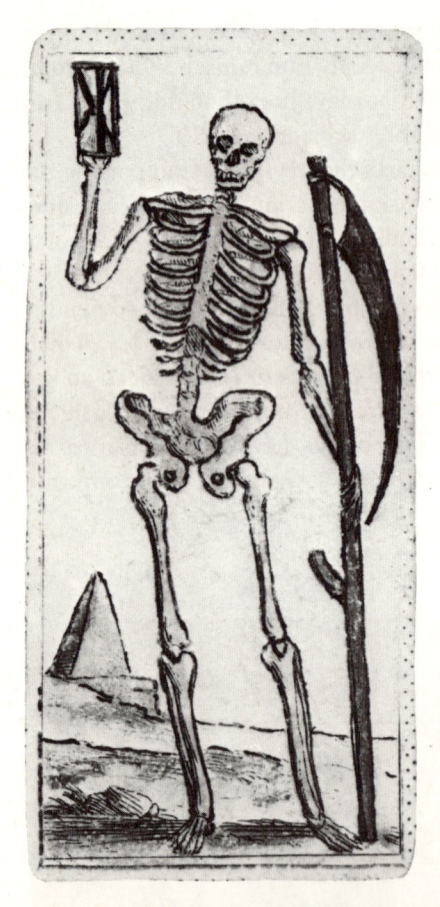

FAR LEFT Death as a skeleton with scythe and hour-glass in an Italian pack of the 17th century, and NEAR LEFT as a horseman armed with a scythe. OPPOSITE The Indian god Shiva, the Destroyer, performing the dance of death.

13 *Death*. The Death card has what is by common popular consent the unluckiest of all numbers, and in many of the older packs it is left unnamed, for fear that to name the grim reaper might be to summon him. Some modern writers prefer to call the card the Reaper. The Marseilles Tarot trump shows a skeleton with a scythe who is busy mowing a field of human heads, hands and feet. One of the two severed heads wears a crown but the other does not, which suggests the theme of death as the great leveller, reducing all human beings to a common nonentity in the grave. Death was frequently portrayed as a skeleton in the later Middle Ages. Like the Wheel of Fortune, he was a warning of the vanity and emptiness of the things of this world. Power, riches, physical strength, beauty, genius – all must yield to him. He was armed with a dart or a crossbow, but he also acquired a scythe and an hour-glass as emblems of time, whose sands run out for every man in the end. The Dance of Death, in which grinning skeletons pranced round graves and sidled lovingly up to clutch the living, was painted on the walls of churches and acted out in miming dances.

Interpreters of the Tarot card, however, all agree that despite its name and appearance it is not a symbol of death. It stands for transformation, for change based on an underlying continuity. The skeleton is the part of the body which is most impervious to the assaults of experience and time. The flesh ages and decays, the bone remains. And so the card is an image of the continuity of life in nature, in which death is part of a cycle of life, death and life renewed. For example, plants grow in the ground and then are eaten by men and animals, who die in their turn and their rotting carcasses give life and growth to fresh vegetation. Life and death, creation and destruction are inseparable twins.

Papus connected the card with Shiva, the Destroyer, not as the terminator of life but as the power which annihilates the forms of things without destroying their essence. Shiva in Hinduism is a god of sexuality and regeneration as well as destruction. He is Nataraja, 'King of the Dance', and his dance is the ordered rhythm of a world in which life changes into death and death into life. It is Shiva who fertilizes the sacred river Ganges, and a river appears in the background of some modern versions of the Tarot card. This is another example of a cycle of transformation: water is drawn up from the sea to form clouds, falls to the earth as rain, and ultimately returns to the sea in rivers and streams. The river has been identified with the Styx, across which the souls of the dead were ferried to Hades, or with the Jordan, which in Christian hymns and spirituals is crossed at death to reach the Promised Land of heaven.

As a symbol of life renewed after and through death, the card has an alchemical parallel in the process called 'putrefaction'. The material in the alchemist's vessel at this point was a black and stinking mass which was believed to be dead and rotting, and so generating new life within itself, a noxious but powerful vitality born of corruption which had to be purified and redeemed by the descent of the 'spirit'. Psychologically, putrefaction means a condition of exhaustion and melancholy, the spiritual rotting away of the old self, from which a new vitality will spring.

The theme of death and new life has erotic connotations and correspondences,

Death on a pale horse, from the
Book of Revelation, by Blake
and OPPOSITE by Dürer.

once again. The card's Hebrew letter is *nun*, 'fish'. The fish is a symbol of the phallus and the sperm, because of its shape and its penetrative motion through the water, and a symbol of fecundity because of its multitudes of eggs. It was also an early Christian symbol of Christ, the Saviour from death. The sign of Scorpio is associated in astrological tradition with death, evil, the serpent of Eden and the genitals, and with ideas of penetration and secrecy. It suggests the dark vitality secretly generated in the alchemist's 'putrefying' material. Scorpio is ruled by Mars, the planet of violent energy. The colour of Mars is red and the name Shiva means 'the Red One'. Crowley linked the Tarot card with the Hindu concept of kundalini, a potent secret energy in the body, closely connected with sex. As a goddess, Kundalini is the consort of Shiva. The ferocious wolf and the scarlet lobster are beasts of Mars. The cactus has a phallic shape, contains a milky fluid, and calls to mind the sting of death. The dung-beetle rolling its eggs along in a ball of muck stands for the life-giving power of the 'dung' or decaying filth of the depths of the mind.

In terms of Egyptian mythology the card corresponds to the evil Seth, the murderer of Osiris. But Seth's crime was the necessary precondition of Osiris's resurrection, with all its implications for man's salvation, just as physical death is an integral part of the cycle of nature. The Golden Dawn drew the conclusion that the evil, animal drives deep in human nature are the essential springboard or launching platform of spiritual progress.

Waite redesigned the card completely, under the influence of the vision in Revelation of Death on a pale horse. The skeleton, in black armour and riding a white charger, bears a great black banner emblazoned with the Mystic Rose, symbolizing life. The rose has five petals, and the Golden Dawn had earlier interpreted the severed heads, hands and feet of the Marseilles trump as an allusion to the number five, standing for the four elements of matter plus the spirit or spark of life. The river runs in the background of Waite's card and the sun of immortality blazes between two pillars. The design has the same meaning of transformation and renewal which other interpreters have seen in older versions of the card.

14 *Temperance*. Temperance is the classical virtue of moderation, self-restraint and reasoned control of one's appetites. Most interpretations of the Tarot card read very oddly indeed in this light. But the figure pouring liquid from one container into another suggests another old and related meaning of temperance as the mingling of different ingredients in due proportion. This was the stock traditional representation of the virtue, though alternatives were a woman grasping a sword or holding the key to a walled town, the Celestial City.

Some writers call the card Time or the Angel of Time and interpret it as a symbol of time flowing from the past through the present to the future. It is time as the equalizer, the evener-out of things, which mixes in due proportion the opposites of death and life, decay and growth, failure and success, sorrow and happiness. To some it suggests the continuity of life flowing from one physical form to another, and so it stands for renewal and reincarnation. This can be linked with Papus's explanation of Temperance, following the Death card of transformation, as a symbol of individual and bodily existence. The flowing liquid is the water of life, pouring into the container of each separate physical body.

Alternatively, the liquid flowing from one jug or vase into the other has been explained as a symbol of the influence of one mind on another. In this case the card means thought-transference, telepathy, the power of suggestion, hypnotism, the influence emanated by saints and holy men or by spiritual healers. Paul Foster Case took the pouring liquid to be 'mind-stuff' and interpreted the card in terms of the vaguely popular, and popularly vague, notion of 'vibrations' – the belief that the fundamental reality of the universe consists of patterns of oscillation or vibration. This idea, which was founded on nineteenth-century scientific discoveries about the nature of light, electricity and magnetism, was developed by the Spiritualists and by Madame Blavatsky and the Theosophists to become part of the common currency of occult speculation around the turn of the century. Case thought that one meaning of the Tarot card was that the vibrations can be tempered, or adjusted, by the human mind. 'There is nothing in the cosmos but vibration, and all forms of vibration may be modified and managed by mental control.'[39]

In the Golden Dawn system Temperance's path on the Tree connects Tifereth and Yesod, the spheres of the sun and moon, or the conscious and the unconscious. The card's number, fourteen, belongs to the moon, which goes from new to full, and full to new, in fourteen days. Some modern designs make one of the vases or cups golden, for Tifereth and the sun, and the other silver, for Yesod and the moon. In the Cabala Yesod corresponds to the genitals and is called 'the spout for the waters from on high', the channel through which divine vital energy floods into the earth and man. In the descent of the Tree the liquid pouring from the higher cup to the lower is the flow of 'the waters from on high'.

Going the other way, up the Tree, the liquid is the flood of a spiritual orgasm in which the soul mounts from a lower plane to a higher. This direct ascent from Yesod to Tifereth is the flight of the arrow of Sagittarius and is called the Path of the Arrow. Sagittarius is the sign of the archer or huntsman and is connected in astrology with fire and burning ardour. It is usually represented as a centaur, a creature half animal (lower) and half man (higher), carrying a bow and arrow, which suggests the union of opposites. Hunting in spiritual terms means ardent aspiration. Artemis and Diana were the classical goddesses of the chase. The horse and the dog are the huntsman's beasts and symbolize the passage from lower to higher because they have been tamed and trained to help man. The card's plant is the rush, not only because its name suggests speed, vibration, ardour and urgency, but as a male emblem, like the arrow. It has hollow, stem-like leaves and its pith was used to make wicks for candles.

In many modern designs the figure pouring the liquid, who in the old Tarot

FAR LEFT to RIGHT Cards of the 20th century in which an angel holds two containers between which flow a liquid in one case and a rainbow in the other. NEAR LEFT to RIGHT Temperance in a Belgian pack holding a sword and again pouring liquid, and Intemperance as a woman drinking.

packs was female, has become androgynous as a symbol of the mingling of opposites. The figure often has one foot on the ground and the other in a pool of water, which has the same meaning and also refers specifically to the bridging of the gap between the realms of the spirit and the flesh, or the conscious and the unconscious. 'If attention is directed to the unconscious,' Jung said, 'the unconscious will yield up its contents like a fountain of living water. For consciousness is just as arid as the unconscious if the two halves of our psychic life are separated.'[40]

If Temperance is the path of the arrow, the bow from which the arrow is shot is formed by the paths of the Moon, the Day of Judgment and the World, whose letters are *qoph, shin* and *tau*, which together make up the Hebrew word for 'bow'. These are the three lowest paths of the Tree, leading up from Malkuth where the spiritual ascent begins. The three Hebrew letters add to 800, and $8 + 0 + 0 = 8$: similarly the letters *he vau he*, Eve, standing for 'woman', add to 17, and $1 + 7 = 8$. The arrow piercing the bow is a symbol of sexual union, which is itself an image of spiritual achievement and delight. When the paths of the bow have been mastered, the initiate is propelled to a higher level on the path of the arrow, which the Golden Dawn identified with the strait and narrow path of Jesus's words: 'strait is the gate, and narrow is the way, which leadeth unto life, and few there be that find it.'[41]

The bow is 'the Rainbow of Promise stretched above the earth', which is a reference to the story of the Flood in Genesis. When the waters had subsided and Noah's Ark had come safely to rest on Mount Ararat, God repeated to Noah and his family the command which he had given to Adam and Eve, to be fruitful and multiply. Then God promised never again to send a flood to destroy the earth and set the rainbow in the clouds as the sign of this promise that life would go on, renewed from generation to generation.

In Waite's version of Temperance the irises growing beside the pool hint at this story. Iris was the Greek goddess of the rainbow, which classical authors regarded primarily as a sign of rain, 'the waters from on high'. Rain fertilizes the earth and some writers said that Iris as the principle of fertilizing moisture was the mother of Eros, the god of love. The weapon of Eros was the arrow of desire, which brings us back again to the erotic symbolism of the card and the theme of ardent aspiration. Waite also added a path leading away to two mountain peaks in the background. Between them is the sun and in it the faint suggestion of a crown. This is because the path of Temperance is continued higher up the Tree by the path of the Female Pope, which leads up to Kether at the summit of the system. The radiant crown of Kether between the two peaks of Hokmah and Binah is both the distant radiance of the divine and the distant promise which beckons man up the path of the arrow.

Temperance's Hebrew letter is *samekh*, which Crowley associated with a ritual that he took over from the Golden Dawn, 'for the Attainment of the Knowledge and Conversation of the Holy Guardian Angel'. This angel, who is the figure in the Tarot card, is the magician's presiding genius, both in the old sense of a guardian spirit and in the modern sense of an individual's own special quality and power. The purpose of the ritual is to summon up the 'angel' from the depths of the magician's inner self and consciously identify with it. Hence the alchemical motto in Crowley's version of the card, which he called Art: *Visita Interiora Terrae Rectificando Invenies Occultum Lapidem*, 'Visit the interior of the earth and by rectifying you will find the hidden Stone.'[42]

Sagittarius the centaur, half archer and half horse, is associated with Temperance in modern interpretations.

THE TWENTY-TWO TRUMPS 117

118 INTERPRETATION

15 The Devil. The card of the Devil varies considerably in different packs, but in most of them he is partly human and partly animal, is standing on a platform to which two smaller demons or a man and a woman are tied, and in one hand is holding something which may be a burning torch or a trident or a pitchfork. He frequently has the horns and legs of a goat, the wings of a bat and the talons of a bird of prey, which are common features of the traditional picture of Satan as an amalgam of noxious and sinister creatures. In the Tarot of Marseilles, where he looks less diabolical than might be expected, the Devil is bisexual and wears a peculiar hat with the antlers of a stag protruding from it. His gestures are the reverse of the Juggler's, and the horned hat may be a parody of Mercury's winged cap. It has sent some writers off on the track of the old Celtic stag god Cernunnos, who is believed by the modern witches to have been one form of their virile horned god, from whom they think the medieval Satan was descended.

The card is generally explained along the obvious lines as a symbol of the power of evil in the world, man held captive by his own animal urges, materialism, the dominance of brute force and ignorance, the exaltation of pride, hatred, cruelty and lust. As the reverse of the Juggler, the Devil stands for the application of creative power and intelligence to selfish and wicked ends, and is sometimes renamed the Black Magician. In many packs, alternatively, he looks like a parody of the Pope or Hierophant, which implies that he is 'the concealer of sacred things', the force which hinders the building of the bridge between man and God. Between the Devil's horns in Waite's pack is the Pope's pentagram reversed, with one point downwards, as a symbol of spirit mastered by matter, man at the mercy of his flesh. The Devil's platform is a cube, which stands for matter and recalls the throne of the Emperor. He is the power which keeps man imprisoned in materialism and in ignorance of his spiritual potential. The inverted torch suggests the flames of hell and the blazing inner fires of man's savage passions.

The card is almost invariably linked with Pan, the Greek goat god, standing for wild nature and untamed sexuality, the overmastering, rapacious and terrifying force of animal desire which pulses through all creation, renewing and perpetuating all species and forms of life (the word *pan* in Greek means 'all'). The goat and the ass in the correspondences are symbols of brutish lust. Capricorn is the sign of the goat, the animal of Pan and by long tradition the animal most closely connected with the Devil. Priapus was the Roman god of the phallus, whose sacrificial animal

FAR LEFT TO RIGHT A design after Court de Gébelin of a hermaphrodite Devil with bat's wings and the antlers of a stag, and the Devil in a modern Italian pack. NEAR LEFT TO RIGHT Waite's version of the Devil, and the Devil of an 18th-century Italian pack, holding a trident and trampling the souls of the damned.

was the ass. The thistle stands for the prickling of desire and is also a plant of sin, because God condemned the ground to bring forth thorns and thistles after Adam and Eve had sinned in Eden. Khem was the ancient Egyptians' name for their country, meaning 'the Black Land' and referring to the black silt deposited by the Nile. Black is traditionally the Devil's colour and black soil suggests night-soil, excrement, which belonged to Satan as lord of matter and in which Aleister Crowley took a consuming interest.

In astrology Capricorn's ruler is Saturn, which has an old reputation as an evil power, linked with the colour black and with death, time and fate. Following Temperance, the Devil is sometimes identified with time in its cruel destroying aspect, with inexorable fate or even with the distressing inexorability of logic. Saturn is the planet of boundaries, limitations and inertia, which has reinforced the interpretation of the two smaller figures in the card as individual lives chained in the prison of time and matter. Again, Capricorn is associated with the knees, and kneeling is a sign of obedience and subjection, suggesting human beings in an inert bondage to circumstances. The same meaning has been drawn from the card's Hebrew letter, which is *ayin*, 'eye' (and one old Tarot trump shows the Devil with eyes all over his body). The eye implies what is seen with it, the surface appearance of things, and so stands for the error of materialism – mistaking appearances for reality and supposing that nothing exists beyond what is plain to the senses.

Crowley, on the other hand, who passionately identified himself with Pan and Satan, connected *ayin* with the 'secret eye' of the phallus and reached the opposite conclusion. 'The formula of this card is then the complete appreciation of all existing things. He rejoices in the rugged and the barren no less than in the smooth and the fertile. All things equally exalt him. He represents the finding of ecstasy in every phenomenon, however naturally repugnant...'[43]

Even apart from Crowley, in most interpretations the Devil is not entirely sinister. He is often linked with the concept of negative evil, the resistance of form to force. For example, when a man walks along he puts one foot after the other on the ground, where he encounters an unyielding resistance. But without this 'evil' resistance of a platform of solid ground – like the Devil's platform in the Tarot card – he would not be able to move forward. Evil, then, is the thrust-block of good. It is by overcoming evil that good occurs, and the Devil has his place in the scheme of things. Similarly, when the Devil is thought of as a 'block' in the sense of a taboo or a mental inhibition, the implication is that good will result from overcoming it.

From this point of view, the evil which the card represents is a potential source of strength. Eliphas Lévi identified it with Pan, the Baphomet of the Templars and the Satanic goat of the witches' sabbath, and described it, much to the annoyance of Waite, as a symbol of 'occult science'. Man must come to terms with the force of Pan in himself, which has to be mastered and turned into a force for good. So transformed, it supplies the driving energy of spiritual renewal. Satan's other, and in legend older, name is Lucifer, 'light-bearer'. He is connected with the serpent of Eden, which appears in some versions of the card, and the Hebrew word for serpent, *nahash*, has the same number-value as *Mashiah*, Messiah, the Saviour. Lucifer or the light-bearer, Madame Blavatsky said, is inside us: 'It is our Mind – our tempter and Redeemer, our intelligent liberator and saviour from pure animalism.'[44]

Saturn, the planet of time and death, shown devouring his own children in the 'Mantegna' card. OPPOSITE An Etteilla Devil.

14 Droit. **FORCE MAJEURE** Droit **14**

LE DIABLE.

FORCE MINEURE. Renversé.

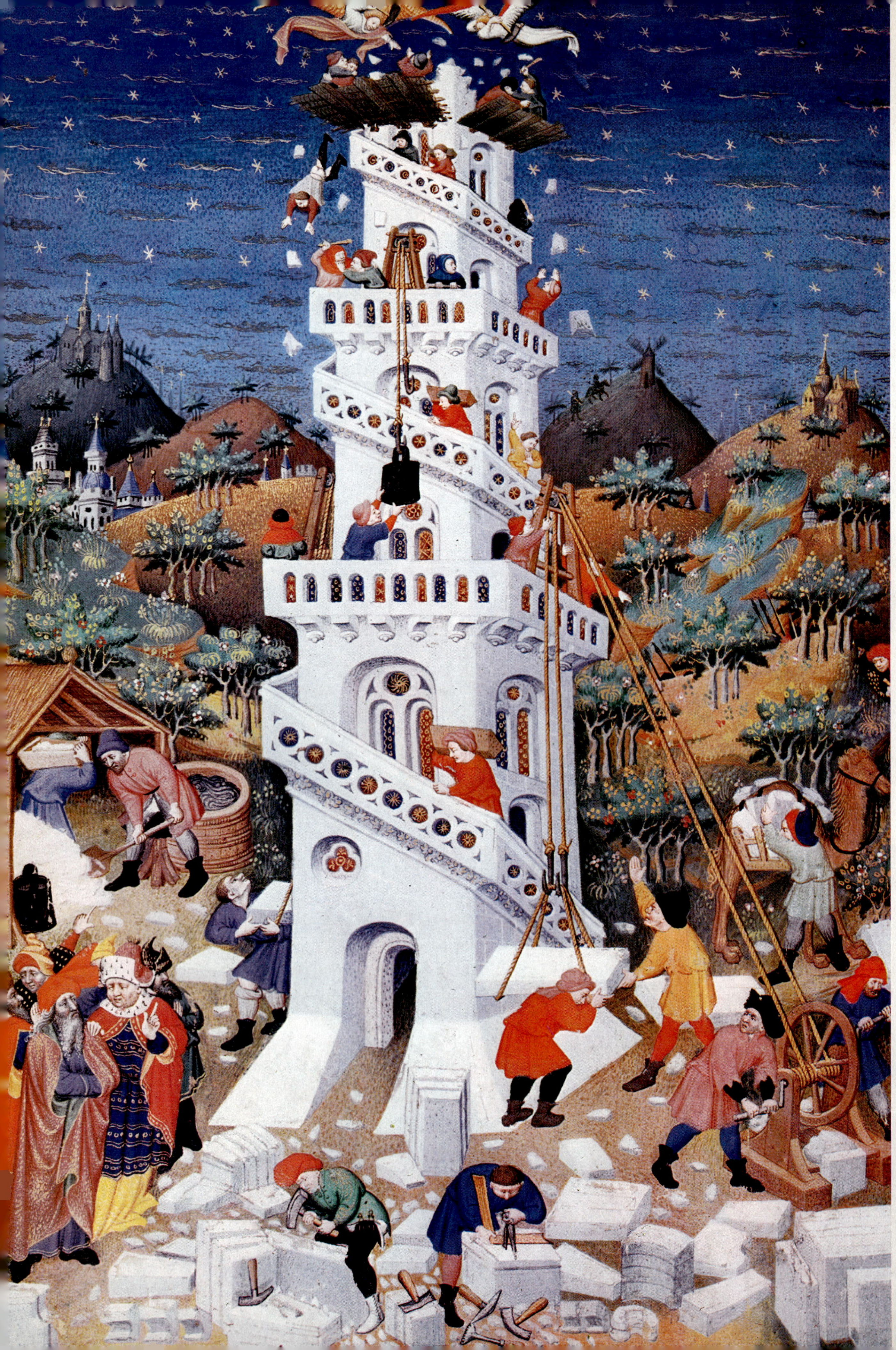

16 *The Tower*. A tower is struck by lightning and the top of it, which resembles a crown, is collapsing. Sparks or drops are falling to the ground and so are two human figures, one of whom is often shaped like an *ayin*, which belonged to the card in the older system of correspondences. In Italian packs it is generally called *La Torre*, the Tower, and in French packs *La Maison Dieu* or House of God, which may be a reference to the Temple in Jerusalem or may simply mean a church. It is also known as the Lightning and in some packs no tower is shown, only the bolt of lightning. Wirth named the card *Le Feu du Ciel*, Fire from Heaven, recalling the words of Jesus: 'I saw Satan fall like lightning from heaven.'[45]

The card obviously shows the destruction of something, but what is destroyed is a moot point. Different writers have related it to the fall of Atlantis, God's vengeance on Sodom and Gomorrah, the destruction of the Temple, and the collapse of the Church of Rome eagerly awaited by the Cathars or other medieval heretics. More often it is connected with the legend of the Tower of Babel, which does seem to be its most likely source. This sky-scaling tower was built by the descendants of Noah, who in their insane pride intended to invade heaven from the top of it and take their revenge on God for having drowned their ancestors in the Flood. God punished the builders by the confusion of tongues, so that ever since men have spoken many different languages to the detriment of communication between them.

The Tower is frequently interpreted in the spirit of this legend as the punishment of pride and over-confidence, or more broadly as the destruction of a false system of values. Many writers have followed up Wirth's hint and related the card to the story of the fall of Lucifer, but for most of them Lucifer is not the victim but the author of the destruction. It is his lightning-flash which destroys error. The Tower's Hebrew letter is *pe*, 'mouth', which is appropriate to the legend of the confusion of tongues. But *pe* transliterated into Greek is the initial letter of *phallos*, which makes the card a symbol of ejaculation in more senses than one. Paul Foster Case, who had a neat way with a pun, explained it as 'the perception that the structure of knowledge built on the foundation of the fallacy of personal separateness is a tower of false science. At this stage the advancing seeker for wisdom suffers the destruction of his whole former philosophy.' Crowley said it meant: 'To obtain perfection, all existing things must be annihilated.' His card contains the murderous third eye of Shiva, the eye whose lightning burned the god of love to ashes. But this eye, like the phallus, is also an organ of creation.[46]

The Tower's path on the Tree joins Netsah and Hod, the opposite spheres of cohesion and flux in the universe. It is the base of a triangle whose other sides are the paths of Death and the Devil, the cards of transformation and renewal, destruction and reproduction, which it links together. Descending the Tree, man is becoming increasingly entangled in matter and individuality, and the card represents the falseness and instability of his resulting intellectual attitudes. The Golden Dawn connected it with descriptions in the Old Testament of the punishing wrath of the Almighty against those who strayed from his service. Ouspensky said: 'If only men could see that almost all that they know consists of the ruins of destroyed towers, perhaps they would cease to build them.'[47]

Conversely, on the way up the Tree from Hod to Netsah, or from the intellect to the instincts, the bolt of lightning is a sudden flash of illumination which reveals

The Tower of Babel, from the Bedford Book of Hours: the Tarot trump is often interpreted in the spirit of this legend.

and demolishes mistaken values. The tower's three cramped windows indicate the narrowness of materialism and rationalism, but they also hint at the three Supernals at the top of the Tree and the possibility of high attainment. The falling drops are manna from heaven, the life-saving food of inspiration. The two falling figures stand for unreconciled opposites, individual separateness, human beings kept apart by lack of communication and understanding.

The Tower is a lower parallel of Strength on the Tree and can also be understood as another emblem of discipline, the painful sacrifice of egotism symbolized by the toppling crown. Absinthe and rue in the correspondences are bitter, and the wolf is a beast of Mars, the planet of war and destruction. In some designs the flash of lightning is drawn to look like the arrow which is the astrological symbol of Mars. The bear, emerging in spring from the solitary sleep of hibernation, represents escape from personal isolation and wrong attitudes. Horus, 'he who is on high', was the Egyptian god of the sky, connected with the fierce and merciless falcon. The son of Isis and Osiris, he avenged his father's murder, and succeeded to the royal throne, and so he stands for the defeat of a false philosophy and the triumph of a true one.

FAR and NEAR LEFT The Tower Struck by Lightning, from Alliette, and an unusual version from a minchiate pack, where the Tower stands intact and Eve is being expelled through the doorway after the Fall. OPPOSITE A statue by Benvenuto Cellini of Ganymede astride Zeus in the form of an eagle: he was carried off to Olympus to be the cup-bearer of the gods.

17 *The Star*. A naked girl is pouring liquid from two containers into a pool, or sometimes onto the ground as well. A great star and seven lesser stars shine in the sky above her. In the background is a tree with a bird perched on it, which is explained as a symbol of the soul's ability to rise to higher things. The bird may be the ibis of immortality, the dove of the spirit, or the owl of wisdom. In Wirth's card it has been replaced by a butterfly resting on a flower, to symbolize the soul's relationship to the ephemeral body.

A star shining in darkness suggests guidance from above, a light to steer by, a saving gleam of intuition in the troubled mind, and the Tarot card is almost invariably interpreted as a symbol of truth and hope. After the destroying storm and lightning of the Tower there comes the tranquil rain, bringing the promise of a greener earth. Or similarly in the ascent of the Tree, after the dangers and terrors represented by the Moon, the gentle dew of hope falls softly into the blackness of the soul's night.

The liquid is not being poured from one container into the other, as in Temperance, but onto the earth's surface as a sign of inspiration and quickening from above. The girl is naked because she is truth unveiled, and young to represent renewal. She is the feminine principle or the mother goddess, pouring out the water of life in springtime to revive an exhausted world. Crowley described the card as a symbol of the continual outflow and reabsorption of energy in the universe. The Golden Dawn, like Court de Gébelin, identified the shining star with Sirius, the star of Isis, which was connected with the coming of the Nile flood that brought new life to the land. In Christian symbolism a star is sometimes an emblem of the Virgin Mary as *Stella Maris*, the Star of the Sea, and some writers have linked the Tarot card with the Star of Bethlehem, which proclaimed to the three wise men the coming of Christ, the hope of the world. As a symbol of the shining possibilities of the future, the card has also been connected with astrology and other methods of divination.

There are eight stars in the card altogether and the principal one is usually eight-pointed or seven-pointed. The card's number is seventeen, and $1 + 7 = 8$, which stands for woman and new life. A seven-pointed star is explained as a reference to Venus and the sefira Netsah, from which the card's path leads, representing the healing force of love which illuminates the soul in its imprisonment in the body. Venus is the morning-star, *lucifer* in Latin, the 'light-bearer' which brings the promise of a new dawn. The early Christians saw in the morning-star a symbol of Christ. Harold Bayley, whose philology consisted of jumping to conclusions, derived French *matin*, 'morning', from Maat, the Egyptian goddess of truth, and 'star' from Istar, or Ishtar, the great Babylonian goddess of fertility and love. Some authors have identified the girl in the Tarot card as Ishtar.

Aquarius is the sign of the water-pourer and is associated with peace and love, beneficence, communication and inspiration. Juno was the Roman mother goddess, whose chariot was drawn by peacocks. The stars are the eyes of the night sky, and the peacock has 'eyes' on its spreading tail and is connected with Lucifer as light-bearer. The eagle means hope and the eventual triumph of the spirit because it soars into the heights. The womanish Ganymede, the cup-bearer of the gods, was carried up to Olympus by Zeus in the form of an eagle. Writers who prefer to avoid Ganymede's unwelcome sexual implications substitute Hebe, his female predecessor as cup-bearer. The liquid she poured out for the gods was the nectar

126   INTERPRETATION

OPPOSITE A 15th-century design for the Star, attributed to Antonio di Cicognara. ABOVE, LEFT The Star in an 18th-century Italian pack and RIGHT a 19th-century painting from northern India, showing the god Vishnu seated in a lotus on Mount Mandara, encircled by the great white serpent Vasuki as a churning rope.

which kept them forever young. Its equivalent in Hindu mythology is amrita, the dew of immortality, which the gods obtained at the beginning of time by churning the ocean like milk. It is symbolized in the correspondences by the milk of the coconut.

The Blazing Star of Masonic temples represents the sun and is surrounded by symbols of the planets. Similarly, the seven lesser stars in the Tarot card are said to stand for the seven planets known to the ancient world, recalling the old idea of rising through the planetary spheres towards God. Alternatively, they are the Pleiades, which stand for immortality because in Greek mythology they were maidens who were translated into the heavens after death. Some classical authors mixed them up with the Hesperides, the nymphs who lived in the beautiful garden in the far west where the golden apples of immortality were guarded by a watchful dragon (and Hesperos was the Greek name of Venus as the evening star, appearing in the west). Or again, the seven stars have been connected with other groups of seven as a number of completeness – the seven ages of man, the seven principal chakras of Hindu occultism, which are centres of psychic energy in the body, the seven constituents of human nature in Theosophical theory – with the eighth star, which goes beyond completeness, as it were, implying the possibility of transcending normal human limitations.

The letter *tzaddi* is the 'fish-hook' which pierces the soul and draws it up out of its accustomed element to a higher level. It has been associated with meditation as a way of angling for truth in one's own mind. Crowley switched the positions of the Star and the Emperor on the Tree, mainly because he wanted to link the Star with *he* as the letter of the Great Mother. He also suggested, unconvincingly, that the Emperor was better suited to *tzaddi*, which he discerned behind imperial titles such as Tsar, Kaiser and Caesar.

18 *The Moon*. In most packs the Moon's card is grim and nightmarish, though there are some less sinister varieties of it. The 'Charles VI' trump, for instance, shows the moon and two men who are making astronomical calculations, and in an Italian minchiate pack of the eighteenth century a man with a pair of calipers is holding a dial marked with the twelve lunar months. In another version of the trump a lover is serenading a girl on a balcony. But in the more common designs the moon hangs in the night sky shedding drops of dew or blood on the ground. Two dogs or wolves are baying at the moon and a narrow path runs between two ominous towers and away into the distance. At the foot of the card is a pool of water with a nasty crawling creature in it – a crayfish, crab or lobster – which in some versions is heaving itself up onto the land.

The symbolism of the moon is wide-ranging and complicated, and so are interpretations of the Tarot card. Its number is eighteen, and $1 + 8 = 9$, which in the Cabala belongs to Yesod, the sphere of the moon. The moon is generally classified as feminine, and the card itself looks like a female symbol. The moon is the mistress of night and the ruler of the waxing and waning rhythms of life, the menstrual cycle and the tides of the sea, and so in modern psychological terms of the deep waters and swirling treacherous currents of the unconscious. The card is connected with imagination and fantasy, with dreams whose fitful and eerie moonlight disturbs the mind in sleep, and with scaly impulses that claw their way up into the conscious mind from the depths below. The moon has an old and close link with madness (hence the word 'lunacy') and many writers have associated the Tarot trump with fear and horror, the Dark Night of the Soul, hidden dangers and enemies, sorcery, witchcraft and the folklore theme of the werewolf, the human being who turns into a murderous beast at night.

In the descent of the Tree, the Moon's path is the first to reach Malkuth, the sphere of the earth and the physical body, and from this point of view the card stands for the formation of the solid from the nebulous, the building up of physical organisms, the fashioning of the child in the womb. But the moon wanes after waxing and it moulds forms which have no permanence, its pale deceptive light is reflected from the sun, and deep water reflects images on its surface while distorting light-rays which penetrate it. And so the card of the Moon is said to stand for the material world as a distorted reflection of reality, a realm of illusion. Papus said that the soul has now fallen to the lowest point of its course and is immersed in the dark world of matter where the divine light no longer reaches it directly. The Golden Dawn connected the card with the entry of the soul into a physical body and the chaotic waste of waters at the beginning of the world in Genesis. 'Before all things are the Waters and the Darkness and the Gates of the Land of Night.'[48]

The two towers stand at the entrance to our world, but they are also conversely the gateway opening out of it into the unknown land of night beyond. In the ascent of the Tree, the path they guard is 'the lunar way', the way of insight, intuition and imagination, associated with the female, as opposed to 'the solar way' of reason, associated with the male. The lunar way is directed inwards, the solar way outwards. The moon is forever changing its shape in the sky and the danger of the lunar path is failure to find the true insight. This failure leads to the swamps of self-deception, illusion, uncertainty and fluctuation, loss of identity, fear and despair at having missed one's way. The dog was the beast of Hecate, the classical goddess of the baneful moon, and the two baying dogs in the Tarot card can stand for the

THE TWENTY-TWO TRUMPS 129

The Moon driving through the sky in her chariot on the 'Mantegna' card. OPPOSITE Two versions of the Moon card: one from an 18th-century minchiate pack, and BOTTOM the disquieting scene of the commoner version.

mixture of fear and longing in the conscious mind's attitude to the unknown.

The parallel in alchemy is the process called 'solution', an attempt to reduce the material in the alchemist's vessel to a watery state which was regarded as an essential early step in the making of the Stone. Psychologically, it is a process of acid self-distrust and self-criticism in which previously accepted certainties and deep-rooted patterns of feeling and reaction are dissolved away in what the alchemists called an ordeal by bitter water. 'It is bitter indeed', Jung said, 'to discover behind one's lofty ideals narrow fanatical convictions, all the more cherished for that, and behind one's heroic pretensions nothing but crude egotism, infantile greed and complacency. This painful corrective is an unavoidable stage in every therapeutic process.'[49] The drops of blood falling from the moon are a menstruum, a fluid in which a solid body is dissolved, and stand for the breaking down of the reassuringly solid structures of accustomed convictions and pretensions. The ordeal carries the dangers of mental collapse, confusion and anguish, but it is a necessary stage of spiritual progress.

Pisces is the sign of the fishes, creatures which live and breed in the depths. It is classified in astrology as a 'mutable' or changeable sign, unstable and nebulous, connected with water, intuition and mystery. The crayfish in the old Tarot trumps presumably stands for Cancer, the sign of the crab, which is traditionally ruled by the moon. As a scavenger, the crab suggests self-criticism which devours the transitory and valueless, and it corresponds to the dung-beetle of Khepera, which here represents the sun making its perilous passage by night through the dark waters of the underworld before its resurrection at dawn. Carved dung-beetles, or scarabs, were used in ancient Egypt as amulets of life-giving and protective power. The amiable dolphin in Christian art carries dead souls across the waters of death to the next world. Opium stands for sleep, dreams and the journey into the underworld of the mind.

Another way of interpreting the crayfish crawling up from the water onto the land is as a symbol of the evolution of species and the long development from amphibious creatures to man. Some writers connect the card with the legendary lost continent of Lemuria, or Mu, in the Pacific. It was thought in the nineteenth century that Lemuria might have been the original cradle of the human race. On these lines the card can be a symbol of three levels of human existence. The water stands for man's dark past and the unconscious mind, the land above it for the conscious mind, the material world and recorded history, and the moon in the sky at the top for the higher world of the spirit and future evolutionary advance.

Processes in alchemy represented as a tree: the various stages are nowadays taken to correspond to some of the Tarot trumps.

THE TWENTY-TWO TRUMPS 131

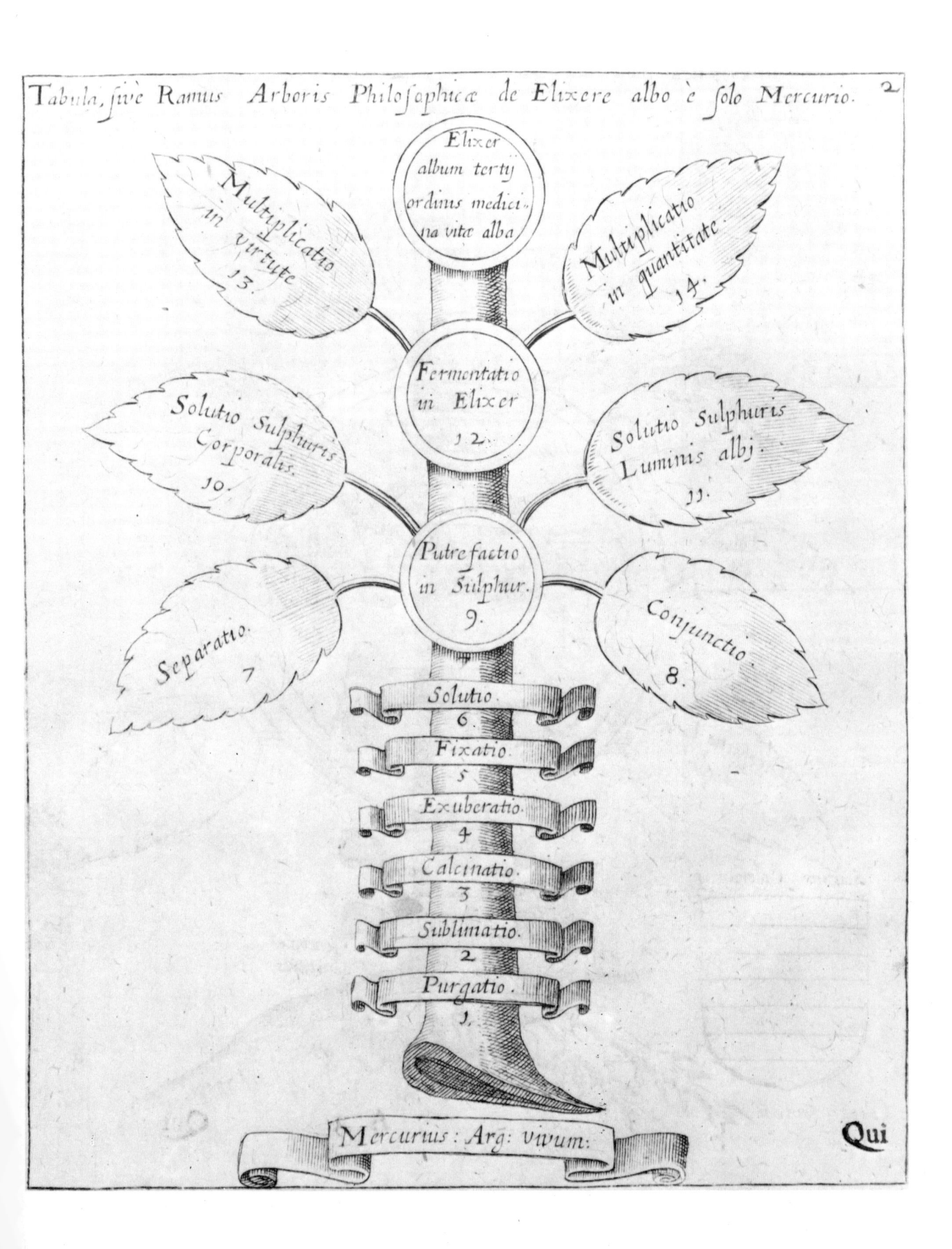

Tabula, sive Ramus Arboris Philosophicæ de Elixere albo è solo Mercurio.

- Elixer album tertij ordinis medicina vitæ alba
- Multiplicatio in Virtute. 13.
- Multiplicatio in quantitate. 14.
- Fermentatio in Elixer. 12.
- Solutio Sulphuris Corporalis. 10.
- Solutio Sulphuris Luminis albj. 11.
- Putrefactio in Sulphur. 9.
- Separatio. 7.
- Conjunctio. 8.
- Solutio. 6.
- Fixatio. 5.
- Exuberatio. 4.
- Calcinatio. 3.
- Sublimatio. 2.
- Purgatio. 1.
- Mercurius: Arg: vivum.

Qui

132 INTERPRETATION

19 *The Sun*. The Sun is a more cheerful card altogether. A sunburst with a human face at its centre, and with drops falling from it, shines on a pair of lovers or on two children who are standing in front of a wall. Following the Moon, night has been dispelled by the glory of sunrise, the children have emerged from the murk of the womb. There are many mythological traditions in which, as in Genesis, night precedes day. Darkness is felt to be older, more primitive and fundamental, and light penetrates a darkness that was there before it. The sun is the giver of light and heat, the maturer of crops, the sustainer of all life on earth. Where the moon stands for the feminine and passive principle, water, the unconscious and instinctive, the sun represents the masculine and active principle, fire, the conscious and contrived.

It is the sun which enables us to see, and so in spiritual terms to recognize a higher goal. The card is frequently connected with alchemy as the search for the true gold of spiritual perfection. The alchemists believed that the action of the sun caused gold to mature in the gound. The sun was therefore the source of the supreme treasure, material or spiritual, and the drops which fall from it in the card have been likened to the shower of gold in which, in Greek mythology, Zeus descended to Danae. The trump has been linked with Mithras as 'the unconquered Sun', whose victory over the powers of darkness is the sign and promise of man's eventual triumph. Or it can be linked with Christ as the Sun of Righteousness and the lord and giver of life.

Preceding the Moon on the way up the Tree, the Sun is the card of daylight which will inevitably be overtaken by night. While it lasts, the daylight is a time of vigorous activity and clear perception. The card's path is 'the solar way', which leads to Hod, the sphere of reason, and it shows the dazzling light of true intelligence which frees the mind from petty worries and concerns. The light burns away conventional and accepted ideas, beginning a process which is continued at a deeper level on the path of the Moon. The Sun's number is nineteen: $1 + 9 = 10$, and in turn $1 + 0 = 1$, which suggests an exercise of will, an act of self-assertion against the demands of the everyday world with its trivial preoccupations and entanglements. The lunar way involves a struggle against oneself, the solar way a struggle against other people.

The occultist here turns his face to the sun in the sense of beginning to identify himself consciously with the light and life of the divine. Like the keen-eyed and predatory sparrowhawk of the correspondences he soars towards the sun, like the heliotrope he follows the sun's course. The lion is the royal beast of the sun and an old symbol of watchfulness because it was believed to sleep with its eyes open. Re and Helios were the Egyptian and Greek sun gods and Apollo, the beautiful Greek god of civilization and philosophy, was frequently identified with the sun. The laurel or bay was sacred to Apollo and is an emblem of victory because laurel crowns were awarded to triumphant generals, athletes and artists.

The letter *resh*, 'head', is associated with intelligence and authority. Like the path of the Moon, the solar way has its dangers – intellectual arrogance, superficiality, a failure to realize the limitations of reason. The sun is the maker of deserts as well as the ripener of vineyards, and reason too can make the mind a barren wasteland. In Greek legend Icarus flew too near the sun and fell to his death in the sea, and the Golden Dawn warned that 'the too-aspiring Icarus may find his waxen wings of Ambition and Curiosity shrivelled and melted by the

Icarus as a child falling from the chariot of the Sun in the 'Mantegna' card. FAR LEFT, TOP The sun rises above two children embracing; BOTTOM in the 'Charles VI' pack the trump shows a young woman alone.

fiery rays of the Sun . . . but approached with humility and reverence, the Sun becomes the beneficent source of life'.[50]

In most versions of the card some of the sun's rays are straight and others wavy. They can represent the sun's double emanation of warmth and light, or the opposites of positive and negative. The wall has been explained in various ways. It can stand for the circle of the zodiac through which the sun appears to run its annual course, or for the physical body in which man is confined on earth, or for the ways in which human beings have brought the natural environment under their control. Or it can be a hint of the importance of self-control.

The two children can again be interpreted as the opposites, but they are more often understood as symbols of joy and innocence, sincerity, freedom, escape from the contamination of the world. At the same time they can imply egotism, greed and inexperience, suggesting that man's spiritual and intellectual powers are at this stage still in their infancy. Jung thought that a land of children in dreams or in art was a symbol of the collective unconscious, with its origins in the dawn of human history. 'We must therefore realize that despite its undeniable successes the rational attitude of present-day consciousness is, in many human respects, childishly unadapted and hostile to life. Life has grown desiccated and cramped, crying out for the rediscovery of the fountainhead. But the fountainhead can only be discovered if the conscious mind will suffer itself to be led back to the "children's land".' In Wirth's design and some other modern packs the young lovers or children are standing inside a fairy ring, which in Jungian terms means that 'the symbol of wholeness is still under the sway of childlike creative powers'.[51]

The children have been linked with the Cabiri, the dwarfish craftsman gods who played an important part in the mysteries of Samothrace, and who are said to represent the powers which the human spirit has in reserve. During their annual festival at Lemnos all hearth fires were put out and new fire was brought from Apollo's temple at Delos, which in relation to the Tarot trump suggests the extinguishing of the 'old fires' of previously accepted ideas and the coming of a fresh divine source of energy. The Cabiri were connected with fertility and they also gave protection against dangers – especially the perils of the sea and shipwreck, which will be encountered on the Moon's path. They were sometimes identified with Castor and Pollux, the heavenly twins who protected sailors and whose relevance here is that they were half mortal and half divine, spending half their time in the underworld and half with the gods on Olympus. They in turn were connected with the sign of Gemini, which is related to both the intellect and the opposites. Gemini corresponds to the Lovers higher up the Tree, which can be taken to imply that the children in the card of the Sun are the separated opposites which must later be reconciled and united.

Waite's card is based on a hint by Lévi and shows a child riding a white horse and carrying a scarlet banner, with the sun shining above him in a clear blue sky. The child stands for a fresh start on the road to spiritual achievement. He is naked because the soul sheds its clothing of matter and the flesh in its ascent. His nipples and navel form a triangle with one point downwards, foreshadowing the sacrifice which will be demanded of him on the path of the Hanged Man. (The worshippers of the Cabiri, incidentally, stood on their heads as a religious rite.) The red banner means vigorous action and the horse is the energy of the sun and the life force. In classical mythology the sun's chariot was drawn by white horses, and Castor and Pollux were great horsemen, sometimes called 'the riders on white steeds'. The child's mount is the same horse which Death rides in Waite's pack.

The Sun shines down on a horse and rider in RIGHT Waite's trump and FAR RIGHT a Belgian card. OPPOSITE Daedalus watching his son Icarus falling into the sea, from a woodcut by Dürer.

20 *The Day of Judgment*. The Judgment, or the Angel, varies comparatively little in most packs. A great winged angel in the sky is blowing a trumpet. Below him coffins are opening and three, or sometimes more, human figures are emerging from them. The card shows part of what the Middle Ages expected to happen at the end of the world on the Day of Wrath. Christ would appear in majesty upon the clouds, the last trump would sound and 'in a moment, in the twinkling of an eye', as St Paul had said, the dead would rise from their graves – dazzled by the light, and some of them clasping their hands in prayer – to be judged and sent to heaven or hell.

The card's Hebrew letter is *shin*, which the *Sefer Yetsirah* connects with fire. Like the sun, with which it is closely linked, fire is creative as a source of warmth and light, but also destructive. Its symbolic connotations include wrath and punishment, ardour and passion, purification and transformation. 'What is that within us which does sound a trumpet,' Waite asked, 'and all that is lower in our nature rises in response – almost in a moment, almost in the twinkling of an eye?'[52] The answer is desire, sensual or spiritual, and the card is a symbol of aspiration, the yearning for higher things. It is another emblem of death and resurrection, of new life gained through the transformation of man's earthly nature. The fiery-maned lion is a symbol of fervour and resurrection. Hades and Pluto were the Greek and Roman gods of death and the underworld. The nettle stands for the sting of death, the poppy for the sleep of death, and the hibiscus is one of the mallow family and represents orgasmic 'death' or collapse.

The alchemical parallel is with the operation called 'calcination', which meant heating the raw material until it was reduced to a fine powder or ash. This was regarded by many alchemists as the first step of their art. Spiritually, calcination seems to have stood for the purging fires of discontent with oneself and one's life in the world and an ardent longing for a better course.

The angel in the card is usually identified as Michael, who was by tradition the angel of the last trump. He was also the leader of the forces of light which routed the Devil and the hosts of darkness in the war of heaven, and this makes him an appropriate symbol of a victory over the lower nature of man. In the Cabala he is the archangel of light and the sun. Medieval Christians believed that he was the guide of souls after death, which had earlier been a function of Hermes or Mercury, and the path of Judgment connects Malkuth, the sphere of the earth, with Hod, which is the sphere of Mercury. The three human figures in the card may originally have had something to do with the Christian tradition that Michael was the angel who preserved Shadrach, Meshach and Abednego from harm in the burning fiery furnace.

For modern interpreters the principal significance of Michael is that his name means 'like God', implying the spiritual potential of humanity. 'We can rise from the grave of our old dead self now, while we are still in the physical body, if our ears are not deaf to the trumpet call from on high.'[53]

In many packs the angel's trumpet has a banner attached to it, on which is an equal-armed cross. Crowley identified the cross as the principal symbol of Christianity and decided that the card, which he renamed the Aeon, depicted the end of the Christian era and the beginning of the new age of which he was the Messiah. But the cross is generally taken to mean that the way of spiritual ascent is through the reconciliation of opposites in a higher unity, which is also suggested

The angel sounding his trumpet, as depicted in ABOVE a 19th-century Italian pack and BELOW a minchiate version.

THE TWENTY-TWO TRUMPS 137

+MICHAHEL+PREPOSITVS+PARADISI+

The Archangel Michael in a 15th-century woodcut, weighing the souls of the dead at the Last Judgment.

by the three human figures, who in modern designs are usually a man, a woman, and a child. These figures are also a hint of the three distant Supernals at the summit of the Tree. They are wholly or partly nude, because naked we come into this world and naked we shall leave it, so that they stand for spiritual aspiration, which casts off the garments of worldliness. The card's number is twenty, and 2 + 0 = 2, which means opposites. This is the number of the Female Pope or High Priestess, who is the gateway to heaven at a higher level on the Tree. The opening graves have been connected with the ancient Egyptian burial ritual of the Opening of the Mouth of a dead man, which was intended to bring him back to life in the afterworld by restoring his ability to breathe and take food.

Shin is the letter of the Holy Spirit, which recalls the experience of the apostles at Pentecost when their human nature was invaded and transformed by the divine, and the words of Joel: 'And in the last days it shall be, God declares, that I will pour out my spirit on all flesh . . .' In the Cabala the component of human nature which makes man potentially capable of understanding the secrets of God and the universe is the 'holy soul', which some authors believed had its origin in the sefira Binah, the divine Understanding itself. The path of Judgment lies at the foot of the left-hand pillar of the Tree, in direct descent from Binah. There is again a link with Mercury, and the sefira Hod, because in alchemy mercury, the metal, was connected with spirit.

Following the Moon and the Sun on the way down the Tree, the Day of Judgment can be interpreted as a symbol of mortality and immortality, showing the balance of opposite forces in nature. 'The scabbard is as deep as the sword is long,' Eliphas Lévi said, 'production is equal to destruction in the movement that preserves life.' *Shin*, 'tooth', here suggests the gnawing bite of death and the teeth which chew up food and so begin the process of transforming it into energy. Opposite the Moon, the card stands for the fiery force which both consumes and renews all material forms. Mercury in alchemy was the fugitive, quickening quality which penetrated matter and without which matter would remain static. The dead rising from their graves are like plants which have died but now are growing again and lifting their heads to light and warmth. 'Unless a grain of wheat falls into the earth and dies,' Jesus said, 'it remains alone; but if it dies, it bears much fruit.' The spiritual corollary is in the next verse. 'He who loves his life loses it, and he who hates his life in this world will keep it for eternal life.'[54]

Four cards from the pack designed by Aleister Crowley; LEFT to RIGHT, TOP the Fool and the Star; BOTTOM the Knight of Cups and the Aeon or Day of Judgment.

0 — The Fool	XVII — The Star
Knight of Cups	XX — The Aeon

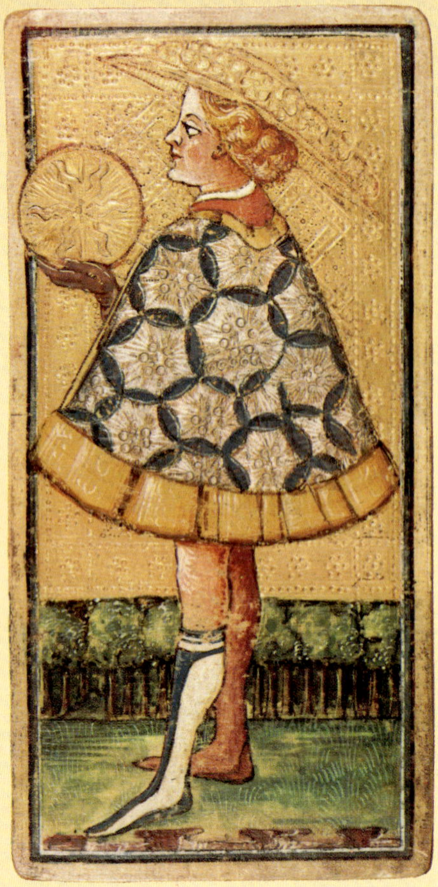
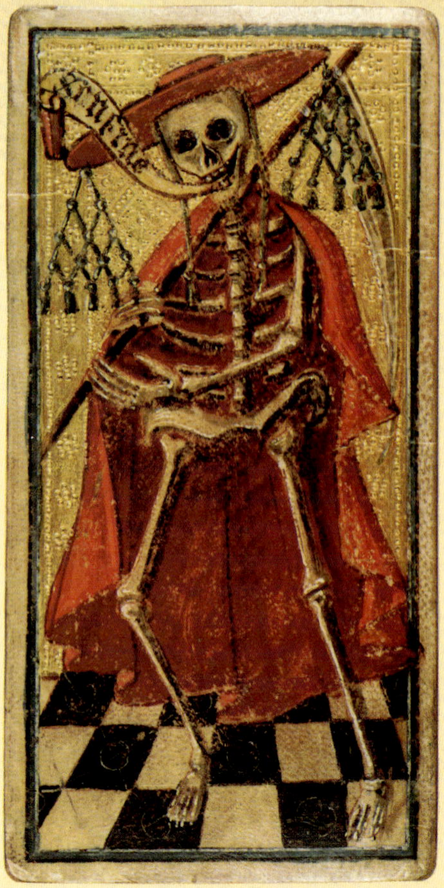
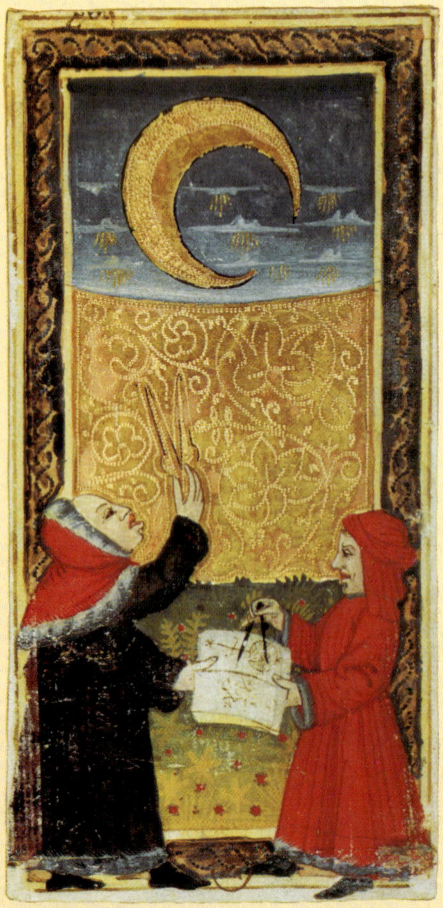
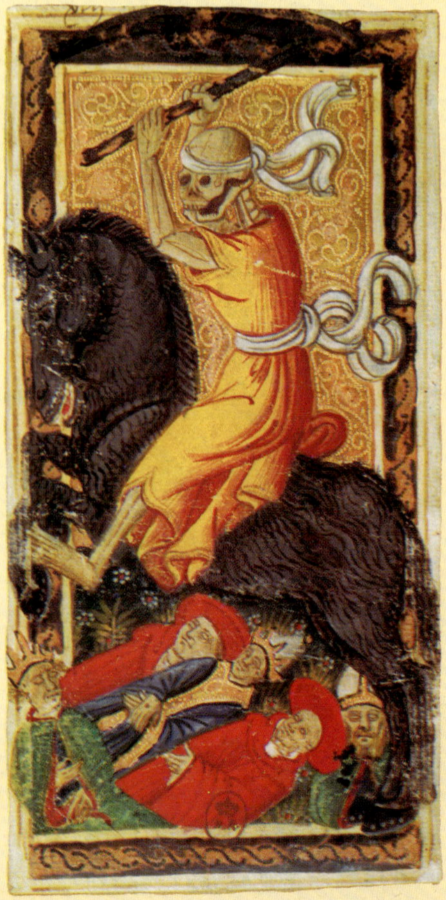

LEFT to RIGHT The Page of Coins and Death, from a late 15th-century Italian pack attributed to Antonio di Cicognara; BOTTOM the Moon, and Death on a white horse in the 'Charles VI' pack.

21 *The World.* The last of the trumps, called the World or the Universe or the System, is generally explained in two opposite but related ways. It is a symbol of the world of ordinary everyday reality, but it also stands for the world of the ultimate spiritual reality. On the Tree its path leads up to Yesod from Malkuth, the sphere of the earth from which man must begin his pilgrimage. But Malkuth is also the earth which receives 'the waters from on high', a distant counterpart of Kether at the summit of the Tree, and in the Cabala it is the whole kingdom of God, which contains within itself the forces of all the sefiroth. The World is the Great Work accomplished by God and at the same time an image of the great work of the spirit which can be accomplished by man.

In most packs the card shows a woman whose nakedness is covered only by a veil, stole or loincloth. She is dancing inside an elliptical wreath (or in one alternative version she is standing on a circle, inside which is a beautiful landscape). Outside the wreath, at the four corners of the card, are the four 'living creatures' of Ezekiel – a man, an eagle, a bull and a lion. They stand for the four elements as the foundations of the material world, the four gospels as the foundations of the Christian message, the four directions and the four seasons, and generally for manifestation, actuality, the solid four-square world. The number-value of *tau*, the card's Hebrew letter, is 400, and $4+0+0=4$. But the four beasts are also taken as a reference to the four letters of the name of the Divine, which in cabalistic theory made the world as a manifestation of itself.

As a symbol of the everyday world, the card has gloomy and ominous connotations. It corresponds to the baleful Saturn, which was the outermost and slowest-moving of the planets known in antiquity and so came to stand for limits, dullness, ponderousness, matter, time and death. The cypress and the yew are graveyard trees. The world-tree of northern mythology was an ash, and through a pun the ash suggests death – 'ashes to ashes, dust to dust'. Sebek was an Egyptian crocodile god and the crocodile is the animal of devouring death.

On the other hand, death can imply the possibility of something beyond it, of translation to a better world. The crocodile can stand for the plunge from the dry land of ordinary earthly life into the flowing water of a more ethereal and spiritual plane of existence. The cypress and yew are evergreens and so stand for immortality. The fruits or 'keys' of the ash are winged, and so suggest ascent. Hellebore root is a drastic purgative which in the ancient world was prescribed as a cure for insanity. The limitations represented by Saturn are also the constraints which drive human beings to seek a way of escape from them.

The woman in the card is dancing, which stands for joy, harmony and the orderly course of the universe and time. 'To the Renaissance mind the dance essentially represented harmony in its capacity as a reflection of heavenly order. It was held that the dance arose through an imitation of the movements of the stars and planets ... Sir John Davies, celebrating Elizabeth I, describes the dance of the elements in creating the measured order of the cosmos:

>   Dancing (bright Lady) then began to be,
>   When the first seeds whereof the world did spring,
>   The Fire, Air, Earth, and Water did agree,
>   By Love's persuasion, Nature's mighty King,
>   To leave their first disordered combating;

> And in dance such measure to observe,
> As all the world their motion should preserve.[55]

Some writers connect the elliptical wreath with the cosmic egg, inside which the woman dances as a sign that chaos has been brought into a harmonious order. Paul Foster Case suggested that the World card stands for 'cosmic consciousness', or what Freud called 'the oceanic feeling'. This is a mystical sense of being utterly at one with nature, of being merged into the sum total and underlying unity of all things, which brings with it, since nature never dies, a conviction of immortality.

The wreath may be made of laurel leaves, standing for high achievement. It is often explained as a symbol of time, of Saturn moving slowly through the circle of the zodiac, with the four beasts as the four cardinal points and the four 'fixed' signs which mark the seasons – Taurus, Leo, Scorpio and Aquarius. In some packs the wreath is replaced by a snake devouring its own tail, an emblem of completion, wholeness and eternity. The ellipse can also be identified as the mystic centre, the still hub of things, the timeless unity, the lost paradise, Jerusalem the golden, which by ancient tradition stands at the centre of the world and is the earthly counterpart of the shining City of Heaven.

In Christian art the ellipse or mandorla is often a symbol of ascent. The Virgin Mary is portrayed inside it in paintings of her Assumption, or translation into heaven, and it sometimes appears in scenes of the Ascension of Christ. Or again, the ellipse can represent the womb and the dancing woman within it is the embryo which will become the newborn child, the Fool, so that the whole procession of the trumps will begin again, revolving like a wheel.

The woman is identified as nature, Eve, the great goddess, or *Anima Mundi*. The cabalists connected the sefira Malkuth with the Shekinah or 'Bride', the feminine aspect of God, which is both the human soul and a part of God which has fallen into matter and become exiled from the Divine. The supreme purpose of human existence, according to the Cabala, is to reunite the Bride with the Bridegroom, to restore the lost wholeness of God. Some writer's say that the dancing woman's stole or loincloth conceals the fact that she is really a hermaphrodite, mingling the two sexes as an image of the restoration of the divine unity, and at the same time representing humanity as male and female. The letter *tau* is also taken to stand for the conjunction of opposites, and as the last of the letters it is an emblem of perfection, salvation and eternal life. In some versions of the card the woman holds two wands, which are again explained as symbols of the opposites and the positive and negative currents in the universe.

The World's number, 21, is the reverse of 12, the number of the Hanged Man. In many packs the dancing woman's legs form a cross, as the Hanged Man's legs also do, but where he is upside down, she is the right way up. Again the implication is that she represents both the Hanged Man's original starting point and his ultimate goal. The card of the World is the universe when it was young, Waite thought, on the day when God established its foundations and 'the morning-stars sang together, and all the sons of God shouted for joy'. It is the world, Ouspensky said, which we always see, but never understand.[56]

LEFT to RIGHT, TOP A decorative Italian card of the World held aloft by two children, and a modern version of the World card; BOTTOM the World held up by the strength of Atlas, in a design by G. M. Mitelli, and a traditional design of a woman dancing within an elliptical wreath of flowers.

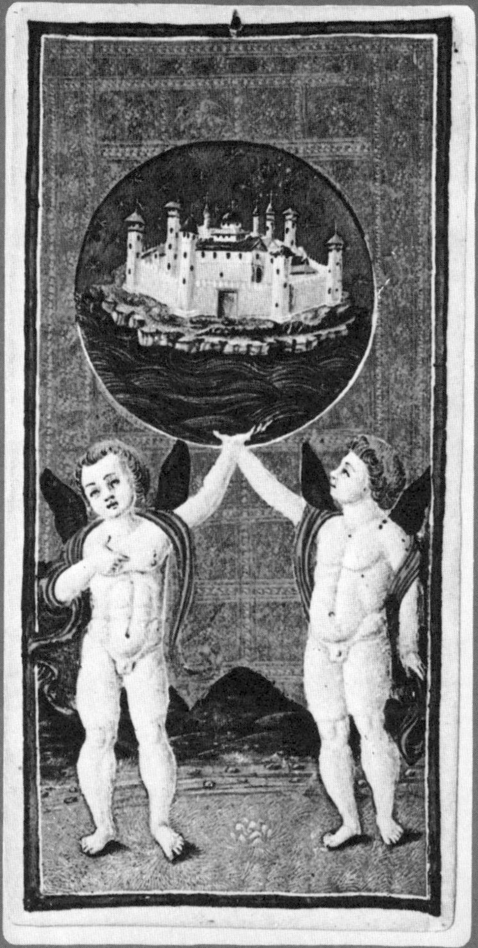

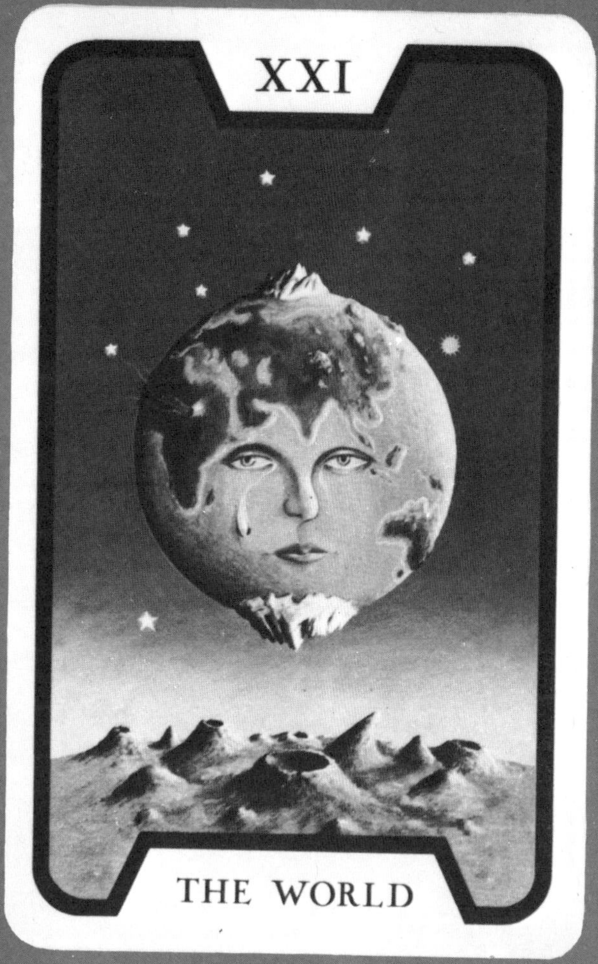
XXI
THE WORLD

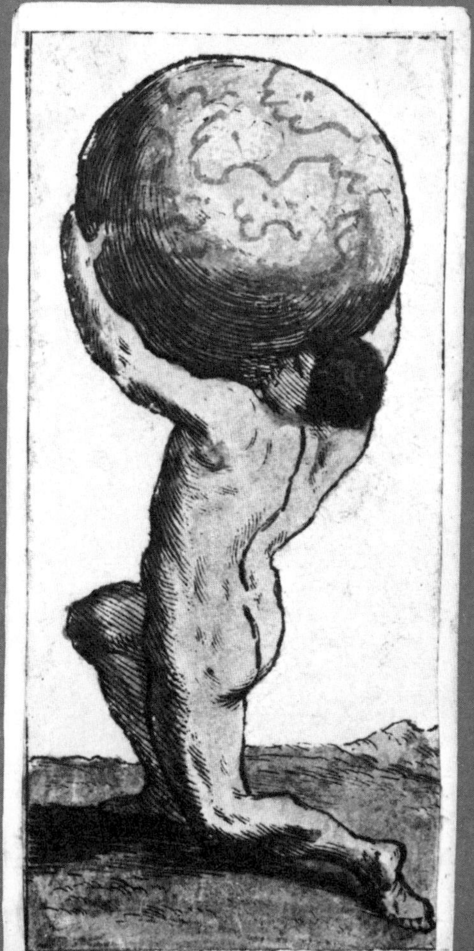

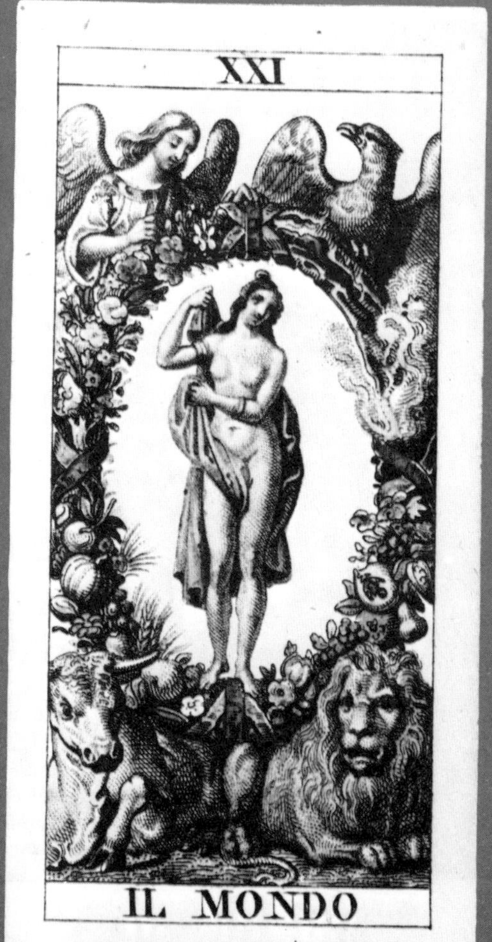
XXI
IL MONDO

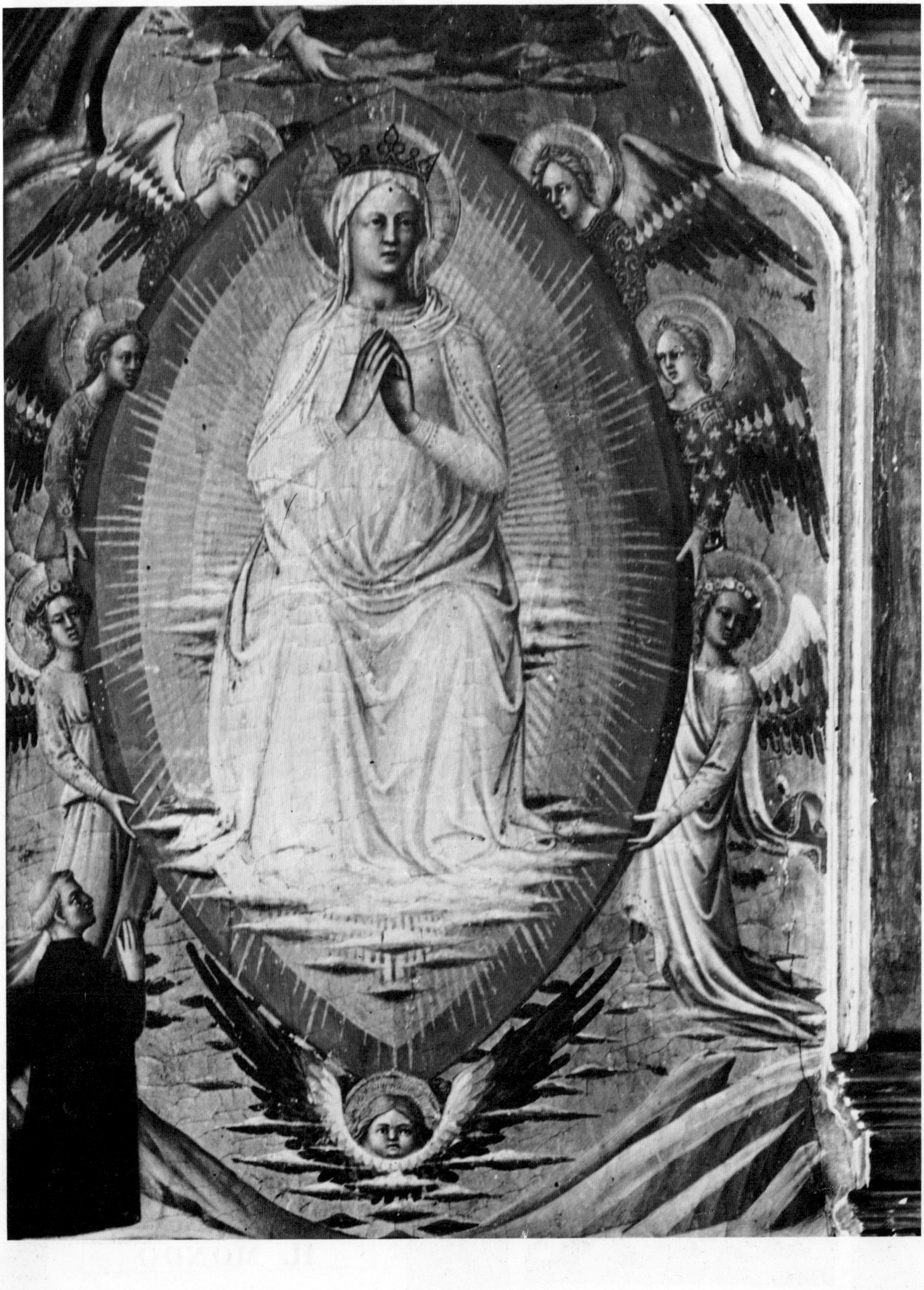

3 MEDITATION

Those who believe that the Tarot trumps are keys to the underlying reality of the universe have naturally tried to use them in meditation as a means of opening the locked doors of that reality. One of the cards is selected, or picked at random, and the meditator concentrates his attention on it, closing his mind to all extraneous thoughts and sense-impressions. Gradually his concentration becomes a reverie in which ideas and images inspired by the card well up in his mind. The experience may end there, or it may go on to a point at which the meditator feels that he has 'entered the scene'. He has left the room and the chair in which he was sitting and has moved, like Alice through the looking-glass, into the environment of the card itself. 'The sensation', according to one account, 'is as though one stepped out through a window into a new world.'[57]

This new world, in occult theory, is the astral plane, the world in which ideas and imaginings have their own independent existence. To explore this world is potentially rewarding but also potentially dangerous. The astral plane contains 'spirits' which lead ill-equipped travellers astray and prey on the unwary, and whether these beings have a separate reality or are imaginary projections of factors inside the explorer's own mind, they can be frightening and harmful to encounter. The symptoms of their unwelcome attentions are said to range in severity from headaches and fainting fits to inability to concentrate, fatigue, nightmares, obsessions, hysteria and mental collapse. The more serious of these psychosomatic symptoms are those which in the old days were put down to possession by evil spirits.

Attempts to explore mysterious levels of reality by meditation are nothing new, of course. The Jewish Merkabah mystics, for example, attempted to make the ascent through the planetary spheres, the heavenly 'palaces' or 'chambers', to the Throne of God. An account of their techniques, written about A.D. 1000, says that the mystic 'must fast a number of days and lay his head between his knees and whisper many hymns and songs whose texts are known from tradition. Then he perceives the interior and the chambers, as if he saw the seven palaces with his own eyes, and it is as if he entered one palace after the other and saw what is there.' It was apparently the bodily posture adopted, with the head between the knees, which caused the mystical ascent to be alternatively called a 'descent' to the Merkabah. Professor Scholem has described it as 'an attitude of deep self-oblivion which, to judge from certain ethnological parallels, is favorable to the induction of pre-hypnotic autosuggestion'.[58]

The members of the Golden Dawn, who regarded themselves as the spiritual heirs of Jewish mysticism, were equally interested in methods of making the mystical ascent of the Tree and exploring its paths through autosuggestion. By contemplating Tarot cards and other symbols they obtained what Francis King has called 'meaningful, extremely vivid, and completely coherent daydreams in which the dreamer retains all his normal powers of choice, will power and judgment'.[59] Descriptions of some of their adventures are included in the lectures and essays to which the Order gave the engagingly daft name of Flying Rolls. Two of the members, for instance, once chose the Empress card to contemplate. Presently they both saw a medieval landscape and found themselves in a Gothic

A detail from the Christian Stories of the Virgin, showing Mary within a mandorla.

temple which contained a beautiful green dragon. Finally, in an idyllic garden they saw the goddess Isis, looking like the figure in the Tarot trump, and she showed them the Holy Grail.

There is no reason to doubt that many of these mental adventures did occur more or less as described. Meditation has recently become far more widely practised and studied, as part of an increasing interest in altered states of consciousness. All systems of meditation depend on closing the mind to most of the external stimuli which usually affect the brain, and it is known that unusual fantasies and hallucinations then occur, which may involve sensations of sound, touch, smell and taste as well as sight. Although these sensations originate within the self, they are generally believed by those who have experienced them to reflect a reality beyond the self. They are said to provide an escape from the limitations of normal consciousness by opening up channels to the absolute, the astral, the soul of the world, the collective unconscious, the cosmic reservoir of memories, or whatever concept suits the believer's theory. In the magical tradition, the explanation given is that since man is a microcosm, a miniature image of the universe, to explore one's own inner world is also to explore the corresponding reality outside.

The Golden Dawn's method of meditation on Tarot cards was well calculated to produce the intended effects. The meditator had an idea of the significance of each trump and its path on the Tree to begin with, and he knew the correspondences – the gods, animals, plants, colours and the rest – which expressed its nature. He was looking for what, in a general way at least, he already expected to see and he was taught to keep strictly on the appointed track by conscious decision. 'In a spontaneous dream,' as Dion Fortune said, 'the symbols are drawn at random from experience; in the Qabalistic vision, however, the picture is evoked from a limited set of symbols to which consciousness is rigidly restricted by a highly trained habit of concentration . . . the untrained person may be able to detach consciousness from the control of the directing personality and thus allow the images to rise, but he has no power to restrict and select what shall appear, and consequently anything may appear, including a varying proportion of subconscious content.'[60]

The corollary is that the Golden Dawn system, like many others, was essentially circular. The successful meditator saw what he expected and wanted to see, which in turn reinforced his belief in the truth of the system. If he did not succeed, he believed that he had missed his way, through some defect of technique or outside interference, and he would try again, harder.

Another, more consciously intellectual way of using the Tarot trumps as keys to the truth is to treat them as if they were figures in a highly complicated dance or pieces moving on the board of a vast and complex game of cosmic chess. Each card represents an idea or group of ideas, and by taking several of them, chosen deliberately or picked at random, and considering their relationships to each other, fresh insights into the dance or game of life can be obtained.

An example is Crowley's exposition of the peculiar word AUMGN, which is an expansion of Aum or Om, the most famous of all the mystic syllables of oriental occultism which are also believed to encapsulate truth. If the letters of Aumgn are turned into Hebrew and then into the corresponding Tarot trumps, the result is: the Fool (A), the Pope (U or V), the Hanged Man (M), the Female Pope (G), Death (N). Briefly, the Fool is the godhead, the Pope is the divine manifested in matter as man, and the Hanged Man means death. So far, the word shows a catastrophe, the incarnation of a god in human form and the slaying of the god. But the apparent death in the Hanged Man is followed by the Female Pope, standing for the knowledge of God, and then by the Death card, implying generation and resurrection. The whole word reveals a circular formula – God becoming man and man eventually resurrected as God. Armed with this word, man has 'a mantra of terrific power by virtue whereof he may apprehend the universe'.

Furthermore, the Hebrew letters of Aumgn add up to 100, which is the number-value of *qoph*, the letter corresponding to the Moon in the Tarot, the card of illusion and reflection. And 100 is made of 20 + 80, or of *kaph* and *pe* (the Wheel and the Tower), which in Greek are the initial letters of *kteis* and *phallos*. This shows, Crowley said, that Aumgn is 'a synthetic glyph of the subtle energies employed in creating the Illusion, or Reflection of Reality, which we call manifested existence' and 'indicates the Magical formula of the Universe as a reverberatory engine for the extension of Nothingness through the device of equilibrated opposites'.[61]

This way of using the Tarot is based on old cabalistic techniques of investigating the reality lying behind surface appearances through the number-values of the Hebrew alphabet. It is on this basis that the name Adam, used to mean 'man', shows that man is potentially divine. Its Hebrew letters *(aleph daleth mem)* add to 45, which is also the total of all the numbers from 1 to 9. These numbers are the foundation of all things because the higher numbers merely repeat and combine them. The foundation of all things is God, and so Adam=45=God, or Adam is 'the name of man as a God-concealing form'. In the Bible, however, it was Adam's sin in Eden which brought death into the world, and if the Hebrew letters are turned into Tarot trumps, the name Adam can be interpreted as revealing this tragedy. The divine (A, the Fool) is born into the world of nature (D, the Empress) and dies (M, the Hanged Man), though with at least the implication of a possible resurrection.

These methods, and techniques of meditation as well, are founded on the belief that the outwardly chaotic and disorderly phenomena of the universe are really segments of a coherent pattern. At the heart of things, if only we could penetrate to it, there is order and design.

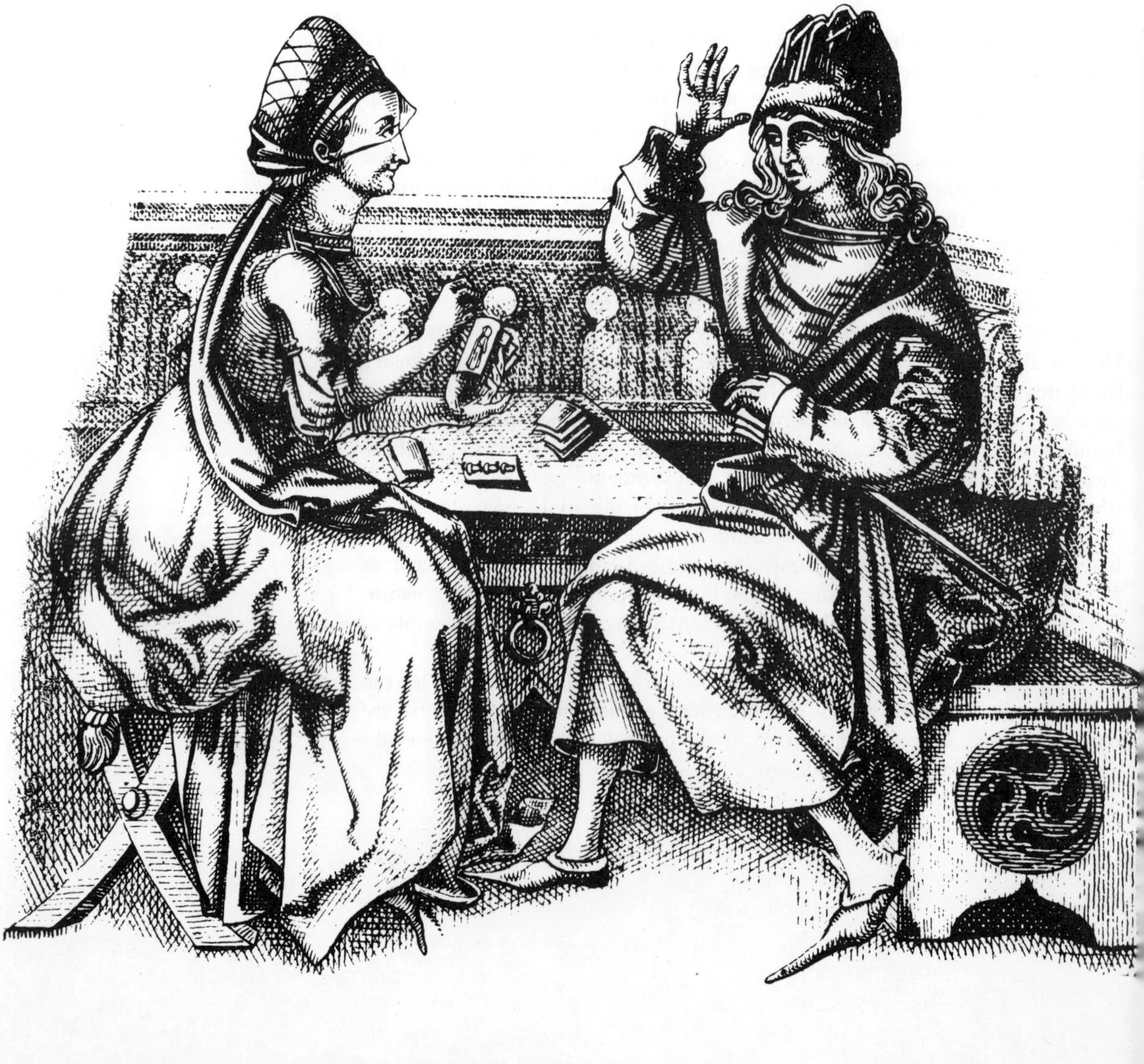

SECTION III

DIVINATION

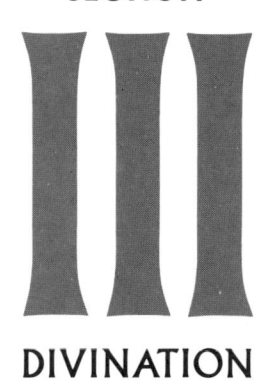

Occult writers of the older generation tended to distinguish between divination, which they approved of, and fortune-telling, which they condemned. The distinction was strongly affected by social attitudes. Divination was a serious-minded effort to penetrate mystery by an enlightened few. Fortune-telling was a shoddy and mercenary activity, catering to women and the lower classes. Its typical setting was the gypsy card-reader's booth at a fairground or the sham clairvoyant's parlour in a back street, next door to the neighbourhood abortionist, where charlatans sold fake readings to superstitious bumpkins and housemaids, and occasionally to ladies gone slumming. It dealt in dark strangers, journeys over water, rivals in love, true and false friends, vulgar ailments, hoped-for legacies and windfalls, dramatic and highly improbable changes of fortune.

Fortune-telling, it was felt, cast pearls before swine and sullied the pearls in the process. Waite said that the history of the use of the Tarot trumps for telling fortunes was 'the story of a prolonged impertinence'. Papus assumed that his women readers would be too feather-headed to appreciate the profound spiritual significance of the cards. He expected them to be interested only in fortune-telling and he simplified the rules for their benefit. Paul Foster Case thought that anyone who debased the Tarot by using it for telling fortunes would cripple himself spiritually. 'Its proper application is to the solution of serious questions, for yourself or others.'[1]

Writers nowadays are less worried about the shady side of fortune-telling, though it still exists, but they agree with the older textbooks that it is not enough merely to learn the supposed meanings of the cards, lay them out in a selected pattern and then read them off by rote. For true divination there must be an exercise of insight and intuition, shading over into genuine psychic ability. To 'divine' in this sense means to acquire knowledge without knowing how one has gained it, without having consciously deduced it or been told it. The knowledge seems to come into the conscious mind direct from some unknown source. It is not necessarily information about the future, but can just as well be concerned with the present or the past.

Although the whole history of divination is replete with folly, credulity and fraud, some people do seem to have a capacity to grasp salient facts about a person or situation by contemplating a layout of cards, the lines on someone's hands, the

A game of cards on the frontispiece of a book describing the Tarot as used in play.

patterns of a horoscope or whatever indicators are used. Modern experimental research in parapsychology suggests that clairvoyance or 'second sight', the ability to see or sense things which are not present to ordinary sight, is a reality: and that people can and do glimpse the future on occasion, if only to a brief and limited extent. There is also evidence, though it is apparently not as strong, for telepathy or direct contact between one mind and another, which could again obviously be an important factor in fortune-telling. There is a growing general tendency now to take intuitions, premonitions and hunches more seriously as possible ways of acquiring knowledge not accessible through the usual channels of the senses. If the modern research is on the right track, it looks as if Tarot cards or other indicators used in divination, though not themselves containers of information, may act as a stimulus and jumping-off point for psychic abilities.

Divination is closely allied to meditation, and Crowley recommended the former as good practice for the latter. The textbooks tell the apprentice Tarot-reader to approach the reading in a calm and peaceful, introspective and rather dreamy frame of mind. He must then focus his attention on both the cards and the question which he wants answered, excluding extraneous thoughts and sense-impressions, and also excluding personal preferences which would sway his interpretations. In effect, he must contemplate a spread of cards with the same sort of concentrated attention that is used during meditation, and recent experiments suggest that clairvoyance and other psychic faculties are sometimes developed or released in meditation.

One phenomenon which may occur in unusual mental states of this kind is psychokinesis, or the direct action of mind on matter: for example, the ability to make dice fall with preselected faces showing by willing them to do so. Psychokinetic ability is more often exercised unconsciously, however, and there is a possibility, though it still seems a remote one, that the shuffling of a pack of cards before they are 'consulted' is sometimes affected in this way. Most writers on the Tarot emphasize that shuffling is important and that while he is doing it the card-reader should concentrate hard on the question he wants answered or the problem that particularly concerns him. Remembering that the reader has the 'meanings' of the cards in his head to begin with, it is conceivable that he might psychokinetically affect the shuffle. The effect would be to arrange the cards, without any deliberate intention of doing so, in an order related to the question or problem at issue, and perhaps unconsciously calculated to produce the answer or advice which the reader would like to obtain. It is interesting that one or two of the textbooks contradict the usual instructions and tell the reader to keep his mind blank while shuffling.

None of this means that anybody who sets up as a Tarot-reader will demonstrate genuine psychic abilities, far from it. But parapsychology does at least raise a strong possibility that there is sometimes more to divination than sceptics have allowed.

Psychic abilities apart, there is another factor which can produce an apparently true reading when the cards are interpreted for someone else – the inquirer or consulter (many writers use the horrible word 'querent'). The inquirer contributes far more to the reading than is generally realized. Even the most amateur and inexpert fortune-teller will quickly discover how much of themselves, their current preoccupations and their hopes and plans, people reveal while having their

Telling fortunes with the cards, in a picture of the late 18th century.

fortunes told. An intuitive card-reader will soon learn to sense when he is on an acceptable track, and how to draw an inquirer out without seeming to do so. And some textbooks say that the reading should quite openly proceed as an exploratory dialogue between the diviner and the inquirer in any case. As a result, much of the blend of character-analysis and prediction which the reader appears to draw from the cards really emanates from the inquirer himself and feeds back to him statements which he already regards as truthful and probable.

This circular process is assisted by the vague and woolly nature of fortune-telling language, which makes it easy for an inquirer to fit himself and his past, present and future into a loosely-worded observation which could apply equally well to many other people and situations. C. G. Leland, the folklorist, discovered some classic examples of artfully worded fortune-telling by gypsies in the nineteenth century. Among the observations which gypsies told him they found it safe to make to almost any inquirer were the following. 'You got yourself once into great trouble by doing a good act.' 'You will soon meet with a person who will have a great influence on your future life if you cultivate his friendship.' 'You will ere long meet someone who will fall in love with you, if encouraged.' 'You had at one time great trouble with your relations (or friends). They treated you very unkindly.' Another was, 'You have been three times in great danger of death', which the gypsies said should be spoken very impressively and was an almost infallible winner with inquirers, who always liked to believe that they had encountered formidable perils. On the other hand, Leland's experiences with gypsies convinced him that there was more to their fortune-telling than mere humbug, and he thought that some of them had 'a very highly cultivated faculty of reading the mind'.[2]

Connected with all this is the phenomenon of the self-fulfilling prophecy, a

A Victorian photograph of gypsy fortune-telling in Epping Forest, London.

prediction which so impresses the inquirer that he unconsciously makes it come true. For example, if he is told to expect trouble at work soon – a forecast which may in reality be based on his own apprehensions – he goes to work with an attitude which soon gets him into trouble. A case of premature death apparently caused by a fortune-teller's prediction was reported in Canada in 1965. A woman of forty-three died in hospital for no discernible medical reason, soon after a minor operation which had gone perfectly well. It turned out that when she was a little girl of five she had been told by a fortune-teller that she would die when she was forty-three. Her birthday had been one week before the operation and she had told her sister and one of the nurses that she was convinced she would not survive it. An hour after the operation she suddenly collapsed, and died the following morning in spite of every effort to save her. 'Post-mortem examination revealed extensive haemorrhage mainly of the adrenal glands, without any other pathology that might explain it.' After a thorough investigation, the surgeons cautiously suggested that the severe emotional tensions caused by her belief in the prediction may have had a bearing on her death.[3]

The moral of this case is that if you attempt to tell fortunes yourself, even light-heartedly and in fun, it is important to be extremely cautious about forecasts of death, illness, financial ruin or impending disaster. People frequently take them far more seriously than they will admit, and real damage can be caused by them.

Card-readers and occultists themselves have naturally welcomed modern evidence for the existence of the psychic abilities which they claim to possess. But they usually do not believe that the Tarot cards act only as a stimulus and contain no information in their own right. Like techniques of meditation, all systems of divination are based on the principle that everything which happens is part of a connected pattern or design. This means that an apparently random event like the fall of a spread of cards is part of the pattern and contains clues to other sections of it, and so to people and occurrences of the past, present and future. There are hidden and generally unsuspected connections beneath surface appearances which make accurate divination possible. Eliphas Lévi stated this belief with characteristic *brio*. 'Caesar was assassinated because he was ashamed of being bald; Napoleon ended his days at St Helena because he admired the poems of Ossian; Louis Philippe abdicated the throne as he did because he carried an umbrella. These are paradoxes for the vulgar, who cannot grasp the occult relations of things.'[4]

Similarly but more soberly, MacGregor Mathers maintained, apropos of the Tarot, that 'the more rigidly correct and in harmony with the scheme of the Universe is any form of Divination, so much the more is it likely to yield a correct and reliable answer to the inquirer. For then and then only is there a firm link, and bond of union, established between it and the Occult forces of Nature.' The same attitude has been expressed by a more recent writer, Richard Gardner, in saying that 'a person who is totally unsympathetic to fortune-telling has an unbalanced mind and has allowed himself to be trapped into the strait-jacket of our time, cutting himself off from the underlying patterns of existence which give life its meaning'.[5]

Another explanation of successful divination, which is again founded on a belief in concealed links between outwardly unrelated occurrences, is C. G. Jung's theory of synchronicity. Synchronous means 'occurring at the same time' and Jung was interested in what he called 'meaningful coincidences' between events which happen close together in time but are not connected by cause and effect. He applied this idea to astrology, which he believed had demonstrated that a human being's personality is affected by his moment of birth. People born under the sign of Aries in the spring, for example, are supposed to resemble each other in certain broad and general ways, and to differ from people born under Leo or Scorpio or any other sign. Jung suggested that personality is not *caused* by the birth-moment, or by the positions of planets and stars, but that it shares the characteristics of that moment. Like vintage wines, he said, we have the qualities of the year and the season in which we were born. A spread of Tarot cards might therefore be a pointer to present situations and trends if in some mysterious way it shares the qualities of the moment at which it is dealt. Whether the theory is right, however, is doubtful.

1 THE CARDS AND THEIR MEANINGS

Conventional playing cards are double-headed, so that they look the same either way up. In most Tarot packs the cards are not double-headed and for divination each card has one meaning when it falls the right way up and a different meaning when it falls upside down or 'reversed'. A few packs are double-headed, however, and if you are using one of these you should arbitrarily mark each card to show which is the right way up. The reversed meaning of a card is not always the opposite of its normal meaning. It may repeat the normal meaning or it may be something quite different.

As there are seventy-eight cards in the pack and each has at least two meanings, depending on which way it falls, the reader has a minimum of a hundred and fifty-six meanings to cope with, plus additional ones for certain combinations of cards – all four Aces appearing in the same spread, for instance, or three Kings close together. But the number of available meanings is really much greater, because in practice a card does not have one significance when it falls normally and another when reversed, but several different meanings in either position. The reader has to make his choice of meanings, influenced by other cards in the spread and by his own intuitive grasp of the inquirer's character and circumstances. Matters are made more complicated by the fact that there is no single set of agreed meanings for the cards. Different textbooks interpret them in startlingly different ways. The reader will have to proceed by trial and error, feeling his way.

It is considered wrong to read the cards repeatedly for the same inquirer or to obtain an answer to the same question for oneself. This betrays a lack of confidence which is inimical to accurate divination, and although it is a mistake to acquiesce in events with a blind and spiritless fatalism, it is no use supposing that a situation can be altered artificially by dealing out a fresh spread of cards.

The meanings allotted to the cards are broad and vague. The Six of Swords, for example, can mean 'success earned by hard work, difficulties overcome, an improved situation'. There are obviously many different circumstances to which this could apply. Or it can mean, more specifically, 'a pleasant journey by water'. Or less specifically again, it can mean 'travel', which might be anything from a trip to the next town to a voyage round the world. A spread of cards provides a number of key-words or key-ideas of this sort which are linked together to 'tell a story'. The vagueness of the language used means that any spread can be interpreted in many ways and can apply to many inquirers. But on the other hand, it is this same vagueness that allows room for the reader's own intuitive or psychic abilities to operate.

This is why the beginner is recommended to memorize the meanings of the cards as soon as he can. Not only will he be more impressive, but reading the cards off by rote from a book cramps his own divining faculties. He needs to get to know his cards well, as if they were people with whom his acquaintance was gradually ripening, until they call up a wealth of ideas and associations almost automatically. Some writers tell him to give his cards special treatment – by wrapping them in silk, perhaps, or keeping them in a handsome box – as a way of symbolizing their importance and so helping him to concentrate serious attention on them. It is also said to protect their 'vibrations' against outside interference.

The four suits of minor cards are frequently linked with the traditional four elements of fire, air, earth and water, but different authors disagree about which element goes with which suit. The system followed here is the Golden Dawn one, in which the attributions are:

Suit	Element
Batons	Fire
Cups	Water
Swords	Air
Coins	Earth

The Queen of Pomegranates, the suit equivalent to Coins, from a copy of a German 15th-century card.

Within each suit the cards from the Ace to the Ten are connected with the ten sefiroth of the Tree of Life. The Ace of each suit corresponds to the first sefira, Kether, the Two to Hokmah, the Three to Binah, and so on to the Ten, which corresponds to Malkuth. These links with the sefiroth have been a major influence on interpretations of the cards.

The court cards are usually taken to represent people – husbands, wives, relatives, friends and acquaintances, people known at work, doctors, lawyers, and so on – who play a role in the inquirer's life. The Queen of Swords, for example, may be a widow, the Page of Batons a rival. One of the court cards is often picked out specially to stand for the inquirer himself. In the old days Kings and Knights were expected to represent men, and Queens women. The court cards of Batons and Swords were supposed to be people with black hair and dark complexions, and those of Cups and Coins people of fair colouring. This is now considered unduly simple-minded. It is the type of personality represented by the card which matters, rather than colouring or even sex. Broadly speaking, however, Kings will generally stand for older men, Queens for adult women, and Knights for younger men. Pages may be young men or women, adolescent boys or girls, or children of either sex.

The types of character associated with the court cards of each suit have been heavily influenced by the element with which the suit is linked. The personalities attributed to the court cards of Coins, for instance, are variations on the theme of earth, which is connected with farmers and agricultural labourers, solidity, dependability, hard work, practical matters and settled routines, inability to see beyond narrow horizons, limitedness, heaviness and worthiness. The Page of Coins is a caricatured country boy, slow, deliberate, solemn and thrifty. The Knight is a rustic 'clod', ponderous, dull and clumsy. The Queen is a Mother Earth figure, warm, secure, comfortable and bosomy, but she is subject to sudden changes of mood, which are the psychological equivalents of earthquakes and eruptions. The King is like a ploughman or farmer, solid and plodding, practical and 'down to earth', but capable of achieving a rich harvest of material success.

There are times, however, when a court card does not represent a person but an event or condition or trend. If the Queen of Swords is not a widow, she may stand for female unhappiness, mourning, or a death. Again, the reader has to decide in the light of other cards nearby and his own understanding of the inquirer's circumstances.

The following list of meanings is drawn from various different systems, but is based primarily on the Golden Dawn interpretations, which were worked out by Mathers and were followed, with variations, by Waite and Crowley. The main general meaning of each card is a blend of the ideas suggested by its design and the sefira and element with which it is connected. Waite gave each of the cards from the Ten to the Ace in his pack its own picture, representing its principal significance, but in most packs the designs on these cards are less pictorial and more emblematic.

Cards from a French pack produced during the Revolution: LEFT to RIGHT, TOP the Liberty or Queen of Cups, and the King of Coins; BOTTOM the Equality or Page of Batons, and the Knight of the same suit.

LIBERTé DE COUPES	GENIE DE DENIERS
EGALITé DE BAATONS	CAVALIER DE BAATONS

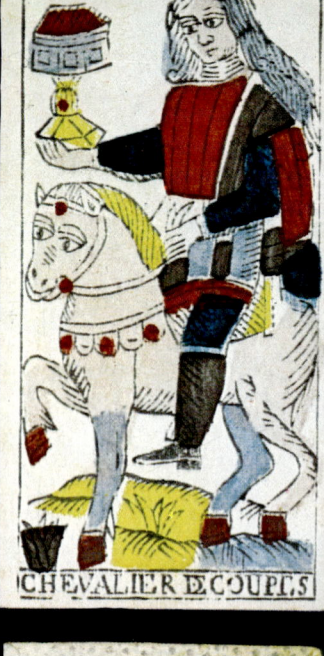

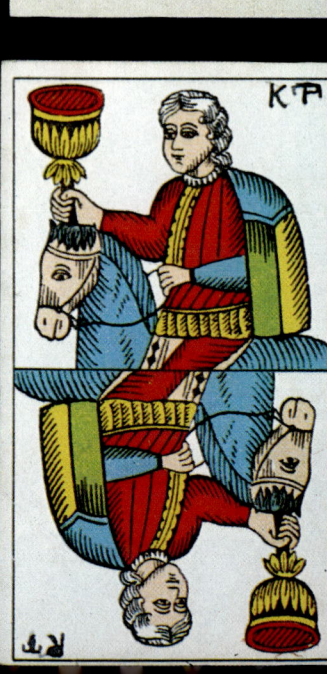

CH.D COUPE	CHEVALIER DE COUPES	CAVALIER DI COPPE
CHEVALIER DE COUPES		CAVALIER DE COUPL.
CAV DI COPPE	CAVALLIER DE COUPES	

Suit of Batons

The suit of Batons (or Wands, Rods, Staffs, Sceptres) is related to the element of fire, the masculine principle and the phallus, and vigorous creative energy. In general it has to do with work and business, enterprise, initiative and pressing on with things.

Ace The beginning of an undertaking or activity, the origin of a situation. A birth, or a fresh start. It is a card of fertile energy, resourcefulness and inventiveness, suggesting that success will be achieved in artistic, social or money matters. It is sometimes connected with ancestry and inheritance. If the Ace of Batons and the Ace of Cups, standing for male and female, are close together in a spread of cards, this is said to indicate an upsurge of vigour and a greater probability of gaining one's objective.
REVERSED. Pride going before a fall. Failure, impotence, sterility, vexation. Ruin and destruction. Persecution and cruelty.

Two Power, authority, influence over other people, splendour and grandeur, wealth and good fortune. On the other hand, achievement may not bring lasting satisfaction, success may turn to dust and ashes in the mouth.
REVERSED. Again there are opposite possibilities, delight and enchantment or astonishment and fear. A surprise, something extraordinary may happen.

Three Manifest and lasting success in business, trade or the arts. It is often connected with the sea, ships, merchandise, voyages of discovery. Partnership and productive cooperation. Hopes realized. Generosity. An established organization or enterprise of some kind.
REVERSED. Arrogance, self-assertion, rudeness, obstinacy, failure of over-ambitious plans. Alternatively, difficulties are overcome, troubles are permanently or temporarily ended.

Four The successful completion of an activity, consolidation of gains, a settled situation. Relaxation after achievement, peace and quiet, restful prosperity. Country life, contented family life, a haven of refuge.
REVERSED. Happiness, prosperity, success, beauty, pleasure.

Five Fierce competition and struggle, a battle for success. The rewards of life are not gained easily. Quarrels, arguments, ordeals, tests.
REVERSED. Legal proceedings, the law, the courts, trickery, fraud. However, disputes may be turned to advantage.

Six Hard work brings its rewards, a well-earned success, a justified triumph. Important news is in the offing.
REVERSED. Fear of successful enemies or rivals, disloyalty and bad faith. There is a traitor in the ranks. Delay.

Seven A challenge which can be overcome by individual courage and strength. A faction fight. A serious threat to your position. You must rely on yourself.
REVERSED. Hesitation, doubts, anxiety. An embarrassing situation. Indecision may be fatal.

Eight A card of speed. Things are moving quickly, perhaps too quickly. Matters coming rapidly to a conclusion, rush and hurry, urgent messages. Possibly, the

The Knights of Cups from nine different packs: LEFT TO RIGHT, DOWNWARDS Galler of Brussels, 1740; Swiss anonymous, early 19th century; Béranger of Nice, c. 1832; Valla of Trieste, 1750; Florentine anonymous, 1650; Müller, Switzerland, 1930; Annannino of Genoa, 1887; Renault of Besançon, 1800; and Grimand of Paris, 1900.

swift urgency of a love affair or other infatuation. For a married person, domestic disputes.
REVERSED. Domestic or internal disputes, quarrels, jealousy, the pangs of conscience. Alternatively, a theft, rapacity.

Nine Strength held in reserve, secure defences, unshakable resistance to vigorous opposition. Resilience. Preparedness. Delay, objectives will be achieved later. Recovery from illness.
REVERSED. Obstacles, delays, adversity.

Ten Oppression, burdens to carry. Energy misused for selfish and materialistic purposes, determination to succeed at expense of others. Cruelty, harsh treatment, injustice. Achievement which turns into a toilsome burden, a surfeit of success, or alternatively, a failure caused by selfishness. Possibly a card of revenge.
REVERSED. Loss, deceit, intrigue, subterfuge.

Page An attractive person who is 'fiery' in the sense of being quick, enthusiastic, energetic, daring and scintillating. A suitor. A faithful lover, a pleasing stranger, a reliable messenger, a trustworthy person. If followed by the Page of Cups, however, the Page of Batons stands for a dangerous rival.
REVERSED. A superficial and shallow person, indecisive, unstable and theatrical. A tale-bearer, a betrayer of secrets. More generally, bad news, unreliable information, gossip. The cards on either side of it should show what the news is about.

Knight An impetuous person, a maker of swift decisions, unpredictable and startling, generous and friendly. Active and alert, he is fiercely energetic but he lacks staying power. If the card does not represent a person, it stands for sudden

departure, flight, moving house, a separation, and conveys a warning against precipitate action. The card following it should make the warning clearer.
REVERSED. A cruel, prejudiced, narrow-minded person. More generally, disagreement, quarrelling, parting, interruptions, discontent.

Queen A warm, affectionate, charming woman, of settled and stable character, practical and calm. A popular person, she is authoritative and determined, kindly and generous, but distinctly intolerant of opposition. Mathers called her 'the lady of the manor'. She may have a tendency to snobbery and is likely to be grasping in financial matters. This is also a card of business success, or a 'good harvest'.
REVERSED. A virtuous woman, an efficient and frugal manager. She can be obstinate, overbearing and unpredictable, quick to take offence, likely to turn suddenly against a friend for no good reason. Obstacles and difficulties.

King A man of strong and admirable character, honourable and honest, fair-minded, generous, romantic and passionate, intensely proud, gifted with courage and endurance. He is often described, in effect, as an old-fashioned country gentleman of the best type. He has a strong sense of humour and is a lover of hard work for its own sake. He is not an intellectual. He jumps to conclusions about minor matters and states his opinions over-forcefully, but is slow to make up his mind about more important questions. The card can also mean a good marriage or a legacy.
REVERSED. A man of strict morality, austere, narrow, intolerant, autocratic, proud. He may have a callous or cruel streak in his nature. More generally, good advice, deliberation.

NEAR and FAR RIGHT The Knight of Batons designed by Bonifacio Bembo and the Ten of Batons from Waite's pack.
OPPOSITE, LEFT TO RIGHT The Ace and Two of Batons, from a 15th-century German pack.

The ace from a 20th-century Piedmontese pack.

Suit of Cups

The suit of Cups (or Chalices) is the luckiest of the four and a preponderance of Cups in a spread is a favourable sign. The cards are connected with the element of water, the feminine principle, love and marriage, feeling and emotion, sensitivity and pleasure.

Ace This is an extremely fortunate card, standing for happiness and fulfilment. Waite's and Crowley's designs represent the Holy Grail. It is also a card of fruitfulness, motherhood, abundance. It may predict a marriage, the climax of a love-affair, the beginning of a love-affair, a happy social occasion or a love-letter.
REVERSED. Change, alterations, instability, unfaithfulness. Something new, unexpected and probably unwelcome.

Two The Golden Dawn called this card the Lord of Love and it stands for loving union, peaceful harmony, friendship, sympathy and affection. It may be a card of marriage, or it can suggest enjoyable occupations and pursuits, leisure activities, hobbies and games.
REVERSED. Foolish behaviour, waste and extravagance, dissipation. Alternatively, the break-up of a relationship, divorce.

Three A card of fruition, abundance and good luck, promising a favourable outcome in any situation. Success is gained without great effort or difficulty. It may refer to a marriage, a birth, a love affair, a promotion, or to healing. It is also a card of general good cheer, hospitality, entertainment, dancing, gladness and sensual enjoyment. There may perhaps be a connection with new clothes.
REVERSED. Quickness, dispatch, expeditious transaction of business, the end of an activity or process. Or it may mean excessive sensual indulgence.

Four A mixture of satisfaction and dissatisfaction. A run of successes is nearing its end and there is uneasiness about the future. 'A stationary period in happiness,' Mathers said, 'which may or may not continue.'[6] The fruit of pleasure, according to Crowley, contains the seeds of decay. Many writers connect the card with surfeit, satiation, boredom, weariness, a disgruntled attitude, a readiness to find fault, familiarity breeding contempt. Or it can mean that an awkward situation is created by other people's kindness.
REVERSED. Something new on the horizon. A new acquaintance or relationship. A foreboding, a premonition.

Five Not an encouraging card. Disappointment in love or friendship, or in relation to a will. A broken engagement. Failure to enjoy an anticipated pleasure. Sadness, regret, frustration. Anxiety and difficulty originating in an unexpected quarter. Kindness and generosity are ill-repaid. Possibilities of deceit and betrayal, friends are being unkind.
REVERSED. News, a surprise, an unexpected arrival or return. Plans and projects which will miscarry.

Six This card has two opposite meanings. It is connected with pleasant memories of the past, nostalgia, a wistful longing for past security and happiness. Alternatively or additionally, it has to do with a new situation. A wish is beginning, but only beginning, to come true. The first precarious steps are being taken on a new

path to achievement, gain or happiness, but there are indications of trouble in store. The situation is not yet fully understood. Beware of being presumptuous and ungrateful. An affront or setback of some kind is indicated.
REVERSED. The future, something which will happen before long, the nature of which is shown by the nearby cards.

Seven A card of vice and guilty conscience, connected with debauchery, dissipation, violence, vanity, prostitution of talent. It also means illusions and mistakes, fantasies, lies. Any apparent triumph is deceptive, any success gained will not be followed up.
REVERSED. A decision or resolution, a plan, a desire. If next to the Three of Cups, success.

Eight Decline of interest, laziness, dissatisfaction with what has been gained, inability to concentrate, aimless wandering about. However, it is not necessarily as bad as it sounds. It may mean the discovery that something previously valued is really worthless, and so imply the abandonment of an old and second-rate objective for a better one.
REVERSED. Happiness, delight, gaiety, conviviality.

Nine A card of good fortune and material happiness. Complete success, an assured future, a wish fulfilled. Physical health and well-being. All obstacles are surmounted. The cup of satisfaction is full and brimming over. A particularly fortunate card for soldiers.
REVERSED. Mistakes, errors, faults, lack of success.

Ten A better card still, since it means permanent success on a higher plane than the Nine, which is related to material and physical well-being. The Ten is connected with spiritual treasure, love which is more than physical, family and domestic felicity, the happiness of friends, peace of mind, a successful end to struggle and competition, the quiet waters of contented achievement. It also suggests reputation, high esteem, someone held in honour. Alternatively, it may stand for a person's home, village, town or country.
REVERSED. Disruption, opposition, disputes, anger, violence.

Page A handsome, perhaps effeminate boy or a pretty girl. A quiet, studious, reflective, gentle, rather vague person, imaginative and much given to romantic dreaming, dependendent on other people but also useful to them. Not a person of strong and definite character, but honest, discreet and with a bent for service. Possibly someone who has been crossed in love. Alternatively, musing and reflection, or news.
REVERSED. A flatterer and deceiver, a selfish person. A jack-of-all-trades. Seduction or deception.

Knight A pleasant, graceful, sensitive, romantic young man, amiable but superficial, enthusiastic if aroused but generally languid and idle, with little depth of character. A dilettante, an aesthete. More generally, a message or arrival, a proposal or proposition. It may announce the appearance of something indicated by the following card.
REVERSED. A sensual and lazy person, a liar, someone who does not keep promises. Possibly, a drug addict or a schizophrenic. Deceit, swindling, fraud.

The Two of Cups, from a pack of the Marseilles type.

Two court cards from the suit of Cups: the Page from a French Marseilles pack, and FAR LEFT the Knight, a 19th-century copy by William Ottley of a 15th-century design.

Queen A good-natured, easy-going woman, calm and tranquil, a good wife and mother, kind to people as long as she is not put to too much trouble on their behalf. She is dreamy, imaginative, fond of poetry, perhaps artistic, flirtatious. She is easily impressed and inclined to take on the colour of her surroundings.
REVERSED. An interfering woman, unreliable and not to be trusted. Someone who changes her mind constantly and is a prey to fantasies. Possibly, a vicious and depraved woman. Villainy, cunning.

King A powerful and immensely ambitious man, probably in a position of responsibility, who is respected and feared. He may be a force for good or evil, but more often the latter. He is 'deep', as water is, and behind an imperturbable exterior he is a man of violent passions, secretive, subtle, crafty, ruthless and totally without a conscience. He will be helpful if it suits him, but is always determined to get his own way. Beware of ill-will in high places.
REVERSED. A profoundly evil man, merciless, dishonest and untrustworthy. Doubt and suspicion.

Suit of Swords

The suit of swords is generally unlucky and a preponderance of these cards in a spread is ominous, basically because the sword as a weapon suggests war, bloodshed and death. The suit is connected with the element of air, which in turn is linked with intellect and instability.

Ace The phallic symbolism of this card, which shows an upright sword topped by a crown, has a good deal to do with its interpretations. It has been explained, for instance, as 'beginning of tense relation'. The Golden Dawn regarded it as a card of great power for either good or evil (Satan is described in the New Testament as 'the prince of the power of the air'). It suggests a tendency to go to extremes, stresses and strains, formidable forces at work. It may be a sign of prosperity and

success achieved against heavy odds, or of anger, punishment and affliction. Some authors say it means death, partly because of its phallic connotations. The Ace of Spades in the conventional pack is in popular tradition the death card.
REVERSED. The meaning is similar but the effects are now definitely bad. Violence, destruction, misuse of power, injustice, love denied, obstacles and hindrances. Or alternatively, conception and childbirth.

Two Harmony, peace and concord. A balance of forces is established. Quarrels are made up and differences reconciled. Pleasure follows or arises from pain. Faithful friendship, or a pacifying feminine influence. Elements of tension are still present, however, and the situation is slightly uneasy.
REVERSED. Treachery, falsehood, pretences. A love of trouble and tension for their own sake. Possibly, a journey to a distant country.

Three Tears and woe. Disruption of relationships, a broken love-affair, separation, parting, divorce. Quarrelling, conflict, selfishness. Someone is making mischief. Or it may merely indicate that something is lost or temporarily mislaid. There is possibly some connection with a nun, or perhaps with singing.
REVERSED. Mistakes, disorder, confusion, mental imbalance. Strife and quarrels, war.

Four A change for the better. Peace after battle, convalescence after illness. Tensions slacken and there is a relaxation of anxiety. The card also suggests solitude and a retreat of some kind, and so possibly compromise, appeasement. There may be some connection with graves and coffins, though the card does not mean death.
REVERSED. Careful economy, sensible management, caution, precautions. Possibly, greed or a will.

Five The Golden Dawn named this card the Lord of Defeat. It stands for failure, dishonour, degradation, discouragement, the triumph of enemies, poverty and anxiety. A spiteful trouble-maker is at work.
REVERSED. Again, failure. Trouble, loss, mourning, a funeral.

Six Success earned by hard work, difficulties overcome, an improved situation. A pleasant journey by water. Travel, a move away from trouble and anxiety to pleasanter circumstances. A messenger, or a risk.
REVERSED. A declaration of love, a confession, a surprise. Publicity.

Seven Uncertainty, a tendency to fail at the last moment through giving up too quickly. Vacillation, unreliability, an untrustworthy person or situation. Compromise and tolerance may lead to bad results. Probably connected with a plan, ambition or desire. A journey by land. There is a possibility of being injured while playing a game or when travelling.
REVERSED. Good advice, wisdom, prudence.

Eight Bad news, a crisis, criticism, illness, isolation, perhaps even hospitalization or imprisonment. Limits and restrictions. Concentration of too much energy on minor matters, over-attention to detail, pettiness, fussiness. Beware of the small print in legal documents, contracts, insurance policies.
REVERSED. An unforeseen event, a surprising incident, an accident. Treachery, frustration, despair. Danger.

Nine An extremely grim card, suggesting serious misfortune. According to Waite, it means utter desolation. It is associated with misery, despair, suffering, miscarriage, failure, disappointment and possibly death. Crowley said that it might imply an attitude of resignation and acceptance of martyrdom, or alternatively an implacable revenge. Others have linked it with clergymen or with people who are unloved.
REVERSED. Justified fear, misgiving and mistrust. Doubt, suspicion. Loneliness. A person of shady character.

Ten This is the worst card in the pack, and even more ominous than the Nine. It is connected with death, ruin and disaster, the failure of all hopes and plans, desolation and grief. Extreme wariness is essential and no one should be trusted. In spiritual matters, however, the 'death' may be the termination of a false belief or attitude. If followed by the Ace and King, it means prison.
REVERSED. Momentary advantage, a false gleam of hope, temporary profit and success.

Page A sharp-eyed, watchful, subtle, acute person, a good negotiator and go-between, tactful and perceptive, graceful and dexterous. A lively boy or 'tomboy' girl.
REVERSED. A spy, or a frivolous person. Someone who is devious and tricky, a false friend. Low cunning is one of the characteristics. Be on your guard against the unexpected. Surprising news.

Knight A forceful, clever and capable person, vigorous and brave, inclined to dominate others and sweep them along with him like a storm-wind. Punctual and punctilious, he may be a soldier. He is not a good person to cross. The card suggests enemies and opposition, and is extremely ominous if it falls close to other unlucky cards.
REVERSED. A fool, impatient and overbearing but inwardly indecisive, as fitful as the breeze. Naïve and conceited, he will never take advice and he lacks staying power. For a woman, it may mean a successful struggle with a rival.

Queen A widow. Also or alternatively, a subtle and intelligent woman, an individualist, highly perceptive. Confident and charming, she is a skilful diplomat, good at managing other people. In general, a card of female unhappiness, sterility, deprivation and mourning. It may have to do with the future loss of a husband or wife.
REVERSED. A thoroughly evil woman, whose attractive exterior conceals hatred, cruelty, treachery, malice and deceit. An accomplished user of lies and half-truths A dangerous enemy. A prude. (In the ordinary pack of playing cards the Queen of Spades has the same reputation.)

King A man in authority, a government official or quite likely a lawyer or doctor. An intellectual. Careful, cautious, mistrustful and suspicious, he is highly intelligent, full of ideas and plans, dedicated to rational solutions but in practice unrealistic and ineffective. According to Crowley, he is quite unable to progress in any direction except by accident, which makes him 'a perfect picture of the Mind'.
REVERSED. An evil man, selfish, obstinate, cold and calculating, cruel, sly and perverse. He is not to be trusted. Do not proceed with a lawsuit.

ABOVE, LEFT TO RIGHT The Nine of Swords from Waite's pack, and the Knight from an early Italian pack. BELOW LEFT the Page of Swords designed by Bonifacio Bembo and RIGHT a 15th-century Three of Swords, in a copy by Ottley.

Suit of Coins

The Coins (or Pentacles, Disks) are connected with the element of earth and are principally concerned with money, property, earning a living, status, worldly influence and security.

Ace A very favourable card. Money and possessions, contented prosperity, material comfort, enjoyment of the good things of life, a secure position in the world, a stable situation.
REVERSED. The same, but now in a less pleasant light. It suggests the corrupting side of wealth – materialism, money-grubbing, selfishness, greed, over-indulgence of physical appetites, smug self-satisfaction, philistine attitudes, putting too high a value on money and social position. Comfortable security has become lack of adventurousness, the stable situation is a rut.

Two The ups and downs of life, the alternation of good and bad luck, profit and loss, success and failure. It implies inconsistency, lack of fixed purpose, passing moods of discontent with the present position, swinging between optimism and pessimism. Difficulties are more imaginary than real. A change may be imminent, possibly a change of job. Or the card may be related to an enjoyable journey, business trip or social occasion.
REVERSED. Pretended enjoyment, simulated cheerfulness, possibly drunkenness. A letter or a message.

Three Constructive work, the building up of something, a gain or improvement. A favourable card for any new project. An increase in income, an acquisition, making a profit. Or higher status, a promotion. Gaining other people's approval, fame, notoriety.
REVERSED. Mediocrity, average performance, weakness, obscurity.

Four Consolidated material success, assured status, power and authority. Substantial material and worldly achievement. A solid and secure position. The successful establishment of a business or enterprise. The card suggests a tendency to cling to what you have and a disinclination to take risks. Or it may indicate a gift, a gambling win, a bonus, something extra. For a bachelor, good news from a woman.
REVERSED. Opposition, uncertainty, delay.

Five Strain and anxiety about money and material things. Poverty, hardship, making economies, a harsh struggle to survive. Loss of money, loss of a job, a decline in status. A card of worry and hard times, which may only be temporary.
REVERSED. Severe financial loss, disorder, a chaotic situation, probably caused by imprudence and extravagance.

Six Prosperity and generosity, gifts, presents, a helping hand, a benefactor. Charity. Gratitude.
REVERSED. Envy, greed, covetousness.

Seven This is not a favourable card, either way up. It suggests a transaction which goes wrong. Disappointment, failure to achieve an expected gain or success. An unprofitable speculation, hard work for little reward, hopes blighted.
REVERSED. Worry, anxiety. An unprofitable loan.

Eight Prudence and skill in business matters, finance and at work, but deployed on a limited scale. Concentration on minor matters at the expense of more important ones, lack of dash and enterprise. Money may be made in small amounts. Greed, hoarding, meanness, low cunning.
REVERSED. Dishonesty in business. Unreliability and hypocrisy. Money-lending.

Nine Good fortune in material matters. Substantial rewards, profits or gains, or perhaps a sizeable legacy. Popularity with others. Foresight, discernment, discretion. Comfort. Safety. Swift fulfilment of what is predicted by nearby cards.
REVERSED. Bad faith, deceit, deviousness.

Ten The card of great accumulations of wealth and property, but it is not entirely a good omen. It stands for the pinnacle of material success, according to MacGregor Mathers, but it implies success reached in old age, with accompanying connotations of exhaustion, boredom, lethargy, pessimism, sharpness about money combined with weary lack of interest or confidence in anything else. It is frequently connected with family wealth, landed estates, business dynasties, or with the family home and family traditions.
REVERSED. Robbery, or heavy taxation. Gambling, unwise speculation, dissipation, loss. A disputed inheritance.

Page A careful, hard-working, rather solemn person, who is slow and deliberate in thought and action, responsible and conscientious, thrifty but not ungenerous. Generally, sound management and administration, economy, thrift.
REVERSED. A waster, a prodigal son or daughter. Luxury, extravagance. Bad news.

Knight A ponderous, dull, slow-moving, heavy-going, clumsy person, conventional, responsible, hard-working and practical, a useful member of society but not a very interesting one. He is not happy in authority and prefers a subordinate position. He likes to know and keep his place. Most descriptions of him are based on a caricature of the peasant or yokel. Usefulness, serviceableness.
REVERSED. An idler. An unemployed person. Laziness, carelessness, greed, suspicion. Petty interference.

Queen A warm-hearted, charming woman, kindly and comfortable, who has all the domestic virtues. Sometimes moody or impetuous, she is generally sensible, practical, busy, truthful, courageous and a tower of strength. She is not an intellectual or especially intelligent but intuitive and understanding. Generosity, security, certainty. A happy marriage.
REVERSED. A spiritless drudge. A silly, capricious, unreliable woman. Fear, mistrust, suspense. An illness.

King A solid, down-to-earth, practical man, steady and trustworthy, a good worker or manager. He may be a businessman or a teacher. Unemotional, insensitive, methodical and plodding, he is not as dull and stupid as he may seem and is capable of achieving considerable material success. Not easily moved, slow to react, he will be a devoted but undemonstrative husband or friend, but he makes an implacable enemy. More generally, energy applied to practical matters.
REVERSED. A brute, a vicious, corrupt and unprincipled man. Danger, fear.

170 DIVINATION

The Trumps: Divinatory Meanings

A preponderance of trump cards in a spread means that powerful forces are at work which are beyond the inquirer's control.

0 *The Fool*: Folly, eccentricity, or even madness. An unexpected appearance on the scene, an unlooked-for influence coming suddenly into play. (*Reversed*: Apathy, turning away from life, carelessness, hesitation, instability.)

1 *The Juggler*: Will-power, initiative. Cleverness, skill, subtlety, adaptability. A choice, a gamble, a risk. Perhaps the beginning of something new and important. (*Reversed*: Loss of nerve. Swindling, cheating, trickery. Uneasiness and confusion, possibly mental illness. There may be some connection with a doctor or psychiatrist.)

2 *The Female Pope*: Secrets. Change, fluctuation. Intuition. Beware of over-enthusiasm. (*Reversed*: Passion, illicit sex. Ignorance, stupidity.)

3 *The Empress*: Happiness, pleasure, good luck. Creativity, fruitful action. (*Reversed*: Inaction, vacillation, disagreement. Dissipation.)

4 *The Emperor*: Success, stability, authority, ambition. Protection, help. Self-control. (*Reversed*: A check, an obstruction. Over-confidence. Death in battle. Serious injury.)

5 *The Pope*: Assistance, good advice, a helpful friend. Inspiration. Religious interests. Marriage, or an alliance. (*Reversed*: Bad advice, lies. Persecution. Weakness.)

6 *The Lovers*: Love, sex, attraction. A choice. Uncertainty. There may be a connection with psychic abilities of some kind. (*Reversed*: Quarrels, parting, divorce. Failing a test. Indecision.)

7 *The Chariot*: Success, triumph over difficulties, self-assertion. Travel, exploration. (*Reversed*: Tyranny. Sudden defeat, misfortune, bad news, accidents.)

8 *Justice*: Balance, equality. Suspense, waiting for a decision. A test, an ordeal. (*Reversed*: Unfairness, legal complications, miscarriage of justice.)

9 *The Hermit*: Caution, prudence, delay. A hiding-place, a place of refuge. Diplomacy, dissimulation, treachery. Old age. (*Reversed*: Secrecy, disguises, fear. Timidity, excessive caution.)

10 *The Wheel of Fortune*: Good luck, wealth, gain. Destiny. (*Reversed*: Bad luck, change for the worse.)

11 *Strength*: Courage, strength, energy, self-discipline, exercise of authority. A reconciliation. The influence of a good woman. (*Reversed*: Despotism, bad temper. Weakness, illness. Disgrace. The influence of a bad woman.)

12 *The Hanged Man*: Sacrifice, submission, suffering, punishment. A setback. Tests and trials. Perhaps an early death. Unconventional behaviour. (*Reversed*: Selfishness. Pain. Defeat. The crowd, the mob.)

13 *Death*: Death, destruction, failure of a project. Change, transformation. Loss of a friend or helper. (*Reversed*: Long life. A birth. Laziness, sleep, inertia.)

Cards from the suit of Coins: TOP LEFT the Ace of Pomegranates, in Ottley's pack, and RIGHT a 19th-century Italian design for the Two of Discs; BOTTOM LEFT to RIGHT the Page of Coins in an 18th-century Swiss and an early Italian pack.

14 *Temperance:* Good management. Cooperation, combination. Partnership. Good health. Escape from a situation. (*Reversed:* Confrontation, disputes, clash of interests. Poor management. Matters to do with priests and churches.)

15 *The Devil:* Material matters. Irresistible impulses, temptation. Obsessions. An unavoidable but fortunate event. (*Reversed:* Blind stupidity, malice. Repression. An unavoidable and unfortunate event.)

16 *The Tower:* Ruin, unforeseen disaster, serious loss. War, battles, conflict. An accident. A sweeping change. (*Reversed:* The same, but less drastic.)

17 *The Star:* Hope, unexpected help, a gift or a promise. Insight. Good prospects, confidence. (*Reversed:* Bad luck, disappointment, hopes unfulfilled. An error of judgment.)

18 *The Moon:* Darkness, danger, fear, bewilderment. Hidden enemies. Illicit love. A crisis, an important change is about to occur. (*Reversed:* Deception, vacillation, minor mistakes.)

19 *The Sun:* Success, prosperity, happiness. A fortunate marriage. (*Reversed:* The same, but to a lesser degree.)

20 *The Day of Judgment:* A decision, the final settlement of a matter. Change, a fresh start. The taking of a definite step. A reunion. (*Reversed:* Suspense, postponement, delay. An unsatisfactory result.)

21 *The World:* Assured success. Travel. (*Reversed:* Failure. Stagnation. Efforts are ill-rewarded.)

Combinations of Cards

A card's meaning is strengthened if it falls between two cards of its own suit in a spread. Its effect is weakened if it falls between two cards of its 'opposite' suit. Batons (fire) and Cups (water) are regarded as opposite suits, and so are Swords (air) and Coins (earth). So for example, if the Ace of Coins, which is a favourable card, falls between two other Coins, this is a highly encouraging sign. But if it falls between two Swords, its favourable meaning is weakened without being cancelled out. When a trump card falls between two cards of the same suit, its meaning is strongly affected by these cards. For example, Mathers interpreted the Death card lying between the Nine of Swords and the Three of Swords as 'Death accompanied by much pain and misery.' When two cards of opposite suits fall side by side, they tend to neutralize each other.

If most of the cards in a spread are court cards, this suggests encounters with numerous people, much human contact, social or business gatherings. The following list of general meanings of other combinations of cards in a spread is drawn principally from Mathers.

Four Aces	– a good sign, strong forces at work
Three Aces	– money, success
Four Kings	– meetings with important people
Three Kings	– high status, a prize, an honour
Four Queens	– much argument

Three Queens	– deception by women
Four Knights	– swiftness, urgency
Three Knights	– unexpected encounters, news
Four Pages	– new plans, new ideas
Three Pages	– the company of young people
Four Tens	– responsibility and anxiety
Three Tens	– commercial transactions, buying and selling
Four Nines	– an extra burden of responsibility
Three Nines	– letters, messages, correspondence
Four Eights	– a torrent of news or information
Three Eights	– much travelling, bustling to and fro
Four Sevens	– disappointments, especially in matters of love
Three Sevens	– agreements, contracts, alliances
Four Sixes	– pleasure
Three Sixes	– gain
Four Fives	– regularity
Three Fives	– disputes, disagreements, quarrels
Four Fours	– peace and quiet, rest
Three Fours	– hard work
Four Threes	– decision, resolution
Three Threes	– deceit
Four Twos	– conversations, conferences
Three Twos	– reorganization

2 LAYOUTS AND READINGS

The cards can be arranged for divination in many different patterns, some of which are believed to have a helpful occult significance of their own. The most complicated layouts use a large number of cards for a reading which may take several hours. Simpler methods use only a few cards. It is obviously sensible to master the simpler layouts first before going on to the more difficult ones.

The usual first step is to choose one of the court cards to represent the inquirer (or yourself, if you are your own inquirer). This card is called the 'significator'. It is removed from the pack and placed on the table, face up. The effect of isolating it at the outset is to simplify matters by preventing it from falling in a random, or apparently random, position in the spread. In more complicated layouts, however, the significator is left in the pack and shuffled with the other cards.

The significator should correspond as far as possible to the inquirer's general character-type and circumstances. Alliette suggested using the Pope as a man's significator and the Female Pope as a woman's, and some readers do this, but like most things connected with Alliette the practice is generally frowned on. If the reading is meant to produce the answer to a specific question, a suitable trump card is sometimes used as the significator: Justice if the question is connected with legal proceedings, for instance, or the Moon if it is to do with an illicit love affair. But usually the significator is a court card.

After picking out the significator, cut the pack into two heaps, turn one of the heaps round and then rejoin the pack for shuffling. The point of this is to make sure that some cards will fall reversed and that it will not always be the same cards.

The next step is to shuffle and cut, which is often done three times in succession before the cards are dealt out. Some writers say that the inquirer should shuffle, and others that both the inquirer and the reader should do it, but the best rule seems to be for the reader to shuffle. Whoever is shuffling, the inquirer should meanwhile concentrate hard on any question or problem that particularly concerns him. After each shuffle, the inquirer or the reader should cut. Cutting is usually done with the left hand into three heaps which are then restacked at random.

Simple Layouts. A very simple type of layout to start practising on uses only three or four cards altogether. Draw the top two cards from the pack and deal them face up next to the significator, which is already on the table. Card 1 stands for the inquirer's present frame of mind and Card 2 for a situation or person looming up in the near future. Alternatively, draw three cards and deal them out in the same way. Card 1 represents something in the inquirer's past, Card 2 something in the present, Card 3 something soon to happen.

Methods like this are too simple to provide anything more than the roughest of indications. As an illustration, however, suppose the inquirer is a married woman who has a worrying but not desperately serious money problem (if it was really serious, you would not insult her by trying to tackle it with only four cards). Suppose you have chosen the Queen of Cups as her significator and the three cards dealt beside it are the Three of Swords reversed, the Page of Cups and the Eight of Coins.

Card 1, for the past, is the Three of Swords reversed, which can mean 'mistakes' or 'quarrels'. It might mean both. Has the inquirer made a mistake over money, by overspending perhaps, which has caused a quarrel? And if so, was the quarrel with the obvious person, her husband? This possibility is raised with the inquirer and proves correct.

Card 2, for the present, is the Page of Cups and the inquirer herself is represented by the Queen of Cups, so it looks as if her problem is concerned with a relative, who is very likely one of her children. Maybe her past mistake is now preventing her from buying something for the child. This turns out to be right. She has set her heart on an expensive birthday present for her daughter, but she has overspent and cannot afford it, and her husband is still annoyed and will not help.

For the future, the Eight of Coins means prudence and skill applied to small-scale financial matters. This suggests that the inquirer can solve her difficulty by sensible management. Perhaps by making careful economies she can save enough for the birthday present. Or perhaps her husband can be skilfully maneouvred into producing the money, though the fact that the Eight of Coins can also mean 'greed, hoarding, meanness' may imply that the prospects on this front are not hopeful.

The obvious problem is that the same spread of cards could perfectly well be interpreted in several quite different ways. Very simple and limited layouts do not provide either enough cards or enough contact with the inquirer for an adequate reading. The learner will soon want to go on to more complicated layouts.

The four Aces from a 17th-century pack designed by G. M. Mitelli: Batons, Cups, Coins, Swords.

VIRTUS ARDUA

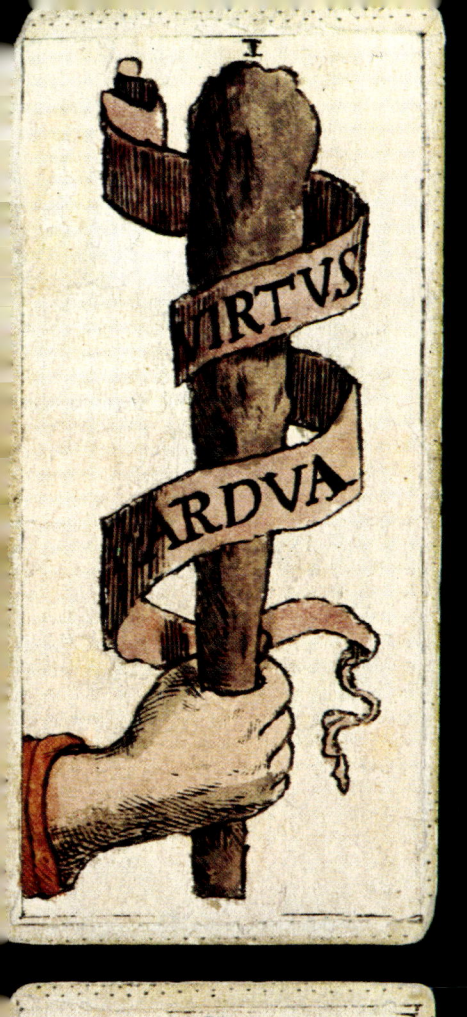

GIOSEPPE MARIA
MITELLI INV:
DIS: E: INT:

OR CVSTOS VSTODIA

ROY·DE·DENIE

The King of Coins, from the 18th-century Belgian pack.

Five Card Spread. This is recommended only for comparatively minor inquiries. After shuffling and cutting, ask the inquirer to pick a number below twenty-two. If he chooses, say, nine, draw the card ninth from the top of the pack and put it on the table, face up. Shuffle and cut again and ask the inquirer for another number. Repeat the process until you have five cards on the table next to the significator. Card 1 stands for positive, constructive factors in the inquirer's situation, and Card 2 for negative, obstructive factors. Card 3 should suggest a way of reconciling the positive and negative factors, leading to Card 4, which indicates the best policy to be adopted. Card 5 shows the probable final outcome.

The Arch or Horseshoe. There is no need for a significator with this spread, which is designed for answering a specific question. After shuffling and cutting, deal out the first seven cards from the pack, face up, in the shape of a semicircular arch. Card 1 goes at the bottom of the arch on the right, and Card 7 at the bottom on the left. Read the cards from right to left, as follows:

Card 1 for the past
Card 2 for the present
Card 3 for hidden or unconscious factors
Card 4 for negative influences, obstacles
Card 5 for other people's attitudes
Card 6 for what the inquirer should do
Card 7 for the probable final result

Suppose the inquirer is a nervous student who wants to know whether he will pass an examination which he has to take soon. The cards in the arch, from right to left, are the Six of Batons, the Hermit, the Six of Cups, the Five of Swords, the Ten of Cups, the Six of Coins and the Sun reversed. At first sight this looks reasonably promising, and three Sixes in the same spread mean 'gain'. Very briefly, and assuming encouraging responses from the inquirer, the reading might take the following track.

Card 1, Six of Batons	– The inquirer has worked hard, which should give him a good chance of success.
Card 2, The Hermit	– He is being cautious about the outcome and is trying to hide his misgivings. He longs for some safe place of retreat from the pressures on him.
Card 3, Six of Cups	– Inwardly, he is retreating from current pressures into nostalgia for past security and happiness.
Card 4, Five of Swords	– He is afraid of failing and his lack of self-confidence will hinder his chances.
Card 5, Ten of Cups	– Those who know him best confidently expect him to succeed.
Card 6, Six of Coins	– He should look for 'a helping hand', either from someone else or more likely from himself. A more generous view of his abilities and prospects will promote self-confidence.
Card 7, The Sun reversed	– The outlook for success is favourable, provided the inquirer adopts the right attitude.

This example, incidentally, illustrates the fact that a great deal of fortune-telling is, in effect, a way of persuading an inquirer to identify his own problems and then helping him to solve them, by giving him more confidence in himself and by appealing to his better qualities and his common sense. In the days before psychiatry and social counselling were common, fortune-tellers did some of the work now attempted by specialists in these fields.

There is a much more difficult form of Arch or Horseshoe layout, the Fifty-four Card layout described later.

The Celtic Cross. This layout, also known as the Grand Cross, is now much in vogue. It was recommended for answering specific questions by Waite, who called it an 'ancient Celtic' method. The significator is placed on the table as usual. After shuffling and cutting, the top card of the pack is turned face up and put on top of the significator, and the reader says, 'This covers him.' This card shows the general atmosphere surrounding the inquirer's question.

Card 2 is placed across Card 1, with the words: 'This crosses him.' It represents the obstacles confronting the inquirer.

Card 3 goes above the significator, with the words: 'This crowns him.' It shows the inquirer's plans and purposes, and the best outcome possible under present circumstances.

Card 4 is placed below the significator: 'This is beneath him.' It indicates the basis or background of the present situation and factors from the past which are influencing the inquirer's attitude.

Card 5 is placed to the left of the significator: 'This is behind him.' It shows an influence which has recently passed, or is now passing, out of the situation.

Card 6 goes to the right of the significator: 'This is before him.' It represents an influence which is beginning to come into play or which will start to operate soon.

Four more cards are now placed in a vertical column to the right of the spread, with Card 7 at the foot of the column and Card 10 at the top. Card 7 shows the inquirer's present position or attitude. Card 8 indicates influences arising from the inquirer's environment and surroundings. Card 9 stands for the inquirer's hopes and fears.

Card 10 is the most important one in the reading. It indicates the final result and it should combine all the influences and factors suggested by the other cards in the layout. If Card 10 is a court card, the inference is that the final outcome depends largely on a person represented by it. In this case, more information about the person concerned can be discovered by using Card 10 as the significator in a fresh layout of the Celtic Cross, with the cards in the new spread applying to him instead of the inquirer.

More recent versions of the Celtic Cross give the cards in the layout meanings which sometimes differ from Waite's. An example is: Card 1 – the present situation; Card 2 – obstacles; Card 3 – conscious factors; Card 4 – unconscious factors; Card 5 – the immediate past; Card 6 – the immediate future; Card 7 – fears; Card 8 – other people's attitudes; Card 9 – hopes, expectations; Card 10 – the probable final result.

There is a more sophisticated way of determining the placing of Card 5 in the layout, depending on which way the figure depicted in the significator is facing.

For example, suppose the significator is the King of Batons in Waite's pack. This king is looking to the reader's left, and so Card 5 is placed to the right or 'behind' him. If the figure in the court card is shown full-face, 'behind' him means to the left. Card 6 goes on the other side of the significator. The same principle can be used in all layouts where cards have to be placed 'before' or 'behind' the significator.

In more difficult layouts, when a row of cards has to be interpreted, the direction in which a king or a page is looking can again be taken into account. Reading is usually done from right to left. Mathers said that if a king is facing against the direction of the reading, he stands for a person or event which is soon to come, but if he is facing with the reading he represents a person or event passing out of the scene. A page facing against the direction of the reading shows that the general opinion about the inquirer or the problem is hostile, but a page facing with the reading shows the opposite.

The Clock or Horoscope. Deal twelve cards in a circle round the significator as if they marked the hours on a clock. Card 1 goes at nine o'clock, Card 2 at eight o'clock, and so on anticlockwise to Card 12 at ten o'clock. One way of interpreting them is to read Card 1 as an indicator of conditions in the month ahead, Card 2 of conditions in the month after that, and so on for a year. If you prefer, do not use a significator, but put a thirteenth card in the middle of the clockface. This card should be read first as a general indicator for the year ahead.

Alternatively, the twelve cards on the clock can be interpreted in terms of the twelve 'houses' into which a horoscope is divided, with Card 1 marking the first house. In this case, the cards apply as follows:

Card 1 – the inquirer himself
Card 2 – money and possessions
Card 3 – mental capacities, self-expression, short journeys
Card 4 – childhood environment
Card 5 – children, love life, pleasures, speculation
Card 6 – health
Card 7 – marriage, close emotional or business relationships
Card 8 – death, legacies, sources of gain
Card 9 – religious and philosophical views, dreams, long journeys
Card 10 – career, status, reputation
Card 11 – friends and social life, hopes, ambitions
Card 12 – enemies, secrets, limitations

The Wheel of Fortune. Imagine that the significator is at the centre of a compass. Take the first three cards from the pack and place them face downwards at the north point, saying, 'Three above you.' Put the next three face downwards at the south point, saying, 'Three below you.' Continue until you have dealt out nine piles of three cards each.

Pile 1 – North   'Three above you.'
Pile 2 – South   'Three below you.'
Pile 3 – West   'Three behind you.'
Pile 4 – East   'Three before you.'

Pile 5 – North-west   'Three for your house and home.'
Pile 6 – North-east   'Three for your hopes and fears.'
Pile 7 – South-west   'Three for what you don't expect.'
Pile 8 – South-east   'Three for what you do expect.'
Pile 9 – Below Pile 2 'Three for what is sure to come.'

Pile 1, 'above you', means the general atmosphere surrounding the inquirer or the question. Pile 2, 'below you', refers to matters within the inquirer's control. Pile 3 and Pile 4 indicate the past and the future respectively. The meanings of the other piles are evident from the list above.

Take each pile in turn and read its three cards together. At the end all twenty-seven cards in the layout should be combined into a coherent reading. If there is any unsolved problem, draw three more cards at random from the pack and consult them.

The Tree of Life. Choose the significator but leave it in the pack to fall where it may. Deal out ten cards, face up, in the pattern of the cabalistic Tree of Life, starting with Kether and ending with Malkuth. Go on dealing until each pile contains seven cards. Put the remaining eight cards aside. The piles apply as follows:

Pile 1 – spiritual matters
Pile 2 – initiative, responsibilities
Pile 3 – sorrows and limitations
Pile 4 – constructive factors, money matters
Pile 5 – opposition, destructive factors
Pile 6 – achievement, reputation, the conscious mind
Pile 7 – love
Pile 8 – business, the arts, communication
Pile 9 – health, the unconscious mind
Pile 10 – home and family

Take each pile in turn and read its seven cards together. The pile which contains the significator is of particular importance in the reading and should identify an area of special interest or concern to the inquirer. When each pile has been read, give a coherent account of the whole layout. If further clarification about any matter is needed, consult the eight cards which you put aside.

This is obviously not an easy layout, because it involves so many cards. The following layouts are also difficult to handle, because the reader is not supplied with many clear-cut points of reference, like 'This crosses him' or 'Three for your house and home.' They are intended for more serious divination.

Twenty-one Card Layout. Choose a significator and remove it from the pack. After shuffling and cutting, draw the top card of the pack, then the seventh card from it, then the seventh from that, and so on, coming back to the top of the pack as necessary, until you have drawn out twenty-one cards. (When counting cards for divination, always *include* in the count the card from which you begin.)

Keeping the cards in order, lay them out face up in three rows of seven cards each, running from right to left. The first row contains Cards 1 to 7, the second Cards 8 to 14, the third Cards 15 to 21. Put the significator to the right of Card 1 and read the cards in the first row from right to left, starting with the significator. Then move the significator down to the right-hand end of the second row and read this row, again starting with the significator. Do the same with the third row.

Next, pair Card 1 with Card 21 and read them together. Pair Card 2 with Card 20 and read them together, and continue in this way until you have read Cards 10 and 12 together. Card 11 is left over. It represents a general influence, for good or ill, affecting this part of the reading as a whole.

As a brief partial illustration of this type of reading, the following is adapted from an example supplied by Mathers. The inquirer is a young business-woman with a financial problem. Her significator is the Page of Batons and the cards in the first row of seven are the Two of Coins, the Five of Coins, the Pope reversed, the Queen of Cups, the King of Coins, the Fool and the Five of Swords. 'The inquirer is making a change in her business (Two of Coins), which is causing her anxiety and loss of money (Five of Coins), through bad advice or deceit (Pope reversed) by another woman (Queen of Cups) and a man (King of Coins), whose foolish recommendations (Fool) are at the root of the trouble (Five of Swords).'

In another example, the inquirer is a man, represented by the King of Cups, and the seven cards in the first row are the Nine of Coins, the Eight of Cups, the Wheel of Fortune reversed, the Page of Batons, the Three of Swords, the Ace of Coins and the Ten of Cups. 'The inquirer's business affairs are prospering (Nine of Coins), but he is losing interest in business (Eight of Cups) and should beware of a change for the worse (Wheel reversed). He has fallen in love with a girl to whom he is not entirely suited (Page of Batons, the opposite suit to the inquirer's own suit of Cups). There is trouble between them, perhaps as a result of malicious gossip (Three of Swords), though his financial success (Ace of Coins) had caused her to regard him with favour (Ten of Cups).'

Forty-two Card Layout. This layout was recommended by Waite for a general reading, when no specific question has been asked. The significator in this method is always the Juggler for a man or the Female Pope for a woman, but it is left in the pack to begin with. After shuffling and cutting, deal out the first seven cards of the pack, face up, in one pile. Deal seven more to form a second pile, and continue until you have six piles on the table, with seven cards in each. Put the rest of the pack aside. Now take the first pile and spread the cards out in a row from right to left. Do the same with the second pile, placing the cards on top of those in the first row. Go on doing this until you have seven new piles of six cards each.

Take the top card from each pile, shuffle them and lay them out in a row of seven cards running from right to left. Take the next two cards from each pile, shuffle them and lay them out in two rows below the first row. Take the remaining three cards of each pile, shuffle them and lay them out in three more rows. You now have six rows of seven cards each.

Find the significator. If it is on the table, take it out of its place and put it to the right of the first row. Replace it with a card drawn at random from the cards which were put aside. If it is not on the table, find it among the cards put aside and put it to the right of the first row. Now read the cards on the table, in succession from right to left, starting at the right-hand end of the first row and ending at the left-hand end of the bottom row.

Fifty-four Card Layout. Leave the significator in the pack and, after shuffling and cutting, deal the cards out face down in two piles, A and B. The top card goes to Pile A and the second to Pile B. The third and fourth cards go to Pile B and the fifth to Pile A. The sixth and seventh cards go to Pile B and the eighth to Pile A, and so on until all the cards have been dealt. Pile A has twenty-six cards and Pile B has fifty-two. Now take Pile B and deal it out again in the same way into two new piles, C and D. Now repeat the process again with Pile D, making two new piles, E and F. You now have four piles: A of twenty-six cards, C of seventeen, E of eleven, and F of twenty-four. Discard Pile F.

The three piles left are all indicators of the near future. Pile A indicates the inquirer's own state of mind, Pile C refers to his job or occupation, and Pile E to his domestic life. Take Pile A, turn it face up and keeping the cards in order, spread them out in the shape of a semicircular arch or horseshoe, running from right to left. Read the whole row from right to left. Then pair Card 1 with Card 26 and read them together, pair Card 2 with Card 25 and read them together, and so on until the row is exhausted. Put Pile A away and do the same thing with Pile C, and finally with Pile E.

Le Grand Jeu (the Great Game). There are several varieties of this. Remove the significator from the pack. After shuffling and cutting, deal out sixty-six cards in the shape of a triangle within an arch, as shown in Diagram Five (page 184).

The cards in the top two rows indicate the present. Cards 1 to 11 and 34 to 44 indicate the past. The rest indicate the future. After a general reading of each set, read them in pairs, Cards 1 and 34, Cards 2 and 35, and so on for the past. Then read Cards 23 and 56, Cards 24 and 57, and so on for the present. Finally read Cards 12 and 45, Cards 13 and 46, and so on for the future.

Next pick the cards up, with Card 66 at the bottom of the pile, Card 1 on top of it, Card 65 on top of that, then Card 2, and so on to Card 33, which goes at the top of the pack. Deal the cards out again in a circle with the significator as its starting point. Card 33 will be the first card to the right of the significator, and Card 66 will be the last card of the circle, to the left of the significator. (Or if the significator is looking full-face or to the left, you can deal the cards round the circle anti-clockwise if you prefer.)

Now read the cards in pairs as follows: first the significator and Card 66; next the cards to right and left of the first pair, which are Card 33 and Card 1; next the cards to right and left again, which are Card 34 and Card 65. Continue in this way until only one card is left. Place this card between two others, drawn at random from the eleven put aside at the beginning, and read this group of three cards together as an indication of a surprise which is in store. 'This mode is rather difficult at first,' said Mathers, with understatement, 'but practice will give facility.'[7]

Opening the Key. This was recommended by Mathers, Crowley and Case, with some variations of procedure. First, choose a significator but leave it in the pack. After shuffling and cutting, cut the pack to the left into two piles. Cut each of these piles to the left again, so that you have four piles. From right to left, these piles correspond to:

Batons – matters of work and business
Cups   – love, marriage, pleasure
Swords – troubles, quarrels, losses
Coins   – money and possessions

Now find the significator. The pile containing it should indicate the general area of the inquirer's question or problem. If it does not, abandon the reading and do not try again for at least two hours (or for a really serious question at least twelve hours).

Otherwise, spread out the pile containing the significator, face up, in a circle with the significator at the top, but without altering the order of the cards in the pile. You must now isolate certain cards in the circle by counting from the significator in the direction in which it is looking (if it is full-face, count to your left). Having counted from the significator to Card 1, count again from Card 1 to Card 2, and so on.

For Kings, Queens and Knights, count 4.
For Pages, count 7.
For Aces, count 11.
For a small card, count its own number.
For the Fool, the Hanged Man and the Day of Judgment, count 3.
For the trumps corresponding to the signs of the zodiac, count 12.
For the other trumps, count 9.

Suppose the significator is a king who is facing to your left. Counting the king as one, count four cards to the left. Suppose this brings you to the Five of Cups. Counting this as one, count five cards to the left. Go on like this round the circle, until you count to a card for the second time. Then stop, and read the cards you have counted, from right to left, paying attention to each card's position in the original spread (for example, whether it falls between two cards of its own suit or the opposite suit in the original circle). Next, pair the cards on each side of the significator, then those to the right and left again, and so on round the circle. The readings at this stage show the origins of the question or problem.

For further development of the question, collect all the cards together, shuffle and cut again, and deal the complete pack out anew in twelve piles, which correspond to the astrological 'houses', as described earlier. The first six piles will contain seven cards each and the others six cards each. Find the pile containing the significator. This pile should be relevant to the question or problem. If it is not, abandon the reading. If it is, make a circle of the cards in this pile, and count and pair as before.

For additional information, shuffle the whole pack again, cut and deal out twelve new piles for the signs of the zodiac. Treat the pile containing the significator as before, counting and pairing.

For the final result, shuffle the whole pack once more, cut, and deal out the cards in ten piles. There will again be different numbers of cards in different piles, but this does not matter. The ten piles correspond to the ten spheres of the Tree of Life, as described earlier. Treat the pile containing the significator as before, counting and pairing.

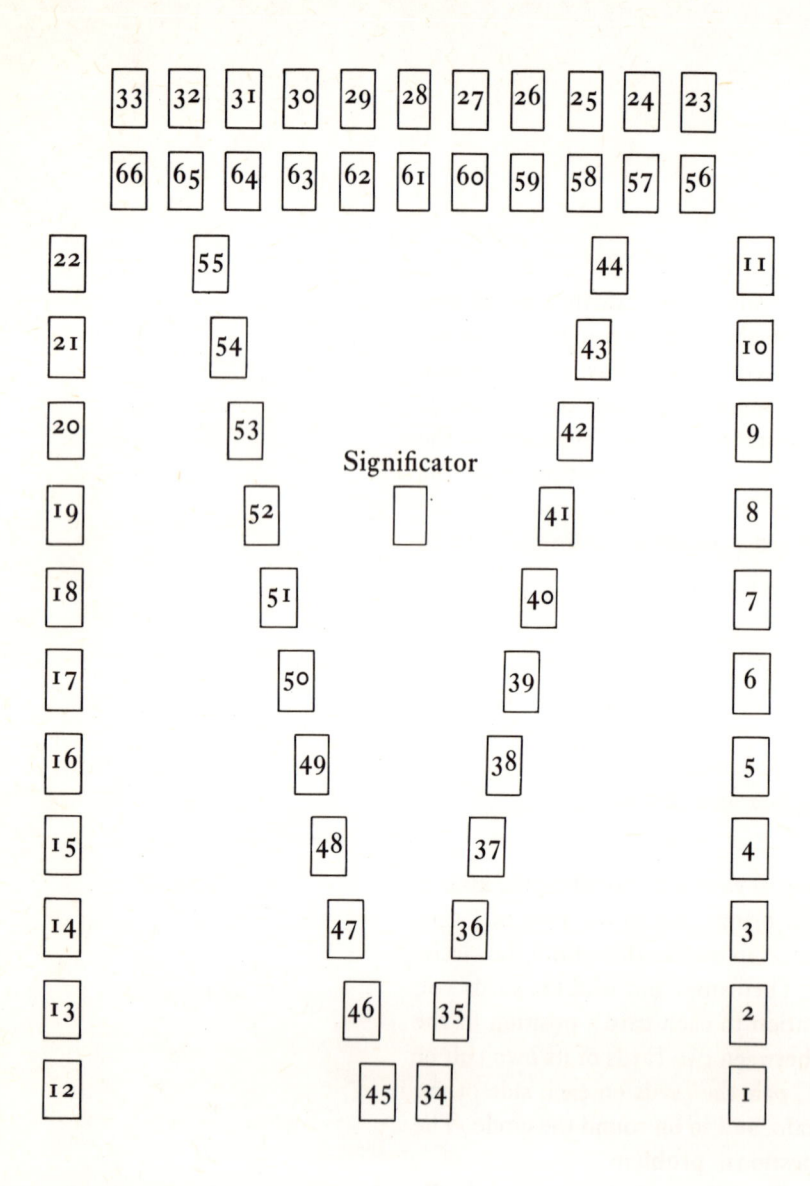

DIAGRAM FIVE: *LE GRAND JEU* (see pages 182–3).

These more complicated layouts should not be handled by beginners. They have been described as causing 'severe psychic indigestion' in inexperienced readers. They demand practised familiarity with the cards, and you should not attempt them until you are ready for them.

It is the fact that the more difficult layouts contain comparatively few pre-established guidelines and signposts, which gives them their value for serious card-readers. The learner inevitably relies on conscious intellectual processes in selecting meanings for the cards in a spread and combining them into a 'story' that makes sense. But it is worth repeating, finally, that this is not what is meant by true divination. It is a necessary stage in learning, but it is eventually a hindrance. For true divination, as Crowley said, ratiocination must be refined to the point at which it becomes intuition or instinct. When divination works, it appears to do so through processes which are principally unconscious and non-rational, and which are still largely unexplored.

Notes to References in the Text

SECTION ONE: HISTORY

1 Tilley, *Playing Cards*, 28
2 Mann, *Collecting Playing Cards*, 28
3 Quoted by many authors, including Hargrave, *History of Playing Cards*, 171
4 See Jeremy Taylor's remarks, for example, quoted in Chatto, *Facts and Speculations*, 297–9
5 See Mann, op. cit., 134 ff.
6 Tilley, op. cit., 112
7 See, for example, Mathers, *Tarot*, 56–7
8 Seznec, *Survival of the Pagan Gods*, 139
9 See Yates, *Giordano Bruno*, 77, and on this whole subject, see Wind, *Pagan Mysteries*
10 See Yates, *Art of Memory*
11 Roberts, *Mythology of the Secret Societies*, 117
12 McIntosh, *Eliphas Lévi*, 51
13 Lévi, *History of Magic*, 76–8
14 For the history of the Golden Dawn and its offshoots, see Howe, *Magicians of the Golden Dawn*, and King, *Ritual Magic*
15 Raine, *Yeats, the Tarot and the Golden Dawn*, 7
16 Waite, *Holy Grail*, 572 f.: Weston, *From Ritual to Romance*, 77–80: Graves, *White Goddess*, 293
17 Runciman, *Medieval Manichee*, Appendix Four: for the Waldensian theory, see Roger Tilley in *Man, Myth & Magic*, VII. 2982
18 Yeats, *Autobiographies*, 90, 249
19 *Man, Myth & Magic*, VII. 3067
20 Yeats, op. cit., 183, 261; Raine, op. cit., 35
21 Yeats, op. cit., 262
22 Quoted in *Encyclopedia of the Unexplained*, 144

SECTION TWO: INTERPRETATION

1 *Le Symbolisme Hermétique*, quoted in Ouspensky, *New Model*, 217
2 Regardie, *Golden Dawn*, I. 193
3 Fortune, *Mystical Qabalah*, 149
4 Poncé, *Kabbalah*, 27–8
5 I Corinthians 2. 14, 3. 18–19: Acts, Chapter 2: Joel 2. 28
6 John 3. 8
7 Budge, *Egyptian Religion*, 114
8 Matthew 18. 3.
9 Crowley, *Book of Thoth*, 57
10 Jennings, *Rosicrucians*, 281
11 Masters and Houston, *Mind Games*, 85–7
12 Papus, *Tarot of the Bohemians*, 106
13 Lévi, *Doctrine and Ritual*, 29–30
14 Cirlot, *Dictionary of Symbols*, 235
15 Jung, *Psychology and Alchemy*, 132
16 Regardie, *Golden Dawn*, IV. 210
17 For Masonic symbolism, see Dewar, *Unlocked Secret*
18 Quoted in Scholem, *Kabbalah and Its Symbolism*, 55–6
19 Reinhold Merkelbach in *Man, Myth & Magic*, IV. 1461
20 Crowley, *Book of Thoth*, 75
21 Wilkins, *Rose-Garden Game*, 129
22 Regardie, *Golden Dawn*, IV. 211
23 Lévi, *Doctrine and Ritual*, 17–18
24 Jung, *Mysterium Coniunctionis*, p. xv
25 Crowley, *Magick*, 332
26 See Strong, *Splendour at Court*, 26
27 See Seznec, *Survival of the Pagan Gods*, 170 ff., 190 ff.
28 Budge, *Egyptian Religion*, 125
29 Regardie, *Golden Dawn*, I. 218: Crowley, *Magick*, 417
30 Waite, *Pictorial Key*, 100
31 Hargrave, *History of Playing Cards*, 35
32 Mâle, *Gothic Image*, 95 n.
33 Jung, *Psychology and Alchemy*, 157
34 Waite, *Pictorial Key*, 119: John 3. 14–15
35 Ussher, *Twenty Two Keys*, 34
36 Regardie, *Golden Dawn*, I. 68
37 Lévi, *Doctrine and Ritual*, 108
38 Jung, *Psychology and Alchemy*, 320–3
39 Case, *Tarot*, 152
40 Jung, *Mysterium Coniunctionis*, 163
41 Matthew 7. 14
42 For the ritual, see Crowley, *Magick*, 355–83
43 Crowley, *Book of Thoth*, 106
44 Quoted in Regardie, *Golden Dawn*, I. 61
45 Luke 10. 18
46 Case, *Tarot*, 164: Crowley, *Book of Thoth*, 108
47 Ouspensky, *New Model*, 235
48 Regardie, *Golden Dawn*, II. 128
49 Jung, *Mysterium Coniunctionis*, 256
50 Regardie, op. cit., IV. 215
51 Jung, *Psychology and Alchemy*, 59, 190
52 Waite, *Pictorial Key*, 151
53 Lind, *How to Understand the Tarot*, 43
54 Lévi, *Doctrine and Ritual*, 34: John 12. 24–5
55 Strong, *Splendour at Court*, 140
56 Job 38. 7: Ouspensky, *New Model*, 229
57 King, *Astral Projection*, 73
58 Scholem, *Major Trends*, 49
59 King, *Astral Projection*, 51
60 Fortune, *Mystical Qabalah*, 96
61 See Crowley, *Magick*, 180–4

SECTION THREE: DIVINATION

1 Case, *Tarot*, 204
2 Leland, *Gypsy Sorcery*, 180–2
3 Jahoda, *Psychology of Superstition*, 8–9
4 Lévi, *Doctrine and Ritual*, 87–8
5 Regardie, *Golden Dawn*, IV. 177: Gardner, *Tarot Speaks*, 22
6 Regardie, op. cit., IV. 176
7 Mathers, *Tarot*, 49

Bibliography

Bayley, Harold, *The Lost Language of Symbolism*, Benn, London, 1968, two volumes in one. (First published 1912)

Benham, W. Gurney, *Playing Cards: Their History and Secrets*, Spring Books, London, no date. (First published 1931)

Budge, Sir Wallis, *Egyptian Religion*, University Books, New York, 1959. (Reprint of 1900 edn)

Case, Paul Foster, *The Tarot: A Key to the Wisdom of the Ages*, Macoy Publishing Co., Richmond, Virginia, 1947

Cavendish, Richard, *The Black Arts*, Routledge & Kegan Paul, London, 1967; Putnam, New York, 1967

Chatto, William Andrew, *Facts and Speculations on the Origin and History of Playing Cards*, Russell Smith, London, 1848

Cirlot, J. E., *A Dictionary of Symbols*, Routledge & Kegan Paul, London, 1962

Crowley, Aleister, *The Book of Lies*, Haydn Press, Ilfracombe, Devon, 1962 reprint

Crowley, Aleister, *The Book of Thoth*, Shambala Publications, Berkeley, California, 1969. (First published 1944)

Crowley, Aleister, *Magick*, edited by J. Symonds and K. Grant, Routledge & Kegan Paul, London, 1973. (First published 1911–29)

Dewar, James, *The Unlocked Secret*, Kimber, London, 1966

Douglas, Alfred, *The Tarot*, Gollancz, London, 1973; Taplinger, New York, 1972

Dummett, Michael, 'The Order of the Tarot Trumps', *Journal of the Playing-Card Society*, Vol. II, Nos. 3 and 4, Feb. and May 1974

Dummett, Michael, 'Sicilian Tarocchi', *Journal of the Playing-Card Society*, Vol. III, No. 1, August 1974

Encyclopedia of the Unexplained, edited by R. Cavendish, Routledge & Kegan Paul, London, 1974; McGraw Hill, New York, 1974

Ferguson, George, *Signs and Symbols in Christian Art*, Oxford University Press, 1954

Fortune, Dion, *The Mystical Qabalah*, Benn, London, 1972. (First published 1935)

Frazer, Sir James George, *The Golden Bough*, Macmillan, London, abridged edn, 1922

Gardner, Richard, *Evolution Through the Tarot*, paperback, no date

Gardner, Richard, *The Tarot Speaks*, Rigel Press, London, 1971

Gombrich, E. H., *Symbolic Images: Studies in the Art of the Renaissance*, Phaidon, London, 1972

Graves, Robert, *The White Goddess*, Vintage Books, New York, paperback, 1958

Gray, Eden, *The Tarot Revealed*, Inspiration House, New York, 1960

Hargrave, Catherine Perry, *A History of Playing Cards*, Dover, New York, 1966. (First published 1930)

Howe, Ellic, *The Magicians of the Golden Dawn*, Routledge & Kegan Paul, London, 1972

Huson, Paul, *The Devil's Picture Book*, Sphere Books, London, 1972, paperback.

Jahoda, Gustav, *The Psychology of Superstition*, Allen Lane, London, 1969

Jennings, Hargrave, *The Rosicrucians, Their Rites and Mysteries*, Routledge & Kegan Paul, 7th edn, no date. (First published 1870)

Jung, C. G. *Psychology and Alchemy*, translated by R. F. C. Hull, Routledge & Kegan Paul, London, 1953

Jung, C. G. *Mysterium Coniunctionis*, translated by R. F. C. Hull, Routledge & Kegan Paul, London, 1963

King, Francis, *Ritual Magic in England*, Spearman, London, 1970

King, Francis, editor, *Astral Projection, Magic and Alchemy*, Spearman, London, 1971

Leland, C. G., *Gypsy Sorcery and Fortune-Telling*, Dover, New York, 1971, paperback. (First published 1891)

Lévi, Éliphas, *Transcendental Magic: Its Doctrine and Ritual*, translated by A. E. Waite, Redway, London, 1896. (Referred to in the text and notes as *Doctrine and Ritual*)

Lévi, Éliphas, *The History of Magic*, translated by A. E. Waite, Dutton, New York, 3rd edn, no date.

Lind, Frank, *How to Understand the Tarot*, Aquarian Press, London, 1969, paperback

Mâle, Emile, *The Gothic Image*, Fontana, London, 3rd edn, 1961, paperback. (First published 1913)

Man, Myth and Magic, edited by R. Cavendish, Purnell, London, 1970–2, seven volumes

Mann, Sylvia, *Collecting Playing Cards*, MacGibbon & Kee, London, 1966

Masters, R. E. L., and Houston, Jean, *Mind Games*, Turnstone Books, London, 1973

Mathers, S. L. MacGregor, *The Tarot*, Occult Research Press, New York, paperback reprint, no date. (First published 1888)

Mayananda, *The Tarot for Today*, Zeus Press, London, 1963

McIntosh, Christopher, *Eliphas Lévi and the French Occult Revival*, Rider, London, 1972

Moakley, Gertrude, *The Tarot Cards Painted by Bonifacio Bembo*, New York Public Library, 1966

Morgan, Lester B., 'Tarot Cards: A Market Analysis', *Journal of the Playing-Card Society*, Vol. II, No. 4, May 1974

Mouni Sadhu, *The Tarot*, Allen & Unwin, London, 1962, paperback

Ouspensky, P. D., *A New Model of the Universe*, Routledge & Kegan Paul, London, 3rd edn, 1938

Papus, *The Tarot of the Bohemians*, translated by A. P. Morton, 3rd edn, Wilshire Book Co., Los Angeles, 1972, paperback. (First published in English 1892)

Poncé, Charles, *Kabbalah*, Garnstone Press, London, 1974, paperback

Raine, Kathleen, *Yeats, the Tarot and the Golden Dawn*, Dolmen Press, Dublin, 1972, paperback

Rakoczi, Basil Ivan, *The Painted Caravan*, Brucher, The Hague, 1954

Rakoczi, Basil Ivan, *Fortune Telling*, Macdonald, London, 1970, paperback

Regardie, Israel, *The Golden Dawn*, Llewellyn Publications, St Paul, Minnesota, 3rd edn, 1970, four volumes in two. (First published 1937–40)

Roberts, J. M., *The Mythology of the Secret Socities*, Paladin, London, 1974, paperback

Runciman, Steven, *The Medieval Manichee*, Cambridge University Press, 1955

Scholem, Gershom G., *Major Trends in Jewish Mysticism*, Thames & Hudson, London, 1955

Scholem, Gershom G., *On the Kabbalah and Its Symbolism*, Routledge & Kegan Paul, London, 1965

Seligmann, Kurt, *The History of Magic*, Pantheon, New York, 1948

Sepher Yetzirah, translated by W. Wynn Westcott, Occult Research Press, New York, paperback reprint, no date

Seznec, Jean, *The Survival of the Pagan Gods*, Harper Torchbooks, New York, 1961, paperback

Strong, Roy, *Splendour at Court: Renaissance Spectacle and Illusion*, Weidenfeld & Nicolson, London, 1973

Tilley, Roger, *Playing Cards*, Octopus Books, London, 1973

Ussher, Arland, *The Twenty Two Keys of the Tarot*, Dolmen Press, Dublin, new edn, 1970, paperback. (First published 1953)

Waite, A. E., *The Holy Grail*, University Books, New York, 1961 reprint

Waite, A. E., *The Pictorial Key to the Tarot*, Rider, London, 1971. (First published 1910)

Walker, Benjamin, *Hindu World*, Allen & Unwin, London, 1968, two volumes

Webb, James, *The Flight From Reason*, Macdonald, London, 1971

Weston, Jessie L., *From Ritual to Romance*, Anchor Books, New York, 1957, paperback (First published 1920)

Wilkins, Eithne, *The Rose-Garden Game*, Gollancz, London, 1969

Wind, Edgar, *Pagan Mysteries in the Renaissance*, Faber, London, 1958

Yates, Frances A., *Giordano Bruno and the Hermetic Tradition*, Routledge & Kegan Paul, London, 1964

Yates, Frances A., *The Art of Memory*, Routledge & Kegan Paul, London, 1966

Yeats, W. B., *Autobiographies*, Macmillan, London, 1955. (First published 1926)

Illustrations Acknowledgments

The producers of this book wish to express their thanks to all those indicated by the list below, who have kindly given permission for items from their collections to be reproduced here.

Abbreviations used are:

- BL By permission of the British Library Board, London
- BM The Trustees of the British Museum, London
- BN La Bibliothèque Nationale, Paris
- HPL Harry Price Library, London
- Mansell The Mansell Collection, London
- RTH Radio Times Hulton Picture Library, London
- SM Sylvia Mann Collection
- V&A By courtesy of the Victoria and Albert Museum, London

A page number in **bold** type indicates a colour plate.

Jacket subjects (front) 'Charles VI', BN; (back) Crowley pack, Warburg Inst. By permission of Gerald Yorke, Esq. Photo: Michael Holford.

Endpapers French, 1440, BN, from *Jeux de Cartes Tarot et de Cartes Numérales*, 1844. HPL.

1–7 The surviving cards of the 'Charles VI' pack, c. 1390, BN, from *Jeux de Cartes Tarot*, 1844. HPL.

8 German woodcut, 1472. Photo: RTH.

10 Two cards from the pack thought to be designed for Charles VI of France, c. 1390. Both BN.

12–13 Swiss Marseilles, c. 1800, SM. Photo: Witty

14 Italian minchiate, 18th c., V&A. Photo: Witty.

16 Double-ended pack, Viennese (G.160) BM. Photo: Freeman.

17 Double-ended pack, German, 1887, (G.118) BM. Photo: Freeman.

18–19 (left to right, top) Old Testament History, Italian, 1748 (I.143); Latin Grammar, Dutch, c. 1670 (D.14); Virtues and Vices, Italian, c. 1700 (I.138). All cards BM. Photos: Freeman. Cavalier Playing cards, English, V&A. Photo: Witty. (bottom) Natural History, Italian, 19th c. (I.9); Follies of James II, English, 17th c. (E.63); Geographical, Naples, c. 1780 (I.27). All cards BM. Photos: Freeman.

20 (far left) Tarocchi di Mantegna, early Italian school (Case 50) BM. Photo: Freeman. (left, above) German, 16th c. Photo: Mansell. (below) German, 1511, BN, from *Jeux de Cartes de Tarot*, 1844. HPL.

22 Tarocchi di Mantegna (Case 50) BM. Photo: John Webb.

23 *Primavera* by Sandro Botticelli, c. 1485. Uffizi Gallery, Florence. Photo: Alinari.

24–5 *Mars and Venus* by Sandro Botticelli, 1485. National Gallery, London.

26 Design from *Le Monde Primitif*, Vol. 8, 1781, by Court de Gébelin. LL.

27 Design from *Le Monde Primitif*, Vol. 8, 1781, by Court de Gébelin. LL.

28 Etteilla pack for cartomancy designed by Alliette, French, 19th c. (F.19) BM. Photo: Witty.

29 From *De Chemia Senioris* by Zadith Senior, Strasbourg, 1566, BL. Photo: Freeman.

30 (top) Cagliostro, HPL. (bottom) Lévi, from *The History of Magic* by E. Lévi, HPL.

32 Photo: RTH.

33 Photo: RTH.

34 Photo: Mansell.

35 Waite's pack, English, early 20th c., V&A. Photo: Witty.

36 Photo: Karsh, Ottawa.

39 Sketch by Augustus John, 1907. Tate Gallery.

41 *The Judgment of Paris* by Lucas Cranach the Elder, 1530. Metropolitan Museum of Art, N.Y., Rogers Fund, 1928.

42–3 Italian minchiate, made up from three packs, 18th c. (I.57) BM. Photo: Witty.

44 *Incontro di Iside con Osiride* by Pinturicchio. Appartemento Borgia, Vatican Museums and Galleries.

46 Designed by Giuseppe Maria Mitelli, Bologna, 17th c. (I.38) BM. Photo: Witty.

49 From *Porta Lucis* by Paulus Ricius, 1516. Copyright G. G. Harrap.

59 German woodcut, (Case 40, Vol. XV) BM. Photo: Freeman.

60–1 Swiss Marseilles, 18th c. (S.6) BM. Photo: Witty.

62 Pentecost from the *Office of the Virgin*, Neapolitan, 15th c. Crown Copyright, V&A.

63 (left) Etteilla (F.19) BM. Photo: Freeman. (right, top) Waite, V&A. Photo: Witty. (bottom) Double-ended pack, Piedmontese, 1943, SM. Photo: Witty

65 Amphora, c. 500–490 B.C., Munich. Photo: Mansell.

66 From the *Codex Urbinus Latinus*, 899 f.85r. Bibliotecca Apostolica Vaticana, Vatican City.

68–9 (left to right) Tarocchi di Mantegna (Case 50) BM. Photo: Freeman. Fortune-telling pack, Italian, early 19th c. (I.32) BM. Photo: Freeman. Italian minchiate, 18th c., V&A. Photo: Witty.

70 Egyptian Sculpture, BM.

71 From *Codex Vossianus* 29 f.87r, by Thomas Aquinas. Bib. der Rijksuniversiteit, Leyden.

73 (above) Galler pack, Belgian, c. 1740–50, SM. Photo: Witty. (below) French, 18th c. (F.18) BM. Photo: Freeman.

75 (above) Egyptian Sculpture, BM. (below) Waite, V&A. Photo: Witty.

77 *Coronation of the Virgin in a Meadow*, School of the Upper Rhine, National Museum, Stockholm.

78 (left) Revolutionary pack by L. Carey, Strasbourg, 18th c. (F.8) BM. (right) Waite, V&A. Both photos: Witty.

79 Terracota. Terme Museum, Rome. Photo: Mansell.

81 (top, left) Tarocchi di Mantegna, BM. Photo: Freeman. (right) Charles VI, BN. (bottom, left) Waite, V&A. Photo: Witty. (right) Revolutionary pack (F.8) BM. Photo: Witty.

82 (far left, top) Galler, SM. (bottom) Waite, V&A. Both photos: Witty. (near left) Study by Albrecht Dürer, BM.

83 Charles VI, from *Jeux de Cartes Tarot*, 1844. HPL.

84 *Papyrus of Ani*. Egyptian Antiquities, BM.

85 *Incontro di Iside con Osiride* by Pinturicchio. Appartemento Borgia, Vatican Museums and Galleries.

86 (left) Waite, V&A. Photo: Witty. (right) Charles VI, BN.

87 German woodcut, from *Spiegel der Menschlichen Behaltius* by Peter Drach, c. 1840.

89 From *Rosarium Philosophorum*, Part II, Frankfurt, 1550, BL. Photo: Freeman.

90 (left to right) Swiss, 18th c. (S.1) BM. Photo: Witty. Tarocchi di Mantegna (Case 50) BM. Photo: Freeman. Charles VI, BN.

91 *God Judging Adam* by William Blake, Tate Gallery.

93 *Hortus Conclusus* (Paradise Garden) by an anonymous Upper Rhenish Master, c. 1410. Städelsches Kunstinstitut, Frankfurt. Photo: Joachim Blauel.

94–5 Italian tarocco design by Bonifacio Bembo, 15th c. (Catalogue 54, M.630) Pierpont Morgan Library.

96 007 pack, designed by Fergus Hall for the film *Live and Let Die*, Eon Productions. Portal Gallery.

98 (left to right) Tarocchi di Mantegna, BM. Photo: Freeman. Waite, V&A. Photo: Witty. 007 pack, Eon Productions.

99 (left) Charles VI, BN. (right) 007 pack, Eon Productions.

100 (left) Etteilla, (F.19) BM. (right) French, 18th c. (F.18) BM. Both photos: Freeman.

103 (left to right) German woodcut, (Case 40, Vol. XV) BM. Photo: Freeman. Italian minchiate, V&A. Photo: Witty. Etteilla, (F.19) BM. Photo: Freeman.

104 (left to right) Vices and Virtues, (I.138) BM. Photo: Freeman. Italian minchiate, V&A. Photo: Witty. Study by Dürer, Koenig's Collection, formerly in Museum Boymans-van Beuningen, Rotterdam.

105 *Papyrus of Ani*, Egyptian Antiquities, BM.

106 Design from *Le Monde Primitif*, Vol. 8, by Court de Gébelin, 1781. LL.

ILLUSTRATIONS ACKNOWLEDGMENTS

107 Galler, SM. Photo: Witty.
108 Charles VI, BN.
109 (left) Detail from the Grabow altar by Master Bertram, 1379–83. St Peter's Church, Hamburg (right) *Crucifixion on the Flowering Tree* by Dürer. Musée des Beaux-Arts, Rennes.
110 (left) Italian tarocco (I.38) BM. (right) Italian minchiate, V&A. Both photos: Witty.
111 Photo: Mansell.
112 *Death on a Pale Horse* by W. Blake. Fitzwilliam Museum, Cambridge.
113 *Death Riding* by Dürer, 1513, BM.
114 (left) Waite, V&A. Photo: Witty. (right) 007 pack, Eon Productions.
115 (left) Virtues and Vices (I.138) BM. Photo: Freeman. (right) Galler, SM. Photo: Witty.
117 From the *Bedford Book of Hours*, Add. MS. 18850 f. 11, c. 1423. BL.
118 (left) Design from *Le Monde Primitif*, Vol. 8, by Court de Gébelin, 1781. LL. (right) Piedmontese, 1943, SM. Photo: Witty.
119 (left) Waite, V&A. (right) Italian tarocco, V&A. Both photos: Witty.
120 Tarocchi di Mantegna, Italian, c. 1470, from *Jeux de Cartes Tarot*, 1844. HPL.
121 Etteilla (F.19). BM. Photo: Freeman.
122 From the *Bedford Book of Hours*, Add. MS. 18850 f. BL.
124 (left) Etteilla (F.19) BM. Photo: Freeman. (right) Italian minchiate, V&A. Photo: Witty.
125 Ganymede by Benvenuto Cellini, 1545–7, Museo Nazionale, Florence. Photo: Mansell.
126 Italian tarocco, attributed to Antonio di Cicognara, late 15th c., V&A. Photo: Witty.
127 (left) Italian tarocco, V&A. Photo: Witty. (right) *The Kachchhawatar*, north India, 19th c. (I.M.221917) Crown Copyright, V&A.
128 (top) Italian minchiate, V&A. (bottom) Italian tarocco, V&A. Both photos: Witty.
129 Tarocchi di Mantegna, (Case 50) BM. Photo: Freeman.
131 From *Mercurius redivivius* by Samuel Norton, Frankfurt, 1630, BL. Photo: Freeman.
132 (left) Tarocchi di Mantegna (Case 50) BM. Photo: Freeman. (right, top) Swiss, 18th c. (S.1). BM. Photo: Witty. (bottom) Charles VI, BN.
134 Woodcut by Dürer. Mary Evans Picture Library.
135 (left) Waite, V&A. (right) Galler, SM. Both photos: Witty.
136 (top) Italian (I.32) BM. Photo: Freeman. Italian minchiate, V&A. Photo: Witty.
137 Woodcut, German school, 15th c.
139 Cards designed by Aleister Crowley, English, early 20th c. Warburg Inst. By permission of Gerald Yorke, Esq. (top left) Photo: Michael Holford.
140 (top) Italian tarocco attributed to A. di Cicognara, 15th c., V&A. Photo: Witty. (bottom) Charles VI, BN.
143 (top, left) Italian tarocco designed by Bonifacio Bembo, in the Accademia Carrara, Bergamo, 15th c., reproductions SM. Photo: Witty. (right) 007 pack, Eon Productions. (bottom, left) Italian tarocco (I.38) BM. (right) Italian tarocco, V&A.. Both photos: Witty.
144 Detail from *Stories from the Life of the Virgin*, School of Fra Angelico, Galleria dell'Academia, Florence. Photo: Mansell.
145 Frontispiece to *Jeux de Cartes Tarot*, 1844. HPL.
151 Drawing, c. 1785. Photo: RTH.
152 Photograph, c. 1860. Photo: RTH.
155 19th-c. copies by William Ottley of German c. 1497, V&A. Photo: Witty.
157 Revolutionary pack (F.8) BM. Photo: Witty.
158 SM. Photo: Witty.
160 Ottley, V&A. Photo: Witty.
161 (left) Italian tarocco in the Accademia Carrara, Bergamo; reproductions SM. (right) Waite, V&A. Both photos: Witty.
162 Piedmontese, 1943, SM. Photo: Witty.
163 Revolutionary pack (F.8) BM. Photo: Witty.
164 (left) Ottley, V&A. Galler, SM. Both photos: Witty.
167 (top, left) Waite, V&A. (right) Sola Busca, Italian (Case 233) BM. (bottom, left) Italian tarocco in the Accademia Carrara, Bergamo; reproductions SM. (right) Ottley, V&A. All photos: Witty.
170 (top, left) Ottley, V&A. (right) Italian, 19th c. (I.16) BM. (bottom, left) Swiss, 18th c. (S.1) BM. (right) Sola Busca (Case 233) BM. All photos: Witty.
175 Italian tarocco (I.38). BM. Photo: Witty.
176 Galler, SM. Photo: Witty.

Index

Page numbers in **bold** type refer to colour plates; page numbers in *italics*, to black-and-white illustrations.

absinthe, 124
abyss, 51, 76, 80, 89, 90
Adam and Eve, 38, 56, 64, 67, 69, 71, 76, 78, 83, 84, *86*, 87–9, *87*, 90, 91, *91*, 98, 101, 103, 116, 120, *124*, 142, 147
Adonis, 100
Aeon, the, *see* Day of Judgment
air, 55, 64, 164; *see also* elements
alchemy, 26, 29, 30, 32, 35, 40, 45, 48, 68, 70, 80, 89, 101, 108, 116, 133, 138; processes of, 83, *89*, 91, 98, 108, 111, 112, 130, *131*, 136
Alliette (Etteilla), *28*, 29, 30, *63*, *100*, *103*, **121**, *124*, 173
almond, 75
alphabet, Hebrew, 26, 30, 35, 38; and paths, trumps, 51, 53–6, 59–142 *passim*, 147
Amon, 103
amrita, 127
angel, 88, 90, 91, 101, 102, 114, 116, 136
Angel, the, *see* Day of Judgment
anima, animus, 72, 79, 81; *Anima Mundi*, 45, 72, 142, 146
ankh, 80
Anubis, 74, 102
ape, 70, *70*
Apis, **44**, 84
Apollo, 21, 24, 35, 92, 133, 135
Aquarius, *14*, 125, 142
Arch layout, 177–8
Aries, *14*, 80, 153
arrow, *see* bow
Artemis, 75, 76, 115
Arthurian legends, 66, 103
'as above, so below', 67, 70, 83, 92
ash, 141
aspen, 64
ass, 66, *102*, *103*, 119, 120
Astaroth, 9
astral plane, 45, 145, 146
astrology, 16, 21, 23, 29, 30, 32, 35, 45, 125, 153, 179, 183; *see also* planets, zodiac
Athene, 80
Atlantis, 123
Attis, 100, 106–7
aumgn, 147

Babel, *see* Tower of Babel
Bacchus, *see* Dionysus
Baphomet, 32, 38, 120
Bastet, 98
bat, 118
Batons, suit of, 9, 15, 17, 35, *35*; in divination, 155, 156, **157**, 159–61, *160*, *161*, 172, **175**, 183
Bayley, Harold, 80, 125
bear, 124
beetle, 92, 112, 130
Bembo, Bonifacio, **94**, **95**, *160*, *167*
Benjamine, Elbert, 40
Bernardino, St, 15, 16

Binah, 51, 52, 67, 69, 76, 92, 116, 138, 156
bitter aloes, 105
Black Magician, the, 119
Blake, William, *91*, 102, *112*
Blavatsky, Madame H. P., 31, 102, 114, 120
Boaz, *see* Jachin and Boaz
Boethius, 101
Bolognese Tarot, 15
Book of Thoth, 30, 32, 38
Botticelli, Sandro, 22–3, *23*, *24*, 25, 67, 78, 86
bow symbolism, 24, 45, 86–7, 110, 115, 116, 124
Brahma, 102
Bruno, Giordano, 23–4, 25, 45
Budge, Sir E. A. Wallis, 92
bull, **44**, 84, *85*, 90, 141
butterfly, 59, 62, 64, 125

Cabala, 9, 22, 24, 25, 29, 30, 31, 32, 35, 48, *49*, 62, 75, 80, 92, 105, 136, 138; outline of, 49–56; *see also* sefiroth, Shekinah, Tree of Life
Cabiri, 134–5
cactus, 112
caduceus, 67, 70
Cagliostro, Count (Giuseppe Balsamo), 26, *30*
Cancer, 92, 130
Capricorn, *14*, 119, 120
Capuchin, the, *see* Hermit
Case, Paul Foster, 38, 114–15, 123, 142, 149, 182
Castor and Pollux, 89, 135
Cathar heresy, 37, 71, 123
Cellini, Benvenuto, 125
Celtic Cross layout, 178–9
Celtic traditions, 9, 37, 75, 118
centaur, 115, *117*
Ceres, 18, 76
Cernunnos, 118
Chalices, *see* Cups
Chariot, the, 10, *12*, *61*, 90–2, *90*, **95**, 97, 98, 102, 108; in divination, 171
'Charles VI' pack, *10*, 11, *81*, *83*, *86*, 90, *90*, 97, 99, 106, *108*, 128, *132*, **140**
Chaucer, Geoffrey, 11, 90
child, symbolism of, 62, 64–6, 67, *74*, 76, *77*, 79, 88, 128, *132*, 133, 134–5, *135*, *143*
Christ, 30, 40, 62, 64, 70, 74, 75, 76, 99, 101, 106–7, 108, *109*, 112, 116, 123, 125, 133, 136, 138, 142
Christian art and symbolism, 48, 49, 55–6, 62, *62*, 70, 101, 102, 105, 130, 141; *see also* Christ, cross, judgment, Mary
Christian, Paul, 30–1
Cicero, 97, 103
Cicognara, Antonio di, *126*, **140**
Circe, 98
clairvoyance, 32, 62, 150
Clock layout, 179
coconut, 127
Coins, suit of, 9, 15, 17, 35, *35*, **140**; in divination, 155, 156, **157**, 168–9, *170*, 172, **175**, **176**, 183
collective unconscious, 9, 45, 51, 72, 134, 146
Constancy, 15
Constant, A. L., *see* Lévi
correspondences (general), 53, 146
cosmic consciousness, 142
counting cards, *see* divination

court cards, 9, 15, *17*, 18–21, *28*; in divination, 155, 156, **157**, **158**, 160–1, *161*, 163–4, *164*, 166, *167*, 169, *170*, 172–3, **176**, 179, 183
Court de Gébelin, Antoine, 26, 29, 30, 31, 99, 106, 125
crab, crayfish, 92, 128, 130
Cranach, Lucas, the Elder, **41**
crocodile, 59, 62, 65, 66, 141
cross, 72, 74–5, 83–4, 106, 108, *109*, 136, 142, 178
Crowley, Aleister, 32, *32*, 35, 37–8, 53, 56, 59, 66, 84, 91, 92, 107, 112, 125, 127, 136, 147; on Justice, 38; Fool, 64, 65; Empress, 76; Lovers, 89; Strength, 97; Temperance, 116; Devil, 120; Tower, 123; and divination, 150, 156, 162, 166, 182, 184; his pack illustrated, **139**
crown, 24, 51, 72, 79, 97, 101, 105, 110, 116, 123, 164
cube, 80, 92, 119
Cupid, Eros, 35, 86, 87, 88, 116
Cups, suit of, 9, 15, 17, 35, **139**; in divination, 155, 156, **157**, **158**, 162–4, *162*, *163*, *164*, 172, **175**, 183
cutting, *see* divination
cypress, 141

Danae, 133
dance, 110, 111, 141
Dante Alighieri, 9
Day of Judgment, the, 10, *13*, 15, 59, *60*, 108, 116, 136–8, *136*, **139**; in divination, 172, 183
Death (trump card), 10, *13*, 27, *60*, 102, 110–13, *110*, 114, 123, 135, **140**, 147; in divination, 171, 172
death and rebirth, theme of, 46, 62, 65, 69–70, 74, 75, 88, 92, 100, 106–8, 110–11, 114, 136, 138, 147; *see also* Osiris, reincarnation
Demeter, 76, 79, *79*
Demiurge, 85, 88, 92
Devil, the (trump card), 10, 15, *46*, *60*, 85, 118–20, *118*, *119*, **121**, 123; in divination, 172
Devil (Satan), 15–16, 17, 68, 70, 88, 118–20, 123, 136, 164; *see also* Lucifer
dharma, 104
Diana, 75, 115
Dionysus (Bacchus), 65, *65*, *82*
Disks, *see* Coins
divination, 9, 16, 18, 26, *28*, 29, 32, 35, 37, 62, 125, 151, *152*; rules for, 149–84; counting cards, 180, 183; cutting, 174; shuffling, 150, 173–4; *see also* astrology
dog, 59, 62, 74, 75, 115, 128
dolphin, 130
dove, *62*, 78, 125
Dürer, Albrecht, *82*, *104*, *113*, *134*

eagle, 64, 76, 103, 125, *125*, 141
educational cards, 18–22, *19*
Egypt, 35, 55, 72, 74, 120, 138; and origin of Tarot, 9, 26–9, 30, 38; judgment of the dead, 74, 75, 102, 104, *105*; *see also* names of Egyptian deities
elements, the four, 15, 84, 92, 102, 113, 141, 155, 156
elephant, 15, 105
Eleusinian mysteries, 79, 83
Eliot, T. S., 37, 40, 106

Emperor, the, 10, *12*, *61*, 80–1, *80*, *81*, 83, 85, 108, 119, 127; in divination, 171
Empress, the, 10, *12*, *61*, 76–9, *76*, *78*, 80, 85, 89, 145, 147; in divination, 171
Encausse, Gérard, *see* Papus
Enchantress, the, *see* Strength
Eros, *see* Cupid
ether, 64
Etteilla, *see* Alliette
Eve, *see* Adam and Eve
eye, 101, 120, 123, 125

falcon, 124
feather, 64, 104
Female Pope, the, 10, *12*, 15, *46*, 71–5, *73*, *75*, 80, 84, 85, 105, 116, 138, 147, in divination, 171, 173, 181
Ficino, Marsilio, 23, 25, 45
Fifty-four Card layout, 182
fig, 103
fire, 55, 62, 72, 80, 98, 107, 108, 115, 133, 135, 136, 159; *see also* elements
fish, 112, 130
Five Card spread, 177
fleur-de-lis, 80, *81*, 85
Florentine Tarot, 15
Fool, the, 10, *12*, 29, 46, 48, 59–66, *59*, *60*, *63*, 67, 70, **139**, 142, 147; in divination, 171, 181, 183
Force, *see* Strength
Fortitude, *see* Strength
Fortune (goddess), 18, 101, 103, *103*
Fortune, Dion, 51, 76, 146
fortune-telling, *see* divination
Forty-two Card layout, 181
Frazer, Sir J. G., 35, 40, 106, 107
Freemasonry, *see* Masonry

Ganesha, 105
Ganymede, 125, *125*
garden symbolism, 45, 69, 78–9, **93**, 108, 127
Gardner, Richard, 153
Geburah, 52, 92, 98, 105, 108
Gemini, 89, 135
gnosticism, 22, 25, 32, 35, 45, 48, 49, 53, 75, 85, 88, 92; *see also* Hermetica
goat, 118, 119, 120
Golden Dawn, Order of the, 32–5, 37, 38, 40, 45, 53, 156, 162, 164, 165; on Kether, 51; and the Fool, 59, 62–4; Female Pope, 71, 72, 74; Lovers, 88; Hanged Man, 107, 108; Moon, 128; Sun, 133–4; other trumps, 67, 76, 79, 83, 85, 97, 105, 113, 115, 116, 123, 125; and meditation, 145–6
Grail, 35–7, 40, 66, 91, 146, 162
Grand Cross layout, 177
Grand Jeu layout, 182
Graves, Robert, 37
Great Beast, 37, 97
Green Man, 66
Guaita, Stanislas de, 31
gypsies, 9, 11, 26, 32, 149, 151, *152*

Hades, 136
Hall, Manly Palmer, 40
Hanged Man, the, 10, *13*, 35, 40, *46*, *60*, 106–9, *106*, *107*, *108*, 135, 142, 147; in divination, 171, 183
Harpocrates, 64, 83
Hathor, 35, 76
Hebe, 125
Hebrew alphabet, *see* alphabet
Hecate, 75, 128
hekhaloth, 53, 92, 145
Helios, 133
heliotrope, 133
hellebore, 141
hermaphrodite, 70, 116, 118, *118*, 142
Hermes, 67, 68, 136; Hermes Trismegistus, 29, *29*, 32, 99

Hermetica, 22, 23, 25, 29, 32, 35, 68
Hermit, the, 10, *12*, *61*, 99–100, *99*, *100*; in divination, 171, 177
Hesed, 52, 98, 99
Hesperides, 108, 127
hibiscus, 136
Hierophant, the, *see* Pope
High Priestess, the, *see* Female Pope
Hod, 52, 123, 133, 136, 138
Hokmah, 51, 52, 62, 76, 80, 116, 156
horns, 72, 81, 118
Horoscope layout, 179
horse, 90, 92, 113, 115, 135
Horseshoe layout, 177–8
Horus, 35, 64, 65, 66, 70, 74, *74*, 76, 80, 83, 124
House of God, the, *see* Tower
Houston, Jean, 66
Hunchback, the, *see* Hermit
hunting symbolism, 115

Iamblichus, 30
ibis, 70, 125
Icarus, 132, 133, *134*
initiation, 74, 75, 100
Insight Institute, 40
iris, 116
Ishtar, 76, 125
Isis, 35, 64, 70, 72, 73–5, *74*, 76, 78, 80, 83, 84, 103, 124, 125, 146

Jachin and Boaz, 72, 74, 75
Jacob, Eugene, *see* Star, Ely
James, William, 45
Janus, 89
Jennings, Hargrave, 66, 85, 103
Jesus, *see* Christ
John of Brefeld, 11, 16, 17, 26
Joker, the, 21, 59
Judas, 107
Jude, St, 99
Judgment, the, *see* Day of Judgment
Judgment of Paris, 22, 41, 86
judgment of the dead, 104, 136–8, *137*; *see also* Egypt
Juggler, the, 10, *12*, 29, 46, 59, *61*, 67–70, *68*, *69*, 71, 75, 80, 85, **96**, 98, 118; in divination, 171, 181
Jung, C. G., *36*, 45, 48, 49, 70, 89, 92, 97, 99, 108–9, 116, 130, 134, 153; *see also* anima, collective unconscious
Juno, *61*, 72, 125
Jupiter, 15, 23, 52, *61*, 64, 72, 80, *82*, 83, 103
Justice, 10, *12*, 18, 21, 38, *61*, 97, 104–5, *104*, 106, 108; in divination, 171, 173

karma, 102, 104
Kether, 51, 52, 62, 67, 69, 74, 116, 141, 156, 180
keys of heaven and hell, 72, 75, 84
Khem, 120
Khepera, 92, 130
King, Francis, 145
Knights Templar, 26, 32, 120
kundalini, 112

ladder symbolism, 17, 21–2, 25, 51, 52, 53, 62, 73
laurel, 133, 142
Leland, C. G., 151
lemniscate, 67, 69, 70, 98
Lemuria, 130
Leo, 97, 98, 142, 153
letter mysticism, 24–5, 55–6; *see also* alphabet
Lévi, Éliphas (Alphonse Louis Constant), 30, *30*, 31, 32, 35, 38, 53, 56, 59, 62, 67, 68, 85, 135, 138; and the Lovers, 88–9; Chariot, 90, 91; Hermit, 99; Hanged Man, 107; Devil, 120; on divination, 153
Libra, 97, 105
Lightning, the, *see* Tower

lily, 100; *see also* fleur-de-lis
lion, 24, 97, 98, *98*, 133, 136, 141
'living creatures', 92, 102, 141
lobster, 112, 128
lotus, 92, *127*
Lovers, the, 10, *12*, *61*, 86–9, *86*, **94**, 99, 135; in divination, 171
Lucifer, 85, 120, 123, 125
Lull, Raymond, 24–5, 29, 32
Lust, *see* Strength

Maat, 35, 104, 125
Mackenzie, Kenneth, 32
Magician, Magus, the, *see* Juggler
magpie, 89
Malkuth, 49, 52, 116, 128, 136, 141, 142, 156, 180
mallow, 84, 136
Mantegna, Andrea, 21, 22; 'Mantegna' cards, *20*, 21–2, *22*, 25, 51, 67, 68, 80, 90, *90*, 97, *98*, *120*, *129*, *132*
Mars, 22–3, *24*, 52, 80, 90, *90*, 92, 105, 112, 124
Marseilles Tarot, *12*–*13*, 15, *26*, *27*, 56, *60*–1, 67, 110, 113, 118, *118*, *163*, *164*
Martinists, 29, 30, 31, 32
Mary, the Virgin, 62, 64, 74, 75, 76–9, *77*, **93**, 125, 142, *144*
Masonry, Masonic symbolism, 26–9, 31, 32, 35, 55, 72, 73, 74, *127*
Masters, R. E. L., 66
Masters, the, 83, 100
Mathers, S. L. MacGregor, 32–5, *33*, 37–8, 45, 53, 59, 89; on divination, 153, 156, 161, 162, 169, 172, 179, 181, 182
meditation, 24, 145–7, 150, 153
memory, art of, 24–5
Mercury, 52, 67, 68, *68*, 118, 136, 138; mercury (metal), 70, 138
Merkabah mysticism, 92, 145
Mesmer, F. A., 26, 29
Michael, Archangel, 136, *137*
minchiate pack, *14*, 15, **42**–**3**, 97, *103*, *104*, 124, 128, *128*, 136
Minerva, 18, 78, 80
Miseria, 15
Mitelli, G. M., *109*, *143*, **175**
Mithras, 9, 66, 108, 133
moon, 52, 72, 74, 75, 79, 83, 89, 92, 101, 115, 128, 130
Moon, the (trump card), 10, *13*, *60*, 116, 125, 128–30, *128*, 133, 135, 138, **140**, 147; in divination, 172, 173
Morgan, Morrigan, 75
Mu, 130
myrtle, 78

name of God, *see* Tetragrammaton
narcissus, 100
Neoplatonism, 22, 30, 49
Netsah, 52, 123, 125
nettle, 136
Northbrooke, John, 15
Nu, Nun, 64
number symbolism, 21, 35, 53–5, 56, 59–142 *passim*, 147

oak, 103
obelisk, 59, 65, 66
Odin, 107
Old Man, the, *see* Hermit
Opening the Key layout, 182–3
opium, 130
opposites, 22–3, *24*, 41, 49–52, 59–142 *passim*, 147
Osiris, 31, 35, 65, 70, 74, 80, 83, 84, *84*, 103, 106, 107, 108, 113, 124
O.T.O. (Order of the Temple of the Orient), 31–2, 38, 66, 97
ouroboros, 70, 142

INDEX

Ouspensky, P. D., 40, 123, 142
owl, 80, 125

palm, 70
Pan, 119, 120
Papus (Gérard Encausse), 31–2, 35, 59, 99, 102, 111, 114, 149; on Justice, 38; Juggler, 67–8, 70; Moon, 128
Parsifal, 66
paths, 51, 53, 59–142 passim, 145–6
Paul, St, 62, 136
peacock, 125
Péladan, Josephin, 31
Pentacles, see Coins
pentagram, 84, 119
Pentecost, 62, *62*, 64, 138
periodicity, law of, 102
Persephone, 75
Perseus, 88, 107
Petrarch, Francesco, 11, 90
Philosopher's Stone, 30, 83, 91, 98, 108, 116, 130
Piedmontese Tarot, 11
pillars, 84, 92, 97, 113; see also Jachin and Boaz
Pisces, *14*, 130
Pitois, Jean Baptist, 30
planets, 21, 52–3, 55, 101, 127, 141, 145; see also names of individual planets
Plato, 22, 23, 40, 66, 92, 97
Pleiades, 127
Pluto, 136
Pollux, see Castor and Pollux
Pope, the, 10, *12*, 15, *82*, 83–4, *83*, 85, 87, 103, 119, 147; in divination, 171, 173, 181
Pope Joan, 71, 75
poplar, 103
poppy, 136
Poverta, 15
Priapus, 119
Primavera, see Botticelli
Prometheus, 107
Providence, 16, 73, 102
prudence, 15, 18, 21, 97, 99, 103, 106
psychokinesis, 150
Purgatory, 104, 105
Pythagoreanism, 22, 25, 53

rainbow, 116
Raine, Kathleen, 40
ram, 80
Re, 103, 133
Reaper, the, see Death
rectification, 10, 48
Regardie, Israel, 108
Reich, Wilhelm, 106
reincarnation, 62, 102, 114
Renaissance art and symbolism, 20, 21–5, *22*, *23*, *24*, 29, 30, *41*, 44, 49, 70, 78, 86, 90, 97, *125*, 141
Revelation, Book of, 30, 37, 56, 79, 97, 113
Rods, see Batons
rose, 64, 78, 92, 103, 113
Rosicrucians, 26–9, 30, 31, 32, 35, 55, 99
rue, 124
Runciman, Sir Steven, 37
runes, 55, 107
rush, 115

sacrifice, theme of, 75, 106–9
Sagittarius, 115, *117*

Saint-Germain, Count of, 29
Satan, see Devil
Saturn, 23, 52, 120, *120*, 141, 142
scarab, see beetle
Sceptres, see Batons
Scholem, G. G., 145
Scorpio, *14*, 112, 142, 153
scorpion, 107
Sebek, 141
Sefer Yetsirah, 53–5, 62, 64, 107, 136
sefiroth, 30, 49–55, *49*, 76, 141, 156, 180, 183; see also names of individual sefiroth
Sekhmet, 98
self-fulfilling prophecy, 151–3
serpent, see snake
Seth, 64–5, 74, 102, 113
sexual symbolism, 37, 38, 46, 51, 52, 59–142 passim, 89, 147, 159, 162, 164–5
sheelagh-na-gigs, 75
Shekinah, 52, 72–3, 74, 142
Ship, the, 15
Shiva, 102, 111, *111*, 112, 123
shuffling, see divination
Sicilian Tarot, 15, 106
significator, choice of, 173, 181
Sirius, 74, 125
skeleton, 110, *110*, 113
snake, 67, 70, 87, *87*, 88, 99, 106, 107, 112, 120, 142
Societas Rosicruciana in Anglia, 32, 53
sparrow, 78
sparrowhawk, 133
spheres, planetary, 52–3, 145; see also sefiroth
sphinx, 90, 92, 102
Spiritualism, 32, 37, 45, 114
Staffs, see Batons
stag, 118
Star, Ely (Eugene Jacob), 31, 35
star symbolism, 72, 74, 125, 127, 141; see also zodiac
Star, the (trump card), 10, *13*, 60, 125–7, *126*, *127*, **139**; in divination, 172
Strength, 10, *12*, 18, 21, 48, *60*, 97–8, *98*, 124; in divination, 171
sulphur, 80, 85, 98
sun, 23, 24, 51, 52, 64, 65, 74, 79, 83, 89, 92, 98, 99, 101, 103, 108, 109, 113, 115, 116, 127, 128, 130, 133–5, 136
Sun, the (trump card), 10, *13*, 60, *132*, 133–5, *135*, **138**; in divination, 172, 177
Supernals, 51, 79, 83, 84, 124, 138
swallow, 70
swan, 78
swastika, 108
Swords, suit of, 9, 10, 15, 17, 35, *35*; in divination, 155, 156, 164–6, *167*, 172, **175**, 183
synchronicity, 153
System, the, see World

Taro river, 11
Taurus, *14*, 83, 84, 142
telepathy, 114, 150
Temperance, 10, *10*, *13*, 18, 21, 27, *60*, 114–16, *114*, **115**, 120, 125; in divination, 172
Temple, the, 72, 74, 75, 123
Tetragrammaton, 30, 100, 102, 141
Theosophical Society, 31, 37, 40, 45, 48, 83, 102, 114, 127

Thief, the, see Hanged Man
thistle, 120
Thoth, 30, 32, 35, 38, 67, 70, *70*, 76
Tifereth, 52, 74, 80, 99, 105, 115
time, 70, 79, 80, 101, 120, 142; and the Hermit, 99; and Temperance, 114
Titans, 65, 66
Tower of Babel, **122**, 123
Tower, the, 10, *13*, 37, *60*, 123–4, *124*, 125, 147; in divination, 172
Traitor, the, see Hanged Man
Tree of Life, 49–52, *49*, 53, 72, 79, 88, 145; see also paths, sefiroth; Tree of Life layout, 180, 183
turtle, 92
Twenty-one Card layout, 180–1

unicorn, 71, *71*
Universe, the, see World
Ussher, Arland, 107

veil, 72, 74, 75, 141
Venetian Tarot, 11, 15, 56
Venus, 18, 22–3, *23*, *24*, 35, 52, 76, 78, 79, 80, 83, 97, 105, 125, 127
vervain, 70
vibrations, 114–15, 154
Virgo, 97, 100
Vishnu, 102, *127*
Vulcan, 97, 105

Waite, A. E., *34*, 35–7, 38, 40; on the Lovers, 88; Strength, 97, 98; Hermit, 99; Hanged Man, 106, 108; Day of Judgment, 136; other trumps, 59, 64, 69, 70, 79, 80, 83, 90, 102, 104–5, 113, 116, 119, 120, 135, 142; on divination, 149, 156, 162, 166, 178, 181; his pack illustrated, *35*, *63*, *69*, *75*, *78*, *81*, *82*, *86*, *98*, *114*, *119*, *135*, *161*, *167*
Waldensians, 37
Wands, see Batons
water, 55, 79, 107, 111, 114, 116, 125, 128, 130, 133, 162; see also elements
werewolf, 128
Westcott, W. W., 53
Weston, Jessie L., 35–7
wheel, 30, 64, 73, 101–2, 104, 142
Wheel of Fortune, the, 10, *12*, 40, 48, *61*, 101–3, *103*, 104, 105, 108, 110, 147; in divination, 171, 181; layout, 179–80
Williams, Charles, 40
Wirth, Oswald, 31, 40, 48, 59, 65, 69, 72, 75, 80, 90, 97, 99, 102, 107, 109, 123, 125, 134
witches, modern, 76, 81, 118
wolf, 24, 112, 124, 128
World, the, 10, *13*, 46, 48, 59, *61*, 109, 116, 141–2, *143*; in divination, 172
wreath, 141, 142

Yeats, W. B., 32, 37, *39*, 40–5
Yesod, 52, 115, 128, 141
yew, 141

Zain, 40
Zeus, 64, 103, 125, 133
zodiac, 15, 52, 53, 79, 88, 101, 109, 134, 142, 183; see also names of signs
Zohar, 73

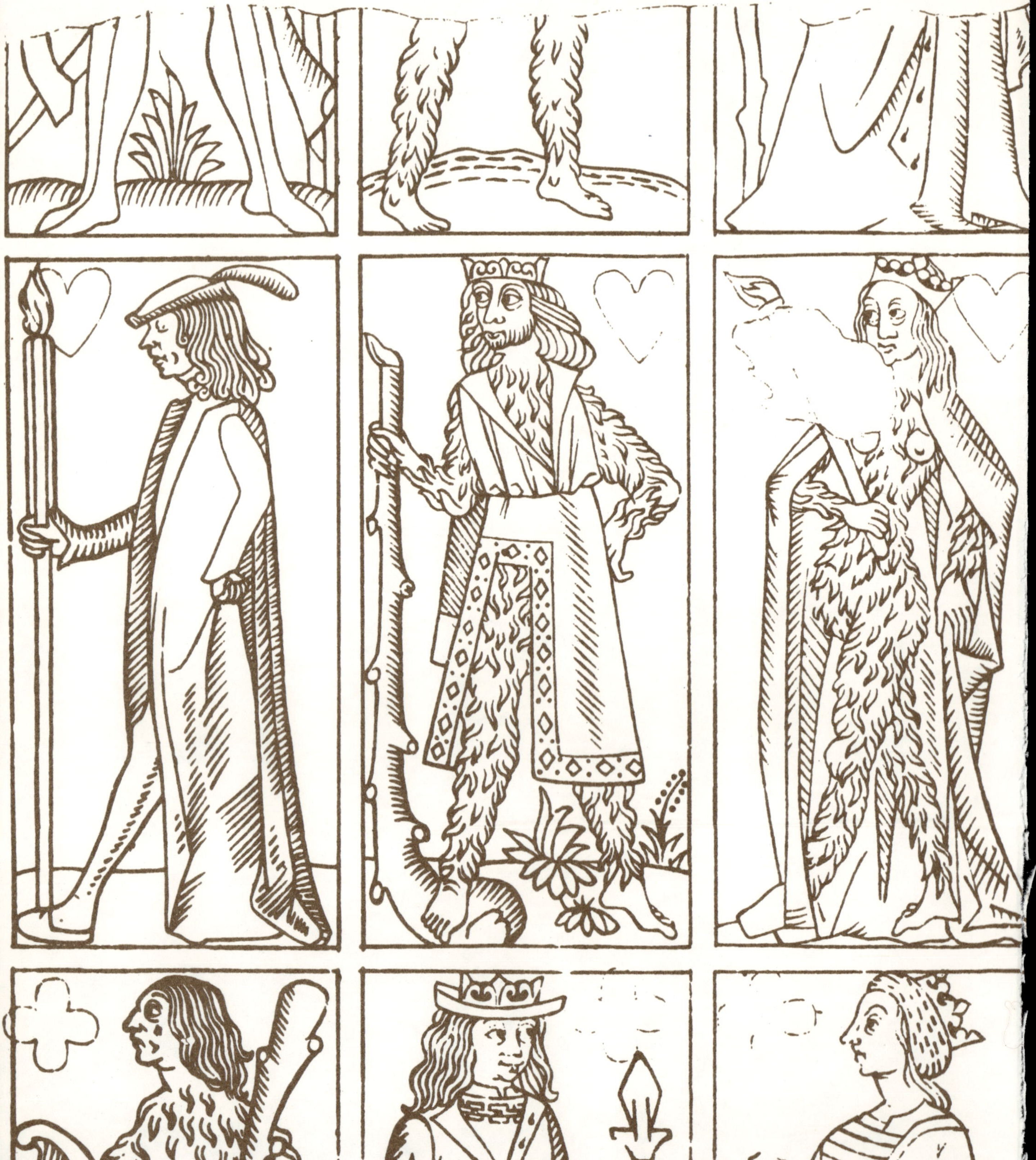